Barcelona
&Catalonia

Barcelona
&Catalonia

Paul Gogarty

Christopher Helm
A & C Black · London

© 1993 Paul Gogarty

Photographs by Paul Gogarty

First published 1993 by Christopher Helm (Publishers) Ltd, a subsidiary of
A & C Black (Publishers) Ltd, 35 Bedford Row, London WC1R 4JH

ISBN 0-7136-8029-6

A CIP catalogue record for this book is available from the British Library.

Typeset by Rowland Phototypesetting Ltd,
Bury St Edmunds, Suffolk.
Printed and bound in Great Britain by
Butler and Tanner Ltd, Frome, Somerset

To Susanna

About this book

This guide is intended to be as useful as possible. It avoids fanning into a thousand different sections on everything from Catalonian pastry-making to treatises on Renaissance architecture. Instead the pages are filled with places: what they're like, what there is to do in them, their history and significance. Quite simply there is more here on Catalonia, the place, than in any other English guide. The organisation is kept as simple and practical as possible. The Barcelona section is followed by an extensive information listing as are each of the tours in the North and South.

The Preface charts my own relationship with the province. The Introduction provides a brief orientation (more is provided in the Barcelona section) followed by a historical outline of Catalonia and its people.

For the sake of simplicity the Costa Daurada section includes the Costa de L'Ebre. Museum opening times for Barcelona are included in the running text and all others are listed at the back. This guide is as accurate as possible but, as opening times change, I would suggest checking with local tourist offices on arrival. Any updates or corrections will be gratefully received. Catalan spellings are employed throughout in preference to Spanish.

Acknowledgements

Thanks are in order to virtually the whole of Catalonia but particularly to Joaquim Amat of the Consorci de Promocío Turistica for providing me with so much help with the book. I'd also like to give special thanks to Inma Felip at the Spanish National Tourist Office in London, Betina Pons, Monica Colomer i Membrado and Maria Luisa Albacar from the Patronat Municipal de Turisme de Barcelona, Miren de Bustinza of the British Institute and Xiquet Sabater i Mecre the delightful host at the Hotel Aiguablava. Thanks also to Brittany Ferries, Iberia and Atesa car hire, Terry Woodman of Private Villas and Madeleine Winship of Interhome. The list is endless but I must also mention by name my friends Jill Rasmussen and John Arnold of the Bar Estudio in Altafulla, Carmen Artigua of Codoniu, the dancers Lydia Azzopardi and Cesc Gelabert, Rowland Norris at the English Centre in Vic, José Alvarez Saavedra at the Vielha tourist office. I am also greatly indebted to Oana Millet in Barcelona for updating information and to a number of guides who provided insight and company at various points on my journey: Antoni-David Jover and Joan Callís in Barcelona, the irrepressible and informative Mercè Mill of Terrassa, Carme Altes and Jordi Carrera in Girona, Manual Blay Saludes in Tarragona and Ramon Alabau Soy in Ripoll. I'm sure this list is incomplete, for which I can only apologise. Lastly I must thank my daughter Larne for pointing out every playground in the province and my son Max for helping test them out.

Contents

Preface

My relationship with Catalonia extends back now more than half my life.

In 1968 I left England with three friends in a beaten up old Cortina seeking adventure. We ended up working out the summer in a bar to the south of Barcelona serving the first big tourist wave as it lapped its way up the littoral.

In my heady role as barman I earned the princely sum of £4 a week. When I left five months later I would do so with £50 in my pocket and a passion for all things Catalan. My boss however had not been satisfied with her bar pickings and had been travelling round villages systematically buying up old wrought iron window grills which she expected to sell at enormous profit back in England. When I visited her farm in Suffolk a year later I saw the grills abandoned and rusting outside the barn.

Perhaps our two financial fates also warmed me to the province. Catalans were generous but no mugs. After all they were the traditional captains of Spanish industry and had once ruled a vast Mediterranean empire. In 1969 their new crop of business entrepreneurs were knocking as loudly as the Catalan Nationalists to be allowed out of Franco's dungeon.

Three enduring images burnt themselves into my memory that summer. The first was of visits to a grand estate just a couple of miles away where my girlfriend would model for a powerful female artist around whom the village had woven intrigue and mystery. Climbing a dusty track past palms, orange groves and vineyards, the wavy red pantiles of her home would suddenly appear. Sometimes we would sit beside the fountain in the courtyard and the señora would paint Donna from under the shade of an orange tree. Sometimes we would sit up in her tower looking out over the country, listening to her declaim the poetry of the province's most famous poet, Jacint Verdaguer, to the accompaniment of the music of Pau Casals who was born and raised just ten kilometres away.

My second enduring memory is of my maiden trip to Barcelona. Standing in an open-back carriage, I gasped with delight as the train suddenly emerged from a tunnel and below us the cliff fell away to a sparkling Mediterranean sea. Even more breathtaking however was the architecture of Gaudí in Barcelona itself and, as soon as I returned to the UK, I smashed up the tiles in my bathroom to re-arrange them trencadís fashion. It was an unmitigated disaster but rather than discouraging me, the experience just triggered a life-long passion for modern architecture's greatest genius.

That summer was unquestionably the summer of my youth and my final memory was also the most momentous historically.

On the night Neil Armstrong did his moonwalk, 20 of us marked the occasion with a sangria beach party. The moon, so huge I strained to make out the footprints, momentarily seemed to release its gravitational pull. The ocean lay unmoving as if not daring to breathe. We sat in the sand in a reverential silence each thinking our private thoughts at being so privileged to witness such an event in such a place.

That summer there was a new optimism among Catalan friends. Many felt the continuing agitation in Barcelona was auguring the dictator's end. He would in fact last a further six years. For the young foreigners amongst us the future seemed boundless.

Franco has gone and no one danced at his wake with more gusto than the Catalans. Few who knew Catalonia then doubted it would survive and outlive the General but even fewer could have anticipated Barcelona's phoenix like ascension to rival Paris and London as the fashionable and artistic centre of Europe so soon after the dictator's death.

I have made many subsequent visits to the province since that first summer and there have been enormous changes even outside its capital. Of course there have been the Costa excesses, of which Catalonia is as guilty as the rest of Spain, but on the whole the changes have been for the better. Developments have become more controlled, living conditions vastly improved and the people are generally more prosperous and better cared for. For those who know and love Catalonia, the best news however is that so much of its inland beauty and ruggedness remains unchanged. This book is intended as a celebration of Catalonia. I may have already known it half my life but hopefully I still have another half life to go.

Introduction

Catalonia is located in Spain's north-eastern corner on the border with France. The province forms a triangle whose base is the Pyrenees; to the west lies Aragón, to the south Valencia and to the east the Mediterranean; its 32,000 square kilometres are divided into four regions, Lleida, Tarragona, Barcelona and Girona. Catalonia is governed under the Spanish Statute of Autonomy of 1979. The ruling body, the Generalitat, has a parliament of 135 elected deputies and a president who holds office for four years. The Generalitat is the ultimate authority in the province but the Diputació, introduced by central government in 1833 to exercise control over the country, still has not been fully dismantled and so – although politically lacking real power – it is still involved in regional projects. The comarques are the organic regional units of the province. They were instituted in 1932 as the lower tier of administration. Within the comarcas are the municipis – the municipal authorities – each governed by a council called the Ajuntament.

The founding of Catalonia dates back one thousand years to 987 when Count Borrell II of Barcelona stopped paying tribute to the French King. The province boasts the oldest flag in Europe and one of the oldest parliaments, established over 600 years ago. It is an autonomous community within Spain with its own language, a Romance tongue related to Provençal. Today Catalan dialects are still spoken in Valencia and parts of southern France, in the Balearics and even in towns in Sardinia.

Catalonia is a 'country' apart from the rest of Spain, despite Franco's attempts to mince it into anonymity; unbelievably diverse and creative, and massively indulged when natural beauties were dealt out. Perhaps most surprising for a land renowned for its 400 kilometres of seaboard is the fact that only five per cent of the province lies below 100m. The countryside is as diverse as its food and people: here we find the palm and the northern fir, the bilberry and the cactus, cork forests and vineyard, volcanoes and honeycomb gorges, churches and church burners. There are exquisite Romanesque chapels and soaring Gothic cathedrals, lush valleys and parched plains, the tight dramatic bays of the Costa Brava and the endless straight golden sands of the Costa Daurada. Catalonia's southern limit is blessed with a near tropical climate in the Delta de l'Ebre's marshlands whilst its northern borders are graced by the snow-clad peaks of the Pyrenees. In these mountains are hidden some of the province's most idiosyncratic towns, its only national park (Aigües Tortes), a dozen ski stations and spectacular alpine scenery. Touring Catalonia from its

3

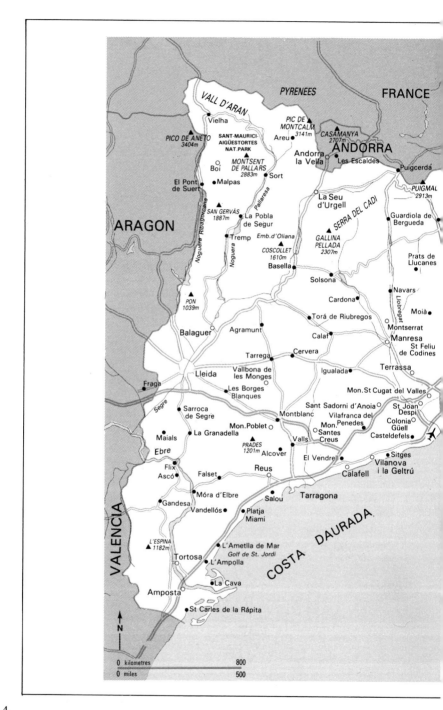

PYRENEES

FRANCE

VALL D'ARAN

Vielha

PIC DE
MONTCALM
3141m

CASAMANYA
2707m

ANDORRA

PICO DE ANETO
3404m

SANT-MAURICI-
AIGÜESTORTES
NAT.PARK

Areu

Andorra
la Vella

Les Escaldes

Puigcerdá

Boi

MONTSENT
DE PALLARS
2883m

Sort

PUIGMAL
2913m

El Pont
de Suert

Malpas

La Seu
d'Urgell

SERRA DEL CADI

Guardiola de
Bergueda

ARAGON

SAN GERVÁS
1887m

La Pobla
de Segur

Tremp

Emb.d'Oliana

GALLINA
PELLADA
2307m

Noguera Ribagorçana

Pallaresa

Noguera

COSCOLLET
1610m

Basella

Prats de
Llucanes

Solsona

Navars

PON
1039m

Cardona

Llobregat

Moià

Torá de Riubregos

Montserrat

Balaguer

Agramunt

Calaf

Manresa

St Feliu
de Codines

Tarrega

Cervera

Igualada

Terrassa

Lleida

Vallbona de
les Monges

Mon.St Cugat del Valles

Fraga

Les Borges
Blanques

Segre

Sarroca
de Segre

Sant Sadorni d'Anoia

St Joan
Despi

Montblanc

Vilafranca del
Penedes

Colonia
Güell

Maials

La Granadella

Mon.Poblet

Mon.
Santes
Creus

Casteldefels

Ebre

PRADES
1201m

Alcover

Valls

Sitges

Flix

Reus

El Vendrell

Vilanova
i la Geltrú

Ascó

Falset

Calafell

Móra d'Elbre

Salou

Tarragona

Gandesa

Vandellós

Platja
Miami

COSTA DAURADA

L'ESPINA
1182m

L'Ametlla de Mar

Golf de St. Jordi

Tortosa

L'Ampolla

VALENCIA

La Cava

Amposta

St Carles de la Rápita

N

0 kilometres   800
0 miles   500

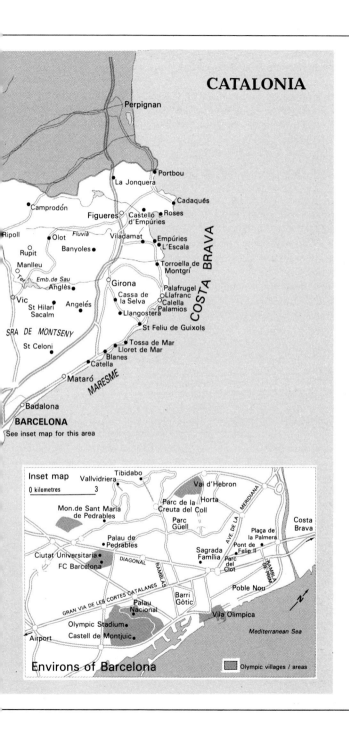

CATALONIA

Perpignan

Portbou

La Jonquera

Cadaqués

Camprodón

Figueres · Castelló · Roses
d'Empúries

Ripoll · Olot *Fluvià* · Viladamat · Empúries
· L'Escala

Rupit · Banyoles ·

Manlleu

Emb.de Sau
· Anglès · · Girona

Vic · · Cassa de · Palafrugel
St Hilari · Angelés · la Selva · Llafranc
Sacalm · Llangostera · Calella
· Palamios

SRA DE MONTSENY · St Feliu de Guixols

St Celoni · · Tossa de Mar
· Lloret de Mar
· Blanes
· Catella

· Mataró *MARESME*

· Badalona

BARCELONA
See inset map for this area

COSTA BRAVA

Inset map Vallvidriera · Tibidabo

0 kilometres ___ 3 ___

Mon.de Sant María
de Pedrables

Val d'Hebron

Parc de la / Horta
Creuta del Coll

Parc
Güell

Costa
Brava

Palau de
· Pedrables

Plaça de
la Palmera

Ciutat Universitaria ·
FC Barcelona · *DIAGONAL*

Sagrada
Família

Pont de
· Felip II
*Parc
del
Clot*

GRAN VIA DE LES CORTES CATALANES

Palau
Nacional

Barri
Gòtic

Poble Nou

Olympic Stadium ·

Vila Olímpica

Airport · Castell de Montjuic ·

Mediterranean Sea

Environs of Barcelona

☐ Olympic villages / areas

somnolent inland dusty plains to its effervescent seaside playgrounds is like travelling through several continents.

The B9 French autoroute becomes the A17 from La Jonquera border post, cutting a swathe down the Mediterranean littoral. From Barcelona westwards, the A2 autopiste leads quickly to Lleida, its westernmost city, before heading across the Spanish heartland to Santander on the Atlantic coast. The roads in Catalonia are generally good and one can tour the whole province never needing to resort to dirt track. There are four grades of road: the motorways; the major national routes (number preceded by N); the main regional (comarcal) routes (number may be preceded by C); and minor roads (unnumbered). If you do divert from the tarmacced roads, however, even here the track will suddenly rise then dip and there will be another small village, tiled roofs invaded by TV aerials as if by a flock of cranes taking a breather on their migratory trail. Despite the fact that half the province's six million population live in metropolitan Barcelona and these inland tracts are sparsely populated, you can never drive for long in Catalonia without coming across some hamlet improbably straddling some impossible ridge, a Moorish fort on one side and parish church on the other.

There are 1437km of railway track linking Barcelona with Girona, Lleida and Tarragona, all part of the national railway grid. There is also an efficient local network linking the capital with the industrial towns of Terrassa and Sabadell.

Catalonia has traditionally been the ecclesiastical and military highway between Europe and Africa and offers vestiges of its distinguished past in Greek settlements, Roman amphitheatres, Islamic fortresses, Crusader castles, Romanesque chapels, Gothic cathedrals, Cistercian convents and Benedictine monasteries. Over the past 100 years however it has been the turn of the province to leave its imprint on the rest of the world through the work of its most celebrated sons, Antoni Gaudí, Pau Casals, Joan Miró, Salvador Dalí, Antoni Tàpies and its adopted son Picasso. Catalonia may have generously bequeathed to the world its artists but it has sensibly retained for itself some of their greatest museums. In Figueres we find the only museum in Europe dedicated to the work of Salvador Dalí and in Barcelona are the superb Miró and Picasso museums. Gaudí also has two small museums in the capital and the Pau Casals Museum is located in the master cellist's old home at El Vendrell. For those with insatiable cultural appetites, Catalonia has a further 300 museums ranging from the wacky (Museu Darder in Banyoles) to the exquisite (Barcelona's Museu d'Art de Catalunya).

Catalonia's four major cities and provinces – Tarragona, Barcelona, Girona and Lleida – each possess a distinctive cultural feel. Barcelona is my, and many others', favourite Mediterranean city, but the balcony and Roman amphitheatre of Tarragona, the Arabic fortress at Tortosa, the imposing Gothic cathedral of Lleida and the cobbled alleyways of Girona's old Jewish Quarter provide each with a unique personality.

A brief historical sketch of the Catalan people

In 1137, following the marriage of Count Ramón Berenguer IV and Petronella of Aragón at the first dawn of the Catalonian Golden Age, the people's constitutional allegiance to the Crown was hardly slavish. 'We who are as good as you swear to you who are no better than we, to accept you as our king and sovereign lord, provided you observe all our liberties and laws; but if not, not.'

With oaths of allegiance like this, it's easy to understand how easily anarchism caught fire in the Catalan mind in the 19th and 20th centuries. But Catalan militancy (like the medieval knights, the province chose St George as its patron) is as dedicated to liberal ideals as it is to its own independence. The Civil War, so well documented in Orwell's *Homage to Catalonia*, spawned the 20th century's most radical crusades for free love, women's rights and vegetarianism. Progressive ethics, fierce independence and idealism tempered by commercial pragmatism (or *seny* – which can be roughly translated as 'savvy' or 'nous') perhaps explains the Catalan people's durability as well as their economic and artistic pre-eminence in Spain.

Catalans do not tire of telling of their differences from the rest of Spain, of their Europeanism, their Mediterraneanism, their progressiveness and tolerance. One Barcelonan friend admitted, 'We are not liked in Spain. The Balearics are our closest friends but they do not like us either.' Outside the province Catalans have a reputation for meanness which is undeserved (their prudence however might explain why their economy is in better shape than other provinces). Throughout Spain the Catalans are derisorily known as *Polacos* (Poles) because of their geographical and cultural distance. There is of course more than a tinge of jealousy that has attached itself to the extraordinary Catalan success story of the past thirty years and quite naturally the Catalans have a few nicknames of their own for their fellow countrymen (denizens of Madrid are known as *chulo* which succinctly expresses a contempt for them as flashy, macho strutters). A reputation for impenetrability may still be deserved by provincial Catalans but in Barcelona a youthful cosmopolitanism has made inroads into the natural reserve.

A fiercely independent spirit has burned throughout Catalonia ever since Wilfred the Hairy (Guifré el Pilós), the Count of Cerdanya-Urgell, founded the House of Barcelona in 878 and set out to unite neighbouring regions liberated from the Moors during Charlemagne's 'Spanish March'. Legend has it that the Catalan flag was born when Charles the Bald smeared blood from Wilfred's mortal wounds down the latter's gold shield. Regardless of the fact the historical rather than mythical flag was

7

not designed until 200 years after Wilfred's death, it still remains the oldest in Europe.

Wilfred's founding of the celebrated Benedictine abbey at Ripoll in 880 (where he is buried) and the convent of Sant Joan de les Abadesses in 885 (where his daughter Emma became the first Abbess) continued the Christian re-conquest of Moorish strongholds. Count Wilfred's reign began a feudal hereditary line of Catalonian count-kings that would last almost 600 years.

Perhaps though, the Catalan character was forged even earlier than this. The Romans stayed 700 years; much longer than they did elsewhere. But even more influential in shaping the nation's values and beliefs was St Paul and the early Christian martyrs who walked the lands seeking converts. Ramón Berenguer IV (1131–62), along with the Cistercian movement, completed the Christian reconquest of New Catalonia.

Expansion northwards into France occurred in the second half of the 12th century and during the 13th and early 14th centuries, the Catalan navy conquered Majorca, Ibiza, Formentera, Valencia, Minorca, Athens, Neopatria (present day Albania) and Sardinia making Catalonia the most powerful sea-trading nation in the Western Mediterranean and forging the nation's Mediterraneanism.

Hubris struck in 1347 when in just two years one quarter of Catalonia's population died from the Black Death. The pendulum continued its downward swing with anti-Jewish witch-hunts and with the Compromise of Caspe which, in 1412, left this proud nation under the yoke of the Castilian crown. A rapid economic decline followed, hastened by Catalonia's exclusion from trade with the New World for two centuries.

Catalonia's relationship with central Castilian rule has never been easy. In 1640 it threw itself under the protection of the French for 12 years and went on to support Charles of Austria against Philip of Bourbon in the War of Succession. In 1715 with Charles' defeat, Catalonia's rights were revoked, its universities closed and its autonomous government dissolved. The next time they had the temerity to declare independence in 1931 (as a republic within the federation of Iberia), it signalled an irreversible chain of events that left the nation decimated by a three-year civil war (1936–9). Catalonia was the stronghold of the Republican resistance following Franco's military coup. With the defeat of the Republicans in 1939, the suppression of the Catalan language and culture was total.

Cesc Gelabert, a Barcelonan dancer who appeared in the successful London run of *Homage to Catalonia* in 1987, told me, 'When something is suppressed, it doesn't die, it just explodes later.' He should know; under Franco his father was imprisoned merely for speaking Catalan. Folk traditions and the Catalan language were outlawed in an attempt to stamp out regionalism and unite the country. Cesc grew up in what he called a cultural vacuum. Not only was there no platform for Catalan art, at the same time artists from abroad were boycotting Franco's Spain. Those that did visit were steered to Madrid under Franco's directives. Franco would never forgive the part played by Catalan socialists, communists and anarchists in the Civil War. Meanwhile Barcelona's artists were leaving in droves for Paris and America. It would be more than 30 years before a sufficiently optimistic climate drew the artists back to their capital (some, such as its adopted son Picasso, never returned).

It is the Civil War more than any other period that epitomises both the heroic and the perverse in the Catalans. When Valentine Cunningham in his lucid introduction to *Writers on the Civil War* asked, 'What on earth was the Spanish Civil War about? The alphabet?' he was not referring to the worlds first media war (pamphlets, speeches, placards and megaphones fought ideologically with the tenacity of any physical trench battle) but to the plethora of factions known by acronyms as – the PSUC, POUM, FAI, CNT, UGT, JCI, JSU – which seemed to be multiplying by the week. These splinter communist, socialist and anarchist groups, though passionately sincere in their idealism, often hated each other more than they did the fascists. It was this factionalism that was probably the most significant single factor in the Republican defeat.

The Civil War was a war of ideas, a moral war and above all a war of words which drew leftists and liberals from every corner of the world to swell the ranks of the Republican army. To outsiders the Spanish Civil War was a moral crusade whichever side you supported. On the right 'the crusade against communism' was just another chapter in the Christian reconquest that started with Charlemagne's Spanish March. The fascists were supported by the likes of Hillaire Belloc, W. B. Yeats, Evelyn Waugh, Ezra Pound, Jean Cocteau and Roy Campbell (to whom is credited the cheap smear 'The Sodomites are all on your side, the cowards and the cranks.' On the left (either in person in the International Brigades or spiritually in newspaper columns) alongside the Republican troops in their crusade against fascism, stood Henry Moore, Paul Nash, Ben Nicholson, Pablo Picasso (who had a violent hatred of Franco and whose mother and sister remained in Barcelona throughout the war), Pau Casals (known outside Catalonia as Pablo Casals), Benjamin Britten, Ernest Hemingway, Stephen Spender, Pablo Neruda, Tristan Tzara, George Barker, Cyril Connolly, Aldous Huxley, C. Day Lewis, Paul Robeson, Benny Goodman, Charlie Chaplin, Errol Flynn, Marlene Dietrich, Bette Davis, Joan Crawford, Thomas Mann, Octavio Paz and of course George Orwell.

As Arnold Lunn pointed out in his *Afterthoughts on the Civil War*, 'The Republicans began the war with almost everything in their favour. They were in possession of all the great centres of industry. The gold reserves were in their hands. The fleet had rallied to their side. The Nationalist risings in Madrid and in Barcelona had failed . . . The Republicans lost because they sacrificed military to political considerations. The war was seen as a means to an end, political revolution. Officers were appointed for political reasons.' Tactical councils of war were replaced by speeches by political commissars on 'the importance of an orthodox interpretation of dialectical materialism,' and morale-boosting soft porn mags such as *La Vie Parisienne* by treatises on 'The phallic origin of Christianity'.

In Barcelona's barber shops, notices dissuaded tipping: 'Do not insult us with tips; we are nobody's slaves now.' Unlike Madrid under the Marxists where only one church was razed, under the anarchists virtually every church in Barcelona was put to the torch. In the burning city they sang 'The pity is not that there should be a convent or four monks less but that there were once so many.' Madrid and Barcelona, though for once on the same side, were as far apart spiritually as ever.

Romance and heroic deeds were legion. Ralph Bates in his *Campanero Sagasta Burns a Church*, tells of the famous battle in Barcelona's Passeig de Colom and

Rambles, when 500 of Franco's troops, fully armed and with four pieces of artillery opened fire on workers who blocked their way. The mob roared up the avenue, 'hundreds falling, the shells tearing lanes through them . . . They reach the military lines and unarmed men leap on the gunners, wrestle with them, strangle them, drag them to the ground and stab them with knives. Men dive at the machine guns like football players and upset them with their hands, kicking, cursing and tearing with nails, hammering out the brains of soldiers with lumps of paving stone.'

There were of course the heroics too of the international volunteers. The British Battalion earned the honorary soubriquet 'The Shock Battalion' for its part in the near-successful attack on Hill 481 outside Gandesa. But the fascists were growing in military might aided by German and Italian troops and artillery.

Bates talks of the 'white mysticism' of the Catalan anarchist measured against whom 'the spirituality of the average priest . . . is a vulgar materialism.' He claims 'the psychology of anarchism is religious. Its tragic courage, its total selflessness, its sense of drama, its worship of Action, its fanatical belief . . . its burning mystical love for its leaders . . . all this, it is evident, discloses anarchism to be a religion. Does one live like that for a wage increase? Does a man leap at discharging cannon for improved lavatory facilities?'

As power passed from the anarchists to the communists so romantic vision was exchanged for secrecy and suspicion. Poetry readings by Rafael Alberti and music recitals by Pau Casals became rarer. Instead pre-revolutionary police forces (whose members were virtually all communists) roamed the streets stamping out other factions. In Orwell's words (*Spanish Nightmare, Collected Essays, Journalism and Letters*), 'political espionage was growing keener and keener.' Political prisoners were mostly shot and often not even told of their crimes and assassinations were commonplace. In 1937 'the atmosphere in Barcelona, what with the ceaseless arrests, the censored newspapers and the prowling hordes of armed police, was like a nightmare.'

Women in the Republican army had travelled a very long way from their traditional Catholic roles (to which they would shortly be returning under the victorious Franco), wearing trousers and practising birth control. One of the most prominent leaders was a woman called Dolores Ibarurri, known as 'La Passionaria', a fish seller, miner's widow and member of parliament. Her eloquent speech at the final stand-down parade for the defeated International Brigades in Barcelona on 15th Nov 1938 was a fitting obituary to those who had chosen to fight a war they did not inherit but instead claimed as their own. 'Mothers! Women! When the years pass by and the wounds of war are staunched: when the cloudy memory of the sorrowful, bloody days returns in a present of freedom, love and well-being: when the feelings of rancour are dying away and when pride in a free country is felt equally by all Spaniards – then speak to your children. Tell them of the International Brigades. Tell them how, coming over seas and mountains, crossing frontiers bristling with bayonets, and watched for by ravening dogs thirsty to tear at their flesh, these men reached our country as Crusaders for freedom. They gave up everything, their loves, their country, home and fortune – fathers, mothers, wives, brothers, sisters and children came and they told us: "We are here, your cause, Spain's cause, is ours. It is the cause of all advanced and progressive mankind." Today they are going away.

Many of them, thousands of them, are staying here with the Spanish earth for their shroud, and all Spaniards remember them with the deepest feeling.'

The Catalan love of freedom, its fiery idealism, 'the extraordinary morale of these people – their courage, good humour and generosity,' (Louis Macneice *Today in Barcelona*) no doubt was what those international volunteers took with them on that fateful day.

NB All writings quoted here are from *The Spanish Front – Writers on the Civil War*, edited by Valentine Cunningham, OUP paperback.

A brief chronology

?–10,000 BC Paleolithic hunter cave dwellings in Tarragona and Girona.

5000–2000 BC Neolithic settlements.

2000–500 BC Celtic tribesmen from north and Iberians from south settle Catalonia. Greeks found Empuries (550 BC).

500–200 BC Carthaginian occupation.

200 BC–412 AD Romans expel Carthaginians. Tarragona becomes the capital of half of Spain, the imperial province of Tarraconensis. St Paul converts first Christians and first martyrdoms occur.

412–711 Visigothic occupation strengthens Christian culture.

712–718 Muslims invade Catalonia and though their hold there is weaker than elsewhere, they remain in the region until 1149. Both Jewish and Christian civil authorities are allowed to remain under their tolerant rule.

782–801 The 'Spanish March' commences in 782, reconquering Old Catalonia for the Christians. Charlemagne's reign as king of the Franks is elevated to Holy Roman Emperor in 800. The Carolingian frontier with the Moors now stretches from Navarre to Barcelona (which Louis the Pious conquers in 801).

814–850 Power is dissipated as the empire is divided among the sons of Louis the Pious.

850–897 Charles the Bald's seeming disinterest in Catalonia provides Wilfred the Hairy (Guifré el Pilós) with an opportunity to declare independence in 878 and unify the counties of Urgel, Cerdanya, Girona and Barcelona.

897–1045 The hereditary line of the count-kings is established in Catalonia and the nominal Frankish suzerainty is completely rejected by Count Borrell in 986.

1045–1093 Ramón Berenguer I (1045–76) establishes the Usatges de Barcelona (drawn up 1064–8) the code of civil liberties which precedes the Magna Carta by over a century. Berenguer goes on to unite the rest of the Catalonian counties. The terms 'Catalunya' and 'Catalans' appear in writing for the first time.

1093–1131 Ramón Berenguer III acquires Provence through marriage and incorporates that part of present-day France into the Catalonian state. He conquers and quickly loses again Majorca and Ibiza from the Moors.

1131–1162 Ramón Berenguer IV, the Count of Barcelona, marries Petronella of Aragón in 1137 creating the Catalan dynasty of the Crown of Aragón. The Christian reconquest of Tortosa and Lleida is completed and the new frontier with the Moors is established along the Ebre. Cistercian monasteries are established and repopulation of New (southern) Catalonia take place.

1213–1336 Catalonia dominates trade in the western Mediterranean through her great years of expansion. Jaume I's long reign (1213–76) brings the conquest in 1245 of Majorca, Ibiza and Valencia. His reign also sees the formation of Barcelona's Consell de Cent (council of 100), one of the world's first democratic parliaments; the first Mediterranean maritime charter, the Consolat de Mar, in 1258 and in the same year the Treaty of Corbeil which frees Catalonia from its status as a French vassal state. Pere II (Peter the Great) conquers Sicily in 1282 (and establishes the Catalan Corts) and Jaume II does the same to Athens and Neopatria before Alfonso III comes to the throne in 1327.

1336–1412 The Black Death kills a quarter of the population in two years (1347–8), the Generalitat (regional government) is formed (1359) and a series of natural and social calamities occur including the first widespread outbreaks of violence against Jews. In 1410 Catalan domination of the union with Aragón ends when the male line of the counts of Barcelona becomes extinct.

1412–1516 With the Compromise of Casp in 1412, the ascendency of the Trastamara dynasty to the throne initiates Castilian hegemony. Ferdinand I unifies Spain with his marriage to Isabella of Castille (1469) and Catalonia goes into a swift decline. A series of peasant revolts are put down, the Inquisition is initiated in the province, and Jews are expelled. Mediterranean trade becomes of secondary importance (and piracy an increasing problem) with the discovery of the New World (with whom Catalonia is forbidden to trade). Catalonia enters its Dark Age.

1516–1700 The House of Austria is established and Charles I continues the suppression of Catalan maritime trade with America. Felip I's reign (1556–98) imposes Castilian viceroys on Catalonia. The holy fire of the Inquisition burns increasingly fiercely and the censorship and suppression of Catalan culture is stepped up. Felip II's reign (1598–1621) and the short reign of Felip III sees the Moriscos (converted Moors) expelled (1618–1648). The War of the Reapers (1640–53) is an unsuccessful revolt by Catalans angered by conscription and the high taxes they were forced to pay for the Thirty Years War (1618–48; the Spanish defeat in the

The monument to Columbus still dominates a waterfront transformed for the 1992 Olympics.

Thirty Years War is largely due to the simultaneous revolts in Catalonia and Portugal against the central Castilian rule). Catalonia audaciously declares itself a republic under the protection of Louis XIII of France. The taste of freedom brought with the War of the Reapers is short-lived and Barcelona finally surrenders to the Spanish army in 1652 but the 'War of the Reapers', the Catalonian national anthem, stirs Catalan blood to this very day.

> Triumphant Catalonia
> Will be again bountiful and rich
> Praise the work of the sickle
> Defenders of our land.

1700–1758 On his deathbed in 1700 Charles, lacking a male heir, chooses Philip of Anjou to succeed him thus making the Bourbons, traditionally bitter enemies of the Habsburgs, the legitimate successors to the Spanish throne. The War of Succession between Philip (supported by Madrid and France) and the Archduke Charles of Austria (supported by Catalonia, Aragón, the Netherlands and England) leaves Catalonia completely subjugated by Philip V in 1714 after the 13-month siege of Barcelona. Philip revokes Catalonia's constitution and privileges with the 'Decrees of Nueva Planta' in 1716, the blackest day in Catalan history, when the once mighty kingdom is dissolved and her political institutions and cultural independence go under the heel of centralising Castile. This day, September 11th, is still marked by a holiday. The economic gloom at least soon starts lifting as Catalonia is finally permitted to trade with Latin America, the cotton industry starts its production in 1746 and viniculture is revolutionised to meet the foreign demand for her brandy. Barcelona's chamber of commerce is founded in 1758.

1759–1812 Charles III brings sweeping changes during his 'Enlightenment'. The textile industry expands when Catalonia is finally granted permission to trade with American colonies (1778) and English looms are introduced. From 1808–1814 Joseph Bonaparte (Napoleon's brother) takes over the throne whilst Ferdinand is incarcerated in France during the Peninsular War. Girona is taken in 1809 after a legendary defence. Catalonia's attempts at regaining autonomy fail despite the new liberal constitution of 1812.

1814–1868 Ferdinand is restored to the throne by the Congress of Vienna (1814) and repeals the liberal constitution. The French invade once more and occupy the country between 1820 and 1826. A liberal revolution (1835) interrupts the First Carlist War (1833–39) and is marked by the 'disentailment' (i.e. taking) of church lands by Mendizábal in 1837, but the eventual defeat of Don Carlos' supporters brings with it further repression in Catalonia under Isabel II's monarchy. Against this backdrop somehow the production of cotton doubles between 1830 and 1840 and the change-over to steam power transforms Barcelona from a port to a factory town. Spain's first railway opens between Barcelona and Mataró in 1848. Revolts continue to be put down and the first general strike occurs in 1855 followed by further repression. The resurgence of Catalanism is underlined with a literary revival in the 1850s and the founding of a Catalan press and theatre. The 'Renaixença' is also marked in 1859 when the Floral Games are re-introduced to celebrate the province's poetry and song.

1868–1876 The Democrats support a coup d'état in 1868 and Queen Isabel is overthrown. In the two years General Prim holds power prior to his premature death, he introduces major reforms including freedom of press, freedom of worship and universal suffrage. The role of both the monarchy and traditional Catholic society is questioned by this revolution. In 1874 a coup d'état by General Martinez Campos restores the Bourbons yet again to the throne. International workers' parties are banned. Alfonso XII (Isabel's son) becomes king. The second Carlist War rages between 1874 and 1876.

1876–1913 After 1876 Catalan nationalism becomes a serious threat when, with the Carlists defeated, the church transfers its considerable weight to the autonomy movement which in return becomes progressively more right-wing. Secret labour organisations flourish. In 1882 Valenti Almirall founds the Centre Català party which seeks to unite 'Catalans of all religious ideas or political affiliations, bringing together all who are interested in the regeneration of our character and betterment of our land.' In 1883 Republicans are calling for a Catalan state within a federal state. 1885 sees the presentation of the Memorial de Greuges (memorandum of grievances) to Alfonso XII. In 1886–87 the economic boom is interrupted with the outbreak of phylloxera disease which ravages the province's vineyards. In 1888 the 'Bases de Manresa' by the Lliga de Catalunya proposes an autonomous state along the lines of Hungary. Separatist feelings, as strong as those in 1640, are also fanned by the loss of Catalonia's traditional colonial cotton trade with Cuba and the Philippines when these islands claim independence for themselves. Anarchist bombings and executions become increasingly common between 1892 and 1897. The 'Tragic Week' in July 1909 sees convents and churches burnt in Barcelona in protest against conscription for the war with Morocco. The anarchist unions in Barcelona enjoy increasing successes at undermining the forces of capitalism (the army, the church and finance).

1913–1936 The revolts and assassinations bring about some elements of home rule. Prat de la Riba becomes president of the Mancomunitat, Catalonia's first regional government in 200 years. These gains are reversed with the coup d'état by Primo de Rivera in 1923 and the abolition of Mancomunitat (1925). His dictatorship lasts seven years. Alfonso XIII however dismisses him in January 1930. The left-wing coalition party Esquerra Republicana wins a sweeping victory in the 1931 municipal elections and two days later its leader proclaims a Catalan Republic. A compromise with central government is found and in September 1932 a statute of autonomy for Catalonia becomes law. With Alfonso XIII having abdicated the throne in 1931, following democratic elections which brought the right-wing to power, the Second Spanish republic is sworn in.

1936–1939 The Spanish left wins the elections. On July 18, 1936, General Franco and General Mola lead a military revolt ('a crusade against communism') and a three-year civil war ensues. Catalonia becomes the Republican stronghold (with its anarchist groups championing 'free-thinking' and turning capitalist based industries into collectives) but the shredding of a united front into mutually hostile factions (innumerable sub-communist and anarchist groups) together with Franco's early control of food producing regions and his military support from Italy and Germany (in arms and mercenaries) gives the fascists ultimate victory. Franco enters Catalonia in April 1938 and Barcelona falls on 26 January 1939. The Catalonian President, Lluis Companys is executed on 15 October 1940. The communists and Prime Minister Negrin favour continued resistance but the war is effectively over. The nationalist forces enter Spain's starving capital on March 28 and two days later the Republican seat of government, Valencia, falls. Many Republicans flee the country for France and America. The days of 'white bread' follow when all manifestations of Catalan culture are suppressed.

1939–1960 Catalan repression is severe. Though 'neutral', Spain sends volunteers to assist Hitler on Russian front and, following their defeat, American bases are established in Spain. In 1944 Republican exiles in France (known as *maquis*) invade and occupy the Val d'Aran. Such sorties and ensuing battles continue into the late 1950s claiming 588 *maquis* lives and 248 of Franco's Guardia Civil. In 1959 the American initiative, the 'Marshall Plan' requires some loosening of the dictatorship in return for economically advantageous trading agreements. US bases remain. The end of the period of *autarchay* (isolation) is signalled by the sudden appearance of foreign products on shelves as Spain's closed economy starts to open up to the rest of the world.

1960–present In 1960, the last anarchist leader of the *maquis* is shot in the street in Sant Celoni (the guerilla resistance had moved from the mountains to the towns). Catalonia's coast becomes a magnet for both tourists and migrant workers from Andalucía. Spain's first motorway from Barcelona to Mataró opens in 1967. A decade of growth and modernisation follows. Repression eases until Franco's death in 1975 when Juan Carlos I ascends the throne thus restoring the Bourbon line. Arias Navarro, one of Franco's old guard, resigns and Adolfo Suarez of the centre-right becomes the first president of the new democracy in 1976. In 1977 the first general elections for 41 years are held. King Juan Carlos makes an important speech in Catalonia praising the people's love of liberty. One million Catalans march demanding autonomy and the return of their president Josep Tarredellas. Tarredellas returns to take up the challenge and head the new Generalitat. Regional rule is permitted in matters of trade, primary education, industry and housing. The Communist Party is legalised. A new liberal Spanish constitution provides for greater regional control and in 1979 the autonomous community of Catalonia is created by the Statute of Autonomy (a similar privilege is granted the Basque country).

In 1980 for the first time in 48 years, Catalonia's citizens are allowed to elect representatives to their governing body, the Generalitat. A nationalist coalition is headed by Jordi Pujol (who, in 1992, was still its President 12 years on). Nowadays though, whilst the province is ruled by the right, Barcelona itself has a socialist council. In the mid 1980s the Generalitat abolishes the individual boroughs that constituted Barcelona's Metropolitan Corporation in an attempt to weaken the socialist cohesive direction. The militant separatist terrorist group Terra Lliure ('Free Land') which sought a totally independent country, finding its support dwindling gives up its armed fight on 5 July 1991. The province may have a tradition for radicalism but its *seny* (common sense) and *pactist* tradition have come to the fore since *autonomia* to create a modern, successful autonomous state.

In 1992, while the rest of Spain celebrates the 500th anniversary of Columbus' discovery of the New World, Catalonia hosts the Summer Olympics. Catalan, after Franco's 40-year ban, is one of the four official languages used throughout the competition.

Food, wine and festivals

Food

Whilst you will undoubtedly have heard of Catalonia's beaches, its great Mediterranean capital, Barcelona, and perhaps even its stunning slice of the Pyrenees; it is less likely, if you are a first time visitor, that you will know anything of its cuisine. The great travesty in this is that the Catalan kitchen is the most diverse and imaginative in Spain.

Geography has played a major part in the shaping of the province's cuisine, located as it is on the shoulder of mainland Europe looking out over the Mediterranean. Its kitchen quite naturally imported aromatic herbs such as laurel, rosemary, thyme, marjoram and mint from Provence and olive oil from the Mediterranean but it was its own practice of cooking with lard that was the most important factor of all in creating the distinctive flavour of many of its traditional dishes.

Perhaps the single most important event in Spanish cooking was the publication in Barcelona in 1477 of the *Llibre de Coch* (the cook's book). Its author, Maestre Rubert de Nola, was chef to King Alfons the Magnanimous. The book, originally written in Catalan, was widely translated and ran into 20 editions offering 243 recipes. Other books on Catalan cooking quickly followed, building up an important sphere of influence outside Catalonia. Today Pyrenean country cooking and Valencian colourful excesses still remain fundamentally rooted in this medieval culinary tradition.

One of the strongest traditions is the mixing of fruit sauces with meat, fish and poultry. Chicken with peach, partridge with grapes, rabbit with almonds, peas with sugar and geese with pears are just some of the culinary experiences you will encounter touring the province. An elaboration came in the 18th century with the invention of chocolate which soon appeared at table as a sauce with rabbit, cuttlefish or lobster.

Of course there are regional variations. The Empordà region (Costa Brava) offers the best mix of 'mar i muntanya', sea and mountain dishes, combining chicken, rabbit or snails with prawns, lobster and other marine delicacies. Barcelona, on the other hand, offers its own distinctive seafood tradition with *la cuina al cava* – sea bass or salmon cooked in Cava (see 'Wines').

Traditional sauces served up with meals include *sofregit* (the Catalan version of *salsa española*), *samfaina* (a kind of ratatouille), *picada* (an almond and toasted hazelnut mix), *romesco* (sauce made from small hot peppers) and *allioli* (olive oil, salt and garlic). Fish and shellfish are of course very important as you would expect of a nation blessed with such a seaboard. *Suquet*, the traditional Mediterranean fish and shellfish stew, is widely available as is the gargantuan *zarzuela* with its greater range of seafare and richer onion, garlic and tomato sauce. *Paella* reaches new heights in Catalonia using rice from the Delta d'Ebre. Red mullet and grouper are the most plentiful fish caught off the coast.

The *escudella*, a vegetable stockpot offered as a soup, is widely available and *carn d'olla* is even more substantial combining black and white sausages, chicken, meatballs, pork, lamb, cabbage and potatoes.

The staple vegetable is undoubtedly the haricot bean or *mongetes* which is often accompanied by the local sausage, *botifarra*. These may also be served with chickpeas or lentils.

Plentiful salads are available everywhere to accompany meals and a popular snack is *pa amb tomàquet i pernil* (country bread spread with olive oil, garlic, salt and tomato) topped with cured ham, one of the great Catalonian experiences. And then of course there are *tapas*. The exotic mushrooms (e.g. fried milky *rovellons*) of the Pyrenees and pre-Pyrenees are particular favourites with Barcelonan *tapas* crawlers. Pastries are an important supplement between late afternoon and evening meals and each region and season has its speciality. Such pastries as *panellets* (a marizpan-like confection made with almonds, pine kernels, sugar and eggs) or *postre de músic* (with almonds, walnuts, hazelnuts, figs and raisins) may also be served as dessert but you will always be offered fresh fruit as an option. Another popular desert is *mel i mató* (fresh cream cheese with honey).

The best meals, outside the capital, are to be found in the country *masies* (vast farmhouses, often fortified). Obviously regional cuisine is more difficult to find where restaurants cater for mass tourism along the coast. But a short inland tour, wherever you are, should reward the adventurous. At a modest hotel restaurant, the Hotel Senglar, in Espluga de Francolí, snails were served as appetizers followed by the most exquisite roasted sweet shallots with a *romesco* dip. Next came a rabbit stew and finally the ubiquitous caramel glazed *crema catalana*. At the Fonda Can Mulleras in the tiny hamlet of Sant Privat d'en Bas, about 15 kilometres from Olot, the vast restaurant was heaving with people enjoying the most exquisite *patates farcides* (painstakingly grated potatoes stuffed with minced pork and veal and fried with beaten egg), *conill amb cargols* (snails with rabbit – Catalonia boasts more than thirty different snail recipes) and *ànec amb peres* (duck with pear). A three course meal with wine cost around £10. Catalonia offers one of Europe's finest unsung cuisines at one of its lowest prices.

Wine

In wine, as with food, Catalonia has not sacrificed quality despite its modest cost. When I once commented at a wine tasting how much Catalan, and indeed Spanish wines generally, had improved over the past two decades, my host replied, 'It is not our wines that have improved but your taste.' He was of course absolutely right; twenty years ago the large supermarkets bought cheap wines in bulk from Spain and our palates expected nothing more than coarse plonk that made you fall over as speedily as possible at student parties. Now however Rioja wines have built a considerable reputation throughout Europe and this is threatened to be eclipsed in the next decade by the wines of the Catalan Penedès region (see Tour 1).

Catalonia has four other major wine-growing regions that play supporting cast to the Penedès heavyweights: the Raimat vineyards to the west of Lleida on the border with Aragón; the Empordà wineries (the deep cherry-coloured rosés account for the lion's share of production but there are some fine simple whites, such as the Blanc Pescador, and full-bodied reds), the Alella region, producing smooth, traditional, fruity white wines (many still kept in wooden casks); and the largest of the wine-growing areas, to the south, in the Tarragona province, where wines range from the light La Conca de Barberà to the heavy, savoury wines of the Terra Alta. There are also of course innumerable small vineyards dotting the province like those found in Sitges that produce the town's sweet sherry-like Malvasia.

The most famous wine to come from Catalonia is Cava, led by Codorniu who introduced the champagne method into its operation in 1872 and revolutionised its technology again this century to become by far the world's largest exporter of sparkling wine (producing twice the quantity of the total champagne production of France).

Catalonia's wineries, and Codorniu's in particular, have deservedly earned the nickname 'wine cathedrals' because of the magnificent Modernist architecture that houses their operations. Inside the Codorniu plant in Sant Sadurní d'Anoia you will find posters advertising Cava by some of the greatest turn-of-the-century artists, Raymon Casas' celebrated Art Nouveau design is one example. A tour through the Penedès is a cultural tour in the widest sense.

Freixenet is the other major exporter from Sant Sadurní and in nearby Vilafranca del Penedès are the brandies and full-bodied reds produced at the Torres complex (their Gran Coronas Etiqueta 1977 was considered superior to even the legendary Chateau Latour by one Paris jury not so long ago). Although most Spanish brandy is now made in Jerez de la Frontera (Andalucia), Catalonia has a much longer tradition of brandy-making and was shipping its produce to Britain as long ago as the 17th century. The Torres distillery and that of Antoni Mascaró, also in Vilafranca del Penedès, are the two most important in Catalonia. Mascaró's brandies are distilled in copper stills similar to those used in Courvoisier operation in the Charente and are then aged in individual oak casks. Black Label, the best of the Torres brandies, is similarly distilled and both products resemble a Cognac or Armagnac.

Catalonia has been a land of good wines since the arrival of the Greeks and Romans but today with its modern technology and vigorous marketing it has become one of the world's most important wine regions.

A brief summary of the main regional characteristics is as follows:
Penedès: white and sparkling; light, young, fruity wines.
Alella: Bright, smooth, white wines.
Priorat: red, full-bodied wines up to 18 per cent proof.

Tarragona: red, substantial wines.
Empordà-Costa Brava: Fresh, fruity rose wines.
Conca de Barberà: white and claret full-bodied fragrant wines.
Raimat-Artesa: young whites and mellow mature reds.
Terra Alta: dry white, fruity strong wines.
Costers del Segre: medium fruity reds.
Wine buffs seeking more detail may care to read *The distinctive wines of Catalonia* by Miguel A. Torres, Servicio Editoriales, S.A., Carrer Aribau 20 pral., 08011 Barcelona. ISBN 84-85646-21-0.

Festivals

Every hamlet, town and city has its annual *festa major* initiating visitors into its ancient traditions. At the Festa de la Llana of Ripoll, shepherds and their flocks come down to a typical country wedding. In Verges each Maundy Thursday the macabre Dance of Death by human skeletons plays out the traumatic events of the 14th century when the Black Death took a quarter of the province's population in less than two years. The three-day Patúm Corpus Christi festival at Berga, complete with fire-breathing dragons, demons and a huge dancing eagle, is even more ancient, dating back to pagan times.

At every opportunity the *gegants* (giants) and *els nans* (dwarfs) will be wheeled out to dance and amuse spectators. In La Garrotxa these folk dances are particularly popular (Olot and Sant Feliu de Pallerols are particularly notable). Without doubt Spain's biggest carnival is now the one that takes place annually at Sitges with its exotic Rio-style costumes and colourful floats. Other important carnivals are held in nearby Vilanova i la Geltrú, Barcelona and Solsona.

Processions are commonplace throughout La Semana Santa, Easter week, when Madonnas and crucifixion scenes bobble on *passos* (floats) carried by local men and women. But the single most enduring expression of Catalan culture is the traditional dancing of the *sardana*. Every week there is *sardana* dancing in Barcelona and in the summer months every village and town hosts its own *sardana*. Hands are held aloft in an unbroken circle and a small rhythmical pattern of steps repeats its tattoo to the music of a *cobla* band made up of wind instruments and a bass which together produce a Moorish haunting, melancholic sound.

Another strong tradition is the singing of sea-shanties, *havaneres*, brought over by seamen from South America in the mid-19th century to the seaside towns. Once the preserve of fishermen's inns, they are often to be heard nowadays sung in Catalan and Castilian at open air concerts when festivities are lubricated by *cremat*, a hot rum and coffee toddy. Some of the best known *havaneres* happen at Calella de Palafrugell, Sant Feliu de Guíxols and Palamós (all located on the Costa Brava). Then there are the performances at different towns of the *castellers* who construct, with enormous strength and agility, human towers up to nine tiers high.

Music festivals are quite simply too numerous to list. Festivals in the Girona province alone occur in Besalú, Calonge, Sant Hilari, Cadaqués, Llívia, Vilabertràn,

21

Sant Feliu de Guíxols, Peralada, Rupià, Torroella de Montgrí, Ripoll and Palamós. The days of each town's festivals are mentioned in the individual tours and more detailed information is provided in the Barcelona information section and in the Further Information section at the back of the book.

Part One: Barcelona

When I first visited Barcelona in 1968, the Catalan capital, like the rest of Spain, had been locked away in Franco's dungeon for 30 years and seemed in the clutches of a terminal depression. The only surviving expression of its distinctive culture and independent spirit was the dancing of the *sardana* outside the churches and the chant of 'Barcelona' at football matches.

Just over a decade ago, it was still prohibited to fly the Catalan flag and anyone caught speaking the language (it is not a Spanish dialect as many suppose) would be told 'Hable cristiano' (speak Christian). It is therefore hardly surprising Barcelonans have celebrated the dictator's death with some gusto. In 1987 whilst *The Face* magazine, self-proclaimed arbiter of style, was electing Barcelona Europe's most fashionable city, the Olympic committee were providing the official seal of approval by awarding it the 1992 Olympics. The city, wisely, took full advantage of this sudden fêting. With the funds made available, it commenced a programme that treated its finest buildings to municipal facelifts, its parks were spruced up and its appalling road congestion reduced by the building of new tunnels and ring roads. As one official put it to me, 'There were a million jobs that needed doing in Barcelona and the Olympics gave us the excuse, and the revenue, to get them done.' The rehabilitation would seem complete: Catalan is the medium of instruction in schools and the Catalonian flag now stands at the top of Everest. Posters across the city rightly proclaim, 'Barcelona – more than ever.'

Barcelona is the heart – both cultural and spiritual – of Catalonia. In *Barcelona and its people** Salvador Giner states, 'To this day the great cosmopolitan Mediterranean city draws its identity and strength from the small nation into which it sinks its roots. Its loyalty to the culture, the language and the long and often difficult past of Catalonia is the source of its inspiration and uniqueness. Far from being a hindrance upon its projection towards the outside world, that loyalty goes a long way to explain the city's remarkable will towards universality, its tireless love of work, its enterprising spirit. These features have blended with its people's cult of the creative. In their thirst for innovation they have built one of the most attractive, complex – and perhaps least known – of the great European cities.'

The first important watershed in the making of modern Barcelona was the acceptance of Ildefons Cerdà's plans for the Ensanche or Eixample (Extension) in

---

* An essay in *Homage to Catalonia*, published by the Arts Council of Great Britain, ISBN 0 7287 04781.

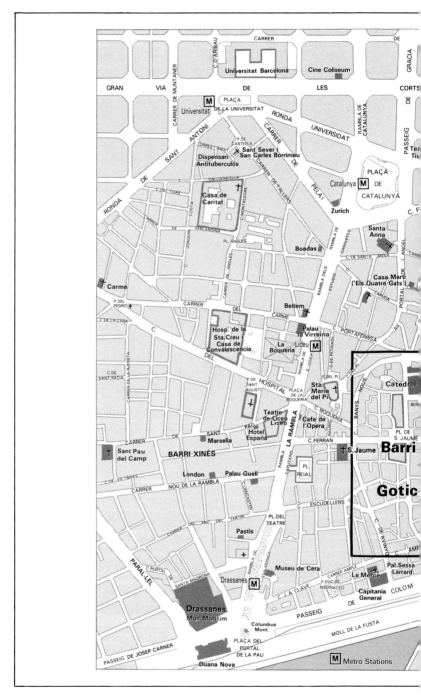

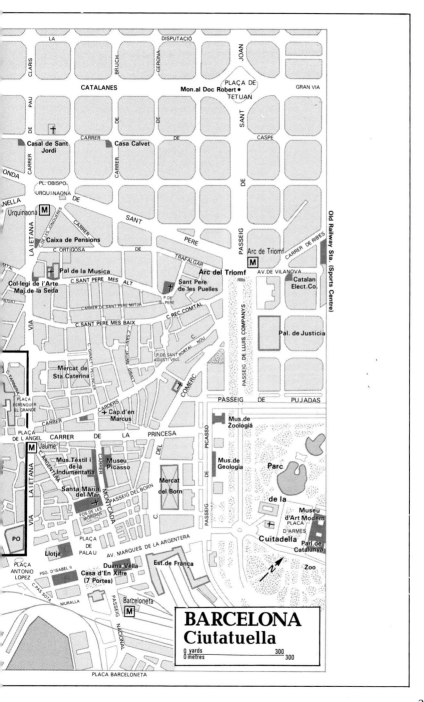

BARCELONA
Ciutatuella

0 yards 300
0 metres 300

1859. The medieval walls that had confined the middle classes to three square kilometres for so long (and bequeathed to the future a perfectly preserved Gothic Quarter) were finally stormed and wide avenues, operating on a grid system, were laid.

At the turn of the century local architects, sponsored by emerging new industrialists, were given licence to create on this fresh canvas a fantasy playground that was the most extraordinary marriage of vision and technical virtuosity. One Spanish guide book (*Spain*, by Dana Facaros and Michael Pauls) boldly states, 'The most compelling reason to visit Spain is to see the works of Europe's most innovative architect, Antoni Gaudí i Cornet.' Certainly to visit Barcelona and not see Gaudí's Sagrada Família, La Pedrera, Güell Park and Güell Palace would be tantamount to visiting Agra and ignoring the Taj Mahal, but Barcelona's favourite adopted son (he was actually born in Reus) was not working alone and Domènech i Montaner, Puig i Cadafalch and others enjoyed similarly riotous successes for their bourgeois patrons. The elegant boulevard Passeig de Gràcia, one of ten roads radiating from the new nerve centre of the Plaça de Catalonia, became the Modernists' pièce de résistance and Barcelona quickly went on to claim the lion's share of the province's Modernist buildings.

For the thirty-odd years that straddled the two centuries, Barcelona aligned itself naturally with the rest of Europe's fin-de-siècle decadence and the huge optimism of the Belle Epoque before it slipped into the cataclysm of the First World War (in which Spain remained neutral, as indeed it did in the Second). These were the great years for Catalan architecture when Modernists turned from classicism back to romanticism to encourage local crafts and skills (much as William Morris had done in England) in decorative ceramics, stained glass and wrought iron. Traditional techniques were also applied to new industrial materials such as reinforced concrete, industrial glass and sheet iron. Together the old and the new created an original flamboyant style using asymmetrical lines and highly coloured floral ornamentation against the sobriety of red brick and graceful Gothic arches.

Running through the new architecture was a strong nationalist philosophy that was also being clearly felt in other areas. In 1879 a Catalan newspaper, *Diari Catala*, was first published, in 1895 football appeared and became the new Catalan religion (with Barcelona FC's Nou Camp its new cathedral) and in 1897 Gelabert made his first cinema films in the capital. Literature of the time recalled the golden age of self-government and in the arts generally Catalanism was dominant.

New industrial centres grew around the city and these, together with some villages in the plain (Sants and Gràcia among them), became incorporated into the city in 1897, increasing the population by 50 per cent (and the city's size by 24 square miles) and thus breaking the million mark for the first time.

Today the city claims over half Catalonia's 2000 classified buildings and indeed boasts more Art Nouveau buildings than any other city in the world. Many not-so-wealthy Barcelonans still inhabit apartments in Modernist palaces in the heart of the Eixample for it wasn't until the 1960s that Modernist architecture became appreciated.

Artistically the city is enjoying a renaissance as flamboyant today as the eruption at the turn of the century but this latest flowering has more to do with its new breed of clothes designers, theatre groups and nightlife. Fashion designers like Lydia Delgado and Tony Miró and new theatre groups such as Els Comediants and La Fura dels Baus have made waves throughout Europe. On London's club circuit, name-dropping New York's fashionable discos like confetti won't win nearly as much kudos as a single mention of Otto Zutz or the KGB.

But the city's character is based on more than idiosyncratic fashion and architecture: there are the magnificent mountain miradors of Tibidabo and Montjuïc, the delicious chill of the Gothic Quarter, the harbour promenade and Ciutadella Park. For a Mediterranean city, Barcelona is reasonably well blessed with parkland and so well endowed with trees it has often been called 'the city of the birds' (some call it 'the city of the dogs' for the same reason). The city also boasts more than 50 museums including one of the three leading Picasso collections and perhaps the world's premier Romanesque collection.

Barcelona is the undisputed natural and political capital of Catalonia with a falling population of 3 million (1,700,000 in its central area). With just under 20,000 inhabitants to the square kilometre, it is said to be the third most densely populated city in the world, though this is mainly concentrated in its dormitory satellites. Migrants from the south however are increasingly returning home whilst other Barcelonans, following the general European trend, are choosing to live outside its perimeters and commute. This, together with the new ring road and strict legislation that is curbing the former excesses of property developers, all bodes well for the future. The healthy trading relationship it has established with Japan (who now have their own school in the city and are providing the bells for the Sagrada Família) should ensure its traditional pole position as Spain's commercial capital. Its major industries are chemicals, textiles, cars, electronics, paper, food processing, iron and steel and machinery.

Hemmed in between the Collcerola Mountains and the rivers Besós and Llobregat, the city enjoys a dry, mild climate with only 90 days of rain a year and temperatures rarely falling between 5 degrees C in winter or above 30 degrees in the summer. Humidity is a problem, often forming a fog over the city. Pollution too, off-shore, found by Kustow in the 1970s, gives a new meaning to the saying, 'Barcelona lives with her back to the sea.'

Of course Barcelona, like all great cities, has its warts. The annual 'Spring Raid' on drugs and prostitution has become an institution almost as ingrained as the *sardana* itself. During one of my recent visits it brought in 300 dealers in 24 hours. Behind the Cathedral are the narrow lanes of the Gothic Quarter leading into the rather tame Barri Xino (China Town), the red light district on the other side of the Rambles. The banners of outraged residents demanding the authorities 'Clean up our city' seem to have been heard but in the summer there are still 30 bag snatches daily, drug trafficking and car break-ins are all too common. Transvestisism chronicled by Genet who could be found down at the waterfront when he wasn't in jail or in Paris, is still popular. Bodega Bohemia and the wonderfully tacky Maria del Mar provide bawdy entertainment. But all major cities have their sex industry and quota of crime and Barcelona, thankfully, has none of the rather intimidating atmosphere one associates with red light districts in some other European cities.

Barcelona has been compared to cosmopolitan Paris, maritime Venice and

27

Unmissables in Barcelona

1 The middle section of **Passeig de Gràcia** starting at the Illa de la de Discòrdia and leading up to La Pedrera. The city's most elegant boulevard with fine Modernist buildings and exclusive shops.

2 The central section of **Rambles** including the Boqueria (also known as the Mercat de Sant Josep), Teatre del Liceu (opera house), Plaça Reial and Palau Güell. Spain's most famous street where Barcelonans still gather daily for the *passeig* (promenade).

3 **Plaça del Rei** and the adjacent **Cathedral** – the heart of the old Gothic quarter.

4 **Picasso Museum** and the **C. Montcada**. One of the most important Picasso museums in the world to which Picasso (who was said to have 'learnt to paint in Barcelona') donated a large number of his works. The museum is housed in three contiguous 13th-century *palaus* (mansions) in one of the city's most beautiful passageways (where wealthy merchants lived in their sumptuous palaces).

5 **Poble Espanyol** and **Museu d'Art de Catalunya** on Montjuïc. Poble Espanyol is a collection of important and typical buildings from different Spanish regions. These are real buildings, not models. Churches, bridges, squares and even regional restaurants serving local dishes cover the vast open-air living museum. The nearby Museum of Catalan Art, housed in the Palau Nacional, has perhaps the most important collection of medieval art in the world and has exhibits covering 68 display halls.

6 **Güell Park**. Gaudí's fantasy garden suburb that became a public park. It contains the Gaudí Museum with the master's delightful, innovative furniture.

7 **Sagrada Família**. The still incomplete new Barcelona Cathedral which was Gaudí's lifework and dominates the city's skyline.

8 **Barceloneta**. 18th-century artificially created peninsula which became the fishermen's district and contains superb seafood restaurants. Unfortunately those that stuck their toes into the sand on the beach were demolished or relocated along the Passeig Maritim in time for the Olympics.

9 **Ciutadella Park**. The city's largest park with important museums, zoo and monumental fountain.

commercial Amsterdam. In reality it is probably a perfect blend of all three. Breakfasting at Pinoccio's in the bustling Boqueria market, lunching on the sands of the Barceloneta, sipping horchata milk (made from almonds that grow underground) in the Passeig de Gràcia, taking tea at Dulcinea's, early evening tapas in the Plaça Reial or a nightcap in the Rambla; one feels perfectly safe at the same time as enervated by the sheer adrenalin of a city that may have only recently re-found its feet, but is dancing beautifully.

Tour 1
The Eixample, Pg de Gràcia and Parc Güell

The layout of the Eixample

The Eixample or Ensanche ('extension') is the modern area fanning out to the north of the old town from the Plaça de Catalunya. Modern Barcelona was born with the Eixample when Ildefons Cerdà's geometric plans were accepted in preference to Antoni Rovira's radial plan in 1859 by the central government in Madrid. Cerdà's design transformed a medieval walled town into a burgeoning city stretching from the mountains to the sea. The wide, tree-lined boulevards contrasted sharply with the narrow Gothic alleyways of the medieval town and quickly became the preserve of the rising bourgeoisie. Nowadays few can afford these private homes and as old tenants move out they are mostly being transformed into offices.

The **Plaça de Catalunya** became the nerve centre from which the major thoroughfares of Cerdà's gridiron radiated. The old Rambles to the south (see next section) and the new Passeig de Gràcia to the north meet in the grand Plaça de Catalunya, gathering place of tourists, locals and statues. Here you will find the biggest department store in the city, El Corte Inglés. The **Rambla de Catalunya** (not to be confused with the old Rambles) cannot compete with the beauty of the Pg de Gràcia that runs parallel with it but there are a few Modernist buildings of interest: the **Casa Pia Batlló** by Vilaseca on the left; **Casa Heribert Pons** on the right at the intersection with Gran Via de les Corts Catalanes; and most notably, Cadafalch's **Casa Serra** (1903) at the head of the Rambla where it meets the Diagonal. This important work, untypically for Cadafalch, seems inspired more by the Renaissance than the Gothic. It is now the headquarters of the Diputació de Barcelona.

The Passeig de Gràcia

In my opinion the **Passeig de Gràcia** is the most elegant street in the whole Mediterranean. It contains many of the city's finest Modernist buildings such as Gaudí's Milà House (known locally as La Pedrera) as well as a number of its most fashionable shops. The wide boulevard is dotted with plane trees and undulating lamp-benches designed by Pere Falqués in 1903 with *trencadís* seats (mosaic of different tiles) and maroon and gilt iron globes. Even the pavement, an ocean of waves on hexagonal-shaped tiles flowing up the wide boulevard, is an aesthetic experience for those used to prosaic flagstones.

29

La Pedrera was originally planned by Gaudí to have the world's first rooftop car park.

The first important buildings you come across as you walk up the left side from Plaça de Catalunya appear at the corner of Calle del Consell de Cent. The **Illa de la Discòrdia** (Block of Discord) is a block of six buildings in which the three most important Modernist architects have their work on display. The first, at No. 35, is Domènech i Montaner's **Casa Lleó Morera** (1903–1905) with its dripping silver sands and onion dome cupola. The building now accommodates the lucky workers of the Patronat Municipal de Turisme de Barcelona on the first floor. If you time your visit between 3.30 and 5.30 in an afternoon outside the peak summer season, you're unlikely to be refused a tour of the building (tel: 215 4477). High points are the Provence sculpted romance tale running across the doorways in eleven carved works and the stained glass tribune and porcelain tiles in the dining room which celebrate simple farm life (the Morera family could thus be reminded of their home farm in Tarragona province whilst eating breakfast). The original furniture is now in the Museum of Modern Art.

Three houses further along at No. 41 you will find Puig i Cadafalch's **Casa Amatller** (1898–1900) whose ceramic crow-stepped gables could be gracing a square in Bruges or Amsterdam. The floral Gothic main gallery and arcaded windows are quintessential Cadafalch. Inside, the Gothic pillars provide regular parking bays for the residents' cars. A magnificent marble stairway sweeps up past wooden scalloped doors to the **Institut Amatller de Cultura Hispanica** whose collection of photographs is the best in the city (Open Thursdays only, 10am–1pm, tel. 216 01 75).

Next door, at No. 43, is Gaudí's **Casa Batlló** (1904–6) with its undulating balconies, iridescent mosaic gallery, button tiled roof and large delicate oval

The rooftop tiles of the Casa Batlló resemble the scales of the dragon which the spear of St George, Catalonia's patron saint, pierces. Note, too, the dragon-faced balconies.

windows split into equal hemispheres by bone-shaped sculpted columns. The organic façade, scaled roof, dragon-eyed balcony and bones of victims make symbolic reference to the legend of Catalonia's patron saint, Saint George (the cross that surmounts the cupola even seems to be piercing the dragon's back). Interestingly Gaudí took out one room to prevent it interrupting Cadafalch's lines next door. Nowadays, like so many other Modernist buildings, Casa Batlló is the property of an insurance company who were recently advertising it for sale. Inside the courtyard the organic cavernous womb is covered with pale blue and white tiles and every detail down to doorbells and postboxes is an aesthetic as well as functional monument. You cannot visit the roof without asking permission on the first floor and this is likely to be refused unless you have applied in writing some time ahead.

From the corner of Carrer d'Aragó looking to No. 255 across the street, we see one of Domènech i Montaner's earliest buildings (1880), the **Editorial Montaner i Simon**. There is a debt to the Mudejar style at the same time as a futuristic anticipation in its cog-shaped symbols and unadorned masonry and ironwork. It was for many years a leading publishing firm and is currently an art research foundation founded by the painter Antoni Tàpies.

The **Dreta del l'Eixample**, between the Pg de Gràcia and the Pg de Sant Joan, is liberally peppered with more examples of Modernist architecture. If you don't have time for an extensive investigation, then you could limit yourself to the area between the streets of Aragó, Valencia and Mallorca. This detour can be worked into our tour of the Pg de Gràcia by crossing to its right side and heading down Carrer d'Aragó. After a couple of blocks you arrive at a delightful small chapel, **Pquia Puríssima Concepció** which had a most melancholic organ playing to an absent congregation when I visited. Beyond the chapel is a small market (**Mercat de la Concepció**) with flower stalls, open 24 hours a day, spilling onto the pavement at its far entrance in the C. Valencia. Turning left and heading back towards the Pg de Gràcia we pass on the next corner the undulating balconies, Gothic arches and vertical glass gallery framed by wooden columns of a cluster of Modernist buildings, one of which is the city's **Conservatori Superior Municipal de Musica**.

Turning right and then left will eventually lead you past the **Palau Montaner** at 278 C. Majorca (begun by the eclectic Domènech i Estapé and completed in 1893 by Domènech i Montaner). The building's most notable features are the ceramic frieze on the façade and imposing staircase inside. The building now houses the central government's Catalonian representative.

Returning to the far side of the Pg de Gràcia, immediately opposite its intersection with C. Majorca, is another Modernist building, the **Casa Enric Batlló** by Vilaseca. A short way further up the Pg de Gràcia we come to the **Boulevard Rosa**, an arcade of boutiques whose tentacles spread to each of the four streets that make up the block. The Boulevard Rosa houses 102 shops and is where many of the city's top designers have outlets.

Across the next intersection is the city's best bookshop **Libreria Francesa** and on the opposite side of the street at 92 Pg de Gràcia is the street's most famous Modernist structure, **La Pedrera** – 'The Stone Quarry' (officially known as Casa Milà). The building dwarfs all around it and is unquestionably Gaudí's most outrageous marriage of Expressionistic imagination and functionalism. Gaudí broke Cerdà's grid plan by utilising chamfered corners to provide a continuity of undulating line stretching round the intersection of the Pg de Gràcia with the C. de Provença. The bush-hammered unadorned stone curtain wall was hung from a steel structure and completed between 1905 and 1911. La Pedrera was declared a world heritage building by UNESCO in 1984.

The public gather inside the inner courtyard beneath the winding stairwell (there's also a ramp to the underground car park – originally Gaudí had planned a futuristic roof car park) on the hour at 10, 11 and 12am and 1pm on Monday–Saturday, before being led up the less impressive service staircase to the roof whose crazed switchback would induce instant seasickness if it weren't for the fixed landmarks of the Sagrada Família and Tibidabo on the horizon. Parabolic brick arches support the bizarre drunken roof terrace which is guarded by abstract ceramic creatures (disguised air vents).

Behind and below you is a perfect example of what Cerdà had originally planned

Antoni Gaudí (1852–1926)

In 1878, the same year that Gaudí completed his architectural studies, he met his wealthy patron Count Eusebi Güell. Astonishingly, just five years later he was appointed chief architect of the city's projected new cathedral, La Sagrada Família. Ironically, the man who symbolises the flamboyance of European Modernist architecture was a deeply religious, conservative man who was a founder-member of the very reactionary Catholic Cercle Artístic de Sant Lluc (who opposed the Modernists). Fortunately Gaudí possessed the vision, audacity and technique to transcend both his own prejudices and the limits of the dominant schools of his time. He lived modestly (in a hut in the Sagrada Família for most of the last 15 years of his life) and died under a tram in Barcelona in 1926 at the age of 74.

Born in Reus in 1852, Gaudí was fortunate to survive his childhood. He was a sickly baby fed on medicinal mushrooms to dull the pains of his rheumatic fever. Catalans have always referred to their eccentrics as those 'touched by the mushrooms'. Perhaps the hallucinogenic mushrooms that grow in the nearby hills go some way in explaining the preposterous visions of this eccentric genius.

Gaudí's unusually long period of architectural study (nine years instead of the usual five) was necessitated not because of dullness as a student but because of a desire to master a wide range of traditional skills and crafts that would then be applied to modern building materials. He became an expert builder, carpenter, ceramicist and iron-worker. Gaudí always designed the first object whether it was a door handle or a church tower before setting his neophytes the task of duplicating the object as many times as the project required.

Perhaps Gaudí's most important teachers, however, were his own parents back in Reus, whose hammering of copper into malleable flat forms for cauldrons and pots provided Gaudí with both the base for his own undulating unbroken organic form and his capacity to visualise the fluid concave-convex space solutions that he later developed (often making his initial models without the use of drawings).

What distinguished Catalonia's greatest architect from his Modernist peers was the extraordinary variety in his work. No two buildings are alike. The unfinished soaring Sagrada Família Cathedral may be the city's most famous landmark, but it is La Pedrera (or Casa Milà), Palau Güell and Parc Güell that have been designated world heritage buildings by UNESCO. What stays constant through his work however is the Pre-Deluvian imagery of spiralling growth through archetypal flora and fauna. Primitive plants and animal-like ferns, palms, snails and armadillos conform to the spiralling principles of growth Gaudí saw as at the centre of creation and which he attempted architecturally to duplicate in an assent towards God (the conch-like towers of the Sagrada Família are a good example of this principle).

Gaudí's principal works are Casa Vicens (1883–5), Finca Güell (1883–7), Palau Güell (1885–9), Colonia Güell (1898–1915), Parc Güell (1900–14), Casa Batlló (1905–7), La Pedrera or Casa Milà (1906–10) and of course his life work, the Sagrada Família.

as the central gardens that each grid of streets would enjoy as a community meeting place. Unfortunately most, predictably enough, soon became workshops and fenced-off individual lots.

The building was recently bought by a local savings bank which has plans to make it a cultural centre when they manage to persuade its inhabitants to be rehoused.

Unfortunately visitors cannot get inside the apartments to have a look round. At **Vinçon**, two doors up, a wallet will cost £40, a small rubber briefcase £230 and a leather holdall £700. Here you might be coaxed in the spending mood with Eno's ambient music, Phil Glass' process music, Stockhausen's silly music or some common or garden classical. There is no crassness at Barcelona's most pretentious store. The interior of this building, once among the finest homes in Barcelona, is extraordinarily beautiful. On the first floor is an exquisitely carved wooden ceiling and open fireplace. It was the house of Ramón Casas at the beginning of the century and his friend and fellow painter Santiago Rusiñol (1831–1881) also supposedly lived here at some point.

At the head of the Pg de Gràcia, you see the **Esglesia de Pompeia** by Enric Sagnier on the left at Number 450 Diagonal (which incidentally is the city's longest street). The church and adjoining Capuchin convent were built between 1907 and 1915 expressing Modernism's Catalan Gothic roots alongside its modern preoccupation with organic architecture. The wooden roof is built on stone arches with highly embellished capitals.

North of the Diagonal, the Pg de Gràcia quickly becomes the C. Major de Gràcia. Before proceeding up it, those with insatiable Modernist architectural appetites may wish to follow the Diagonal eastwards past Salvador Valeri's Gaudíesque **Casa Comalat** (Diagonal 442 – home to the fashionable Si Si Si club) and opposite it Puig i Cadafalch's **Casa Quadras** (Diagonal 373), present home of the **Museu de la Musica**. This largely unvisited building (we were the only ones there mid-morning in August) charts the world's musical history from primitive wind instruments through to the present. There are guitars made from armadillos, trombones that grow into demonic serpent heads and an instrument with concrete blocks whose function and execution are known only to its inventor. The museum is open Tuesdays–Sundays from 9am to 2pm. The window balcony offers a fine view of the street's most important building, **La Casa de le Punxes** (another Puig i Cadafalch design known variously as The House of Spires, The Pincushion or officially as Casa Terrades) a further block along sitting in the triangle formed by three inter-connecting streets at 416–420 Diagonal. It was built between 1903 and 1905 and displays a highly idiosyncratic medievalism with slim conical spires and towers soaring heavenward. Triangular spikes and severe arches underscore the Gothic vision.

A right turn here would lead you back into the Dreta de l'Eixample and through to the Sant Pere district and the Palau de la Musica that is covered in Tour 4 (waterfront section). Instead retrace your steps to the intersection of the Pg de Gràcia and head northwards through the gardens and children's play areas that separate the one-way traffic. At number 132 you will find the **Casa Fuster**, originally an apartment block built by Domènech i Montaner between 1908 and 1911.

The Carrer Gran de Gràcia narrows to burrow through what used to be the village of Gràcia whose atmosphere has been bottled in squares such as the **Plaça del Sol** despite the influx of trendies and yuppies. Here there are some good clubs, restaurants and tapas bars such as El Dorado.

Just before the bewildering roundabout at the head of Gran de Gràcia, take a left down C. Carolines to the very early Gaudí building at Number 22. **Casa Vicens** (1883–88) was commissioned by a wealthy tile manufacturer and shows Gaudí's fascination with North African architecture in its mosaic of brick and tile (a postcard of a house in Tunis found in Gaudí's possessions after his death bears a strong resemblance to Casa Vicens). The iron gate with its fanning dwarf palms reaches full fruition at the Pavellons Güell (see Pedralbes, Tour 8).

The C. Gran eventually leads you to Parc Güell but be warned – it's a long haul and it might be better to catch a train from Metro Lesseps (walk 400 metres up Travessera de Dalt then left up C. Labrand) or, if your budget allows, hail a cab.

Parc Güell (Carrer d'Olot)

Parc Güell (1900–1914) is a children's paradise with a dragon slide, womb-like subterranean passageways, a hundred drunken pillars, and 'gingerbread' houses. The greatest surprise is that it was never designed for children.

Again it was Eusebi Güell who commissioned Gaudí to build a garden city with 60

Parc Güell's gingerbread houses and dragon slides have been requisitioned by Barcelona's children.

35

homes. Only two were ever completed and in 1922 the complex became a public park. One of the two completed buildings was Gaudí's residence, though surprisingly it was built by one of his disciples, Francesc Berenguer. It has now been converted into the **Casa Museu Gaudí** (Tel: 284 64 46; open daily 10am–2pm and 4–7pm except Saturday). The exquisite furniture on display was designed by Gaudí for the Palau Güell, Casa Calvet and Casa Batlló. There are also numerous items made by his apprentices.

Gaudí was responsible for the basic design and structure of the park, its paths and entrances and the main square with its superb mirador on the lip of the Montanya Pelada overlooking the city. Skirting the dustbowl that is the upper playground is an uninterrupted serpentine bench whose mosaic of broken tiles (Gaudí's own invention) create the illusion of a fairground wurlitzer spinning out of control. The bench's ceramic back ingeniously forms the scalloped roof of Gaudí's Hall of a Hundred Columns below. In fact only 86 fluted columns totter in different directions imitating nature's own lack of uniformity. This organic grotto was planned as a market hall before it was hijacked by children who re-invented it as a primeval forest in which to play hide-and-seek.

Many of the memorable ceramics in the park were the work of J. M. Jujol. Particularly noteworthy is the brilliant ceramic dragon that separates the two stairways to the entrance. Here we find a wrought gate similar to that at Casa Vicens and two 'gingerbread' houses with polychrome ceramic towers.

Tour 2
Around the Rambles

Rambles is an old Arabic word for riverbank and Spain's most famous Rambles was once one of the streams that flow from the Collcerola to the sea. Now the only tide is human but it is just as tireless, turning and turning again 24 hours a day. I have a suspicion that Barcelona's Rambles invented street life. For over a hundred years it has been Barcelonans favourite spot for the *passeig*, the evening procession. Apart from the café terraces where late revellers often meet for a last brandy before bed, there are the bookstalls, flower stalls and cacophony of exotic birds complaining from their cramped cages. The Mediterranean light flickers through a leafy canopy of plane trees down a central walkway that separates two opposing streams of traffic.

The Rambles run from the Plaça de Catalunya down to the waterfront for 1.5 kilometres. It is divided into five sections, each with its own distinctive atmosphere. At the head, in the **Rambla de Canaletes** crowds gather to mourn defeats or celebrate victories after each Barcelona FC league match. The Canaletes is a short tacky stretch leading into the **Rambla des Estudis** whose start is signalled by the wonderful Modernist Bar Viena on the right. This section of the Rambles gets its name from the university that stood here in the 16th century. There are a number of spruced-up hotels, such as the opulent Monte Carlo and imposing commercial architecture from the 18th and 19th centuries (e.g. Tobacos de Filipines). The bird market also commences its march down the Ramblas here, giving this section its nickname of **Rambla del Ocells** (boulevard of birds). The name has stuck despite the fact they'll also sell you mice, terrapins or a tortoise. On the right are the buttresses of the delapidated **Esglesia de Betlem** (Church of our Lady of Bethlehem) and opposite it the 18th-century **Moja Palace** which signals the start of the **Rambla de Sant Josep** (also known as Rambla de les Flors because of its profusion of flower stalls). Half way down it is the **Virreina Palace** (named after the widow of the Viceroy of Peru), a Louis XIV-style palace that houses contemporary art exhibitions. Before proceeding here however, as we are now in the heart of the Rambles, detours on both sides are worthwhile.

First, head left (north-east) along the C. Portaferrisa and take the second right, the Carrer Petritxol. This used to be a jewellery centre and is now the most important art gallery in town. Particularly alluring is an exquisite cake shop, Dulcinea, which if succumbed to often enough, may create difficulties for one exiting this narrowest of alleyways. The street leads into the **Plaça del Pi**, the first of two delightful squares littered with artists selling their work, street performers and those who prefer to simply sit at café terraces and watch. Next to this entrance into the Plaça del Pi is one of Barcelona's only *ganiveteria* (knife shop) and beyond it a new covered shopping arcade (mostly gift shops) which connects back with the shoe shops along the Portaferissa. The **Santa Maria del Pi** church (its double bell tower is clearly visible from the Rambles) has a rose window – claimed to be the world's largest – set in an austere Gothic façade (the church is thought to date back even earlier to the 10th century). It is a fine example of Catalonian Ogival architecture, built with only one vast nave and seven ribbed and vaulted sections creating both harmony and simplicity. The church connects the Plaça del Pi with the **Plaça Sant Josep Oriol** (where the Bar el Pi is popular). If you were to continue out of the far square you would come to the pedestrianised shopping street Carrer de la Palla (one of several in this area) which in turn would lead you into the Plaça Nova and the Gothic Cathedral.

Instead, exit from the southern end of the Plaça Nova, via the C. Casanyas, and across the Rambles for the second detour, along the C. de l'Hospital. If you need sustenance before the detour, you can pop into the bakery Forn de Sant Agustí for a Majorcan *ensaimada dell angel* (an almond pastry that is a meal in itself and all for a mere 80 pts). This street is a good place to be at 4pm on Easter Friday when two *cofradias* are hauled over the cobbles and the *saeta* rings out, perhaps more a lament for lost Andalucia, than for the departing Son of God. If you can't be in Seville for Holy Week then Barcelona is as good a place to be as anywhere (because of its large southern migrant population, it is sometimes called the capital of Andalucia). The **Hospital de la Santa Creu** complex is an enclosed Gothic world of its own offering a haven for those feeling numb from the bustle of the Rambles. Notable features are the Renaissance façade and Gothic cloister. The Royal Academy of Medicine with its neo-Classical façade and ancient operating theatre (with 18th-century dissecting table) is also worth visiting as is the Casa de Convalescencia with its important 17th-century polychrome tiles depicting the life of St Paul. The first floor leads to a chapel and to the Central Library (which claims to be the most important in Catalonia), housed in the 15th-century hospital wards.

The Boqueria is Barcelona's favourite market: a fairground palace of chrome.

Retracing your steps in the direction of the Rambles, by taking a left up the Carrer de Jerusalem, you pass one of the city's most deservedly lauded little restaurants, Egipte and a very popular bar, the Jerusalem. This area is always lively, particularly when the Opera House opens its doors. You can now enter Barcelona's most famous market, the **Boqueria**, through its back entrance. The vast steel-girded fruit, vegetable and fish market is a chrome fairground delight that was built on the site of a former convent. Here the Garduña restaurant (on the right as you enter), offers excellent value: the menu de día can be had for around 1000 pesetas. Alternatively you may choose to breakfast on a spinning stool at Pinoccio's (immediately on the left as you are about to exit back onto the Rambla Sant Josep) and watch the stallholders setting up. Free entertainment is provided by Juan, the irrepressible bar owner who speaks no English but has invented an idiosyncratic Esperanto that acknowledges no national boundaries. The Plaça de la Boqueria on the Rambles is paved with tiles designed by Miró and has a neo-classical fountain. In the 18th century this was the first section of the Rambles to be settled. One particularly noteworthy building beautifully restored recently is an extraordinarily Modernist Oriental umbrella shop that has now, sadly re-opened as a bank.

As you enter the Rambla Caputxins you arrive at the **Teatre del Liceu**, Spain's premier opera house with a seating capacity in excess of 2,700 – reputedly the largest in Europe and second biggest in the world. It opened in 1847 on an old monastic site, and became the city's most visible symbol of the gross inequalities of wealth distribution, a constant reminder to the poor of the exclusivity of the new institutions of the Catalan bourgeoisie. It was the only opera house in Europe not to have been built with public or state funds. It is therefore hardly surprising that during the Civil War it became a training ground for Proudhon's anarchist fire-bombers (in fact it was bombed as early as 1893). Somehow the Liceu limped on and has undergone countless facelifts, leaving it with an exterior that is nothing special, though the inside is decidedly sumptuous with six tiers of gold necklaces hanging heavy around a Baroque inlaid ceiling. As no pillars are used in the theatre, the boxes have an unusually uninterrupted view.

The opera season is augmented by a concert season at Easter and ballet season in May. Tours are possible around the theatre on Monday and Friday mornings at 11.30 and 12.15 and commentaries in English are available.

Opposite is the almost equally legendary **Café de l'Opera**, one of the city's favourite meeting points and usually the earliest to open for breakfast and the last to close.

On the **Rambla Caputxins** you pass cane tables and chairs along the central promenade of the Hotel Orient where waiters risk life and limb skipping between the river of snarling cars that separates the customers from the source of their drinks. The Hotel was originally a Franciscan convent.

You are now below the Rambles' waist and off to the right things begin to look decidedly sleazy as hookers start to outnumber hawkers. **Barri Xino** (Chinatown), however, so celebrated by Genet, hardly lives up to its sinister image nowadays and a night stroll through the triangle formed by the C. Unió, Rambles and Avda del Parel-lel is a depressing rather than exhilarating experience with the terrible poverty of migrants from Andalucia all too evident and drug and drink casualties staggering in the alleyways. The further you descend the triangle towards the seafront the more beleaguered this modern urban wasteland becomes.

On the left of the Rambles, the Carrer de Colom leads us into the arcaded **Plaça Reial**, the city's most infamous and beautiful square where pickpockets vie with local stalls, tapas bars and shoeshines to separate tourists from their money. At the centre of the square is a fountain with a statue of the Three Graces. Towering mature palms and street lamps designed by Gaudí dot the large rectangular ochre-coloured square.

The Plaça Reial, designed by Daniel y Molina in the mid-19th century, is becoming a battleground between those wishing to retain its cosmopolitan flavour and community feel (it is densely populated by gypsies, Africans and Andalucians) and those who wish to gentrify them out by attracting back the Catalan bourgeoisie who left in droves at the end of the last century for their new residences in the Eixample. It is feared this programme of gentrification may create a wedge between the Plaça Real and the old city of which it is still so much a part.

At night several jazz clubs open their doors and on every Sunday morning a philatelic and numismatic market is held. The Rambles can be rejoined via the alleyway Bacardí (the city's first covered terrace, dating from the 18th century).

Crossing the Rambles once more, take the Carrer Nou de la Rambla to visit Gaudí's stunningly beautiful earliest masterpiece, **Palau Güell** (1886–1888). The basement stables show his love of simple unclad brick whilst the staircase takes us through progressively more enchanting, celestial worlds until we open out to a vast star-dotted cosmos that is created by light streaming through small holes in the parabolic cupola.

The roof terrace, for the first time, introduced the irregular mosaic of glazed tiles known as *trencadís* that would become the hallmark of the Modernist movement. The building now houses the Museu del Teatre.

The C. Nou de la Rambla continues to burrow through the heart of Barri Xino leading into the Avinguda del Paral-lel (so named because it lies exactly on the earth's parallel 41 degrees 44′). On the left are theatres, such as the Arnau, where many of Catalonia's most famous performers started their careers and where many of them return in advancing years to drink. The area used to be known as Little Broadway and though hardly glamorous, it's still where many go to see shows. It is also the cabaret area where the city's most famous revue at **El Molino** does its own delightfully tacky thing.

The lower section of the Rambles, Santa Monica, is mostly taken up with gambling, fortune telling, fakirs and impressive pavement fakes of El Grecos and Botticellis. The short Passatge de la Banca leads to the **Museu de Cera** (wax museum) which is open 11am–1.30pm and 4.30–7.30pm Monday–Friday; on Saturday and holidays the museum stays open until 8pm. Eventually you arrive at the statue of Colom (Columbus) which signals the start of the Waterfront section of Tour 4.

Tour 3
The Gothic Quarter

Within the Barri Gòtic's 4th-century Roman walls are found the delicious Gothic chills of Hammer Horror sets – a perfect counterbalance to the idiosyncratic excesses of the Eixample. The narrow cobbled alleyways are dotted with startling gargoyles, medieval convents and palaces. Punctuating this history tour of Barcelona's 13th- and 14th-century nobility are converted gourmet restaurants, cafés and bars.

The centre of the Gothic Quarter is Mons Taber, once a far more impressive hill than it is today, around which Iberians and Carthaginians built settlements before the Romans dedicated it to Jupiter and built their Temple to Augustus.

When Barcelona FC football fans chant 'Barsa, Barsa' it is not in tribute to the Carthaginian, Hamilcar Barça, (father of Hannibal) who is said to have given his name to the city. They are simply continuing the tradition for shortening names that locals have pursued ever since the Romans had the pomp to re-christen their home-town Colonia Favencia Julia Augusta Paterna Barcino in 133 BC.

The Gothic Cathedral

The Barri Gòtic starts at the Catholic Cathedral. I was recently fortunate enough to have a room in the Hotel Colón overlooking the Plaça de la Seu on Palm Sunday

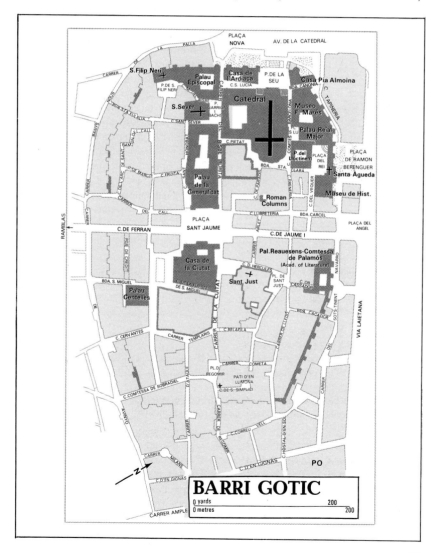

BARRI GOTIC

when the square was filled with five large circles of people dancing the *sardana* around discarded coats, bags and even babies in buggies. Old-timers in suits that had not grown with them sat on chairs making music in front of the soaring Gothic Cathedral of the Holy Cross and Santa Eulàlia. Crowds watched, grasping large palm fronds like centurions beneath the Roman ramparts. This spectacle is repeated (without the palms) every Sunday from noon till 4pm and Wednesday evening from 7pm to 9pm.

To make a proper entrance to the square and indeed the cathedral, approach from the Plaça de Catalunya through the Portal de l'Angel. Having negotiated the street hawkers selling bangles, bags and belts, and stared up at El Corte Inglés' major department store competitor, Galerias Preciados (a surprisingly beautiful building by night when its columns, balconies, wide glass fronts and drapes are gently illuminated), make a brief pilgrimage along the Carrer de Montsió to Barcelona's most famous cafe, **Els Quatre Gats**. The cafe opened in July 1897 on the ground floor of the Casa Martí building. Once the 'gran saló' hosted poetry recitals, concerts and collaborations of all sorts. They published their own journal, *Quatre Gats*, and gave the young Picasso, who spent a good deal of time there, his first exhibition in February 1900. Once the mecca of Modernist bohemians, the cafe is now an elegant restaurant but has managed to retain its artistic ambience with paintings and drawings from those heady days (Rusiñol and Casas are prominent) alongside furniture and fittings by Puig i Cadafalch. To create confusion another El Quatre Gats opened a little further down the alleyway in 1927.

Return to the Portal de l'Angel, which leads into the **Plaça Nova**, abutting the Plaça de la Seu. Here one arch from the Roman aquaduct is still on view alongside the **Collegi d'Arquitectes** (the folk mural of dancing Catalans on the wall is the work of Picasso). Roman stone from the wall will also be seen built into the houses as you proceed on your tour.

Opposite is a narrow alleyway (a former gateway), the Portal del Bisbe leading out of the square between two Roman towers. On one side is the **Palau Episcopal** (Episcopal Palace) with its 13th-century towers, 18th-century façade, Romanesque gallery and triforium windows (beyond it the Carrer Montjuïc del Bisbe leads to the **Plaça Sant Felip Neri**, a delightfully somnolent square whose church stands on the site of a former 18th-century Oratory).

Across the alleyway from the Episcopal Palace on the corner of Carrer de Santa Llucia, is the **Casa de l'Ardiaca**, the 15th-century Renaissance-Gothic residence of Archdeacon Desplà. At the beginning of the century it was used by the Professional Association of Lawyers whose legal wizardry was clearly matched by its wit. On the wall is a letterbox depicting The Scales of Justice. Alongside, five birds in flight show the speed of justice but below them a most lethargic tortoise shows how slowly the court's decisions reach plaintiffs via the city's postal system.

In front of the Casa de l'Ardiaca is the 13th-century Romanesque chapel, **La Capella de Santa Llucia** which contains the tomb of Canon Francesc de Sant Coloma and communicates with the cloister and the cathedral itself.

The **Cloister** of the **Cathedral of the Holy Cross and Santa Eulàlia** is, as you might expect, far from peaceful with every visitor to the city passing through its portals at some point. Because of this it is a very different experience to that offered at Poblet,

The cathedral of Santa Eulàlia in the Gothic quarter stands on the site of the Roman Temple of Augustus.

Lleida, Tortosa or Tarragona. Fortunately, in recompense for lost tranquillity it offers far more attributes to engage the mind than its more meditative cousins.

Obese geese waddle through the magnolias, palms and medlar trees and occasionally risk a shower in the pools beneath the fountain. Skirting the vaulted arcade are small chapels mostly dedicated to patron saints of various guilds (the most memorable being that to the 'Verge de la Llum Patrona de l'Electricitat' – 'The Virgin of Electricity'), decorated with Gothic and Baroque panels and fronted by wrought iron gratings. You may notice that several of the tombs you are walking over have a skull-and-crossbones sculpted on them. During Corpus Christi the fountain beside the Pieta doorway (which also leads into the cathedral) is adorned with cherries and broom and on its jet of water dances the shell of an egg (L'ou Com Balla'). The far side of the cloister offers a fine view of the main dome of the Cathedral and the back of an octagonal bell tower. The **Cathedral Museum** (open daily 11am–1pm), which contains the golden throne of Martin I and a host of reliquaries, is also located off the cloister.

The cathedral rests on the dust of 4th- and 6th-century primitive Christian chapels. The 14th-century Gothic basilica still shows traces of an earlier Romanesque basilica which in turn had been built over the Paleochristian one. The cathedral has three vaulted naves whose slender arches and radiating ribs are unusually beautiful. The choir is the work of Bartholomé Ordoñez, a disciple of Michelangelo, and has a valuable collection of medieval and Renaissance carvings alongside the coats of arms of each knight of the Order of the Golden Fleece who met here in 1518.

In front of the great altar, steps lead down to the crypt where a white alabaster sarcophagus, carved in Pisa in the 14C, contains the relics of Santa Eulàlia, the traditional patron saint of the City. The tomb depicts her trial, martyrdom and crucifixion at the hands of the Romans. Facing the choir at the main entrance is a sado-erotic 16th-century depiction of the thirteen different martyrdoms she is said to have suffered (she was burnt, beaten and then rolled down the nearby Baixada de Santa Eulàlia in a barrel perforated with knives).

Other mysteries of this Catholic church include a 16th-century Black Christ, Cristo de Lepanto, which resides in the large chapel of Sant Oleguer (there are 29 chapels in all) immediately to the right of the main entrance, but which in Lent goes on vacation to the chapel on the left. The mysterious bend in its body is accounted for by a quick swerve to avoid a Turkish cannon ball when the statue served on Don Juan's flagship in the Battle of Lepanto (80,000 mortal bodies were less fortunate). In front of its holiday home is a fine 15th-century Florentine marble font in which the first six Indians brought back by Columbus from the Caribbean were baptised. Another interesting chapel is 'Our Lady of the Good Delivery' which shows the Virgin breast feeding a less than eager Christ. And so it goes on. Beneath the organ was a Moor's head that reputedly spewed sweets in the Middle Ages.

The Catholic Church continued to move in mysterious ways one hundred years ago when the Vatican decided to 'promote' St Eulàlia to the position of Patron of the Bishopric. This cleared the way for bringing in La Verge de la Mercè as the City's official Patron. It is sworn by Barcelonans that four years out of five since that fateful day it has rained the tears of Santa Eulàlia on 24 September, the Festa Major of La Verge de la Mercè.

A favourite busking spot in the Gothic Carrer de la Pietat.

Around the Plaça Sant Jaume

The Sant Eulàlia doorway (particularly beautiful from the street) gives onto the Carrer de la Pietat and thus to the 14th-century Gothic **Casa del Canonge** (House of Canons) (restored in 1929) which now serves as the Presidential office. The alleyway leads into the Carrer Paradís where at Number 10, columns from the **Roman Temple** dedicated to Augustus are preserved. This was the city's highest point, Mons Taber, where the Forum also stood. A hundred yards further on is one of Barcelona's best restaurants, La Cuineta. Retracing your steps past the Portal de Sant Eulàlia, return to the Carrer del Bisbe Irurita where a most delicate overhead passageway connects the House of the Canons with the grotesque gargoyles and medallion of St George on the side façade of the **Palau de la Generalitat** (now the Catalan regional parliament), in the 14th-century this was already the seat of parliament and it was in its Golden Hall that the proclamation of the Republic was signed. It now serves as government offices and hosts ministerial receptions.

The main 16th-century Greco-Roman style façade is in the Plaça de Sant Jaume, which gives entry to the city's loveliest Gothic courtyard with its bone-thin columns and intricate capitals. Also worth a mention here is the filigree work in the 15th-century Flamboyant Gothic Chapel of Sant Jordige (St George). Its prized possession is a 15th-century statuette of Catalonia's patron saint. The back of the building houses the 16th-century Orangery Courtyard whose Carrar marble paving was originally of white and blue tiles. Towering above is the belltower on whose carillon tunes are played at noon. Written requests to visit should be sent three weeks in advance to Gabinet de Protocol i Relacions Externes, Palau de la Generalitat, Plaça de Sant Jaume, 08002 Barcelona.

Across the square, the **Ajuntament, Casa de la Ciutat** or City Hall, is open to visitors every day. Unlike the Palau it does not grace the square with its finest façade but instead has it tucked round the corner facing the Ciutat. Fate has seen to it that the Centre-Right Catalan government office should lie on one side of the square and the 19th-century neo-Classical façade of the Socialist City government office directly opposite.

Here there is another most exquisite courtyard. To the left of the main entrance is the doorway to the ancient scribes' office with a ceiling that dates from 1401 painted by Pere Arcayna. Sculptures by Josep Clarà and Frederic Marès stand on either side of the door. A broad marble stairway leads from the courtyard past the original city coat of arms and Joan Miró's sculpture 'Femme'. The staircase is from this century and decorated with allegorical murals of Catalan life. At the top of the staircase is a Madonna and Child by Josep Viladomat. On the first floor is the sumptuous Hall of the Hundred, a mixture of Gothic, Baroque and modern (begun in 1369 and completed in 1929) and draped in Catalan colours. The semi-circular domed Hall of the New Council with presidential table was built in 1860 and has receptors' and public galleries at the back. Adjoining the Hall of the Hundred are the pointed arches of the 16th-century Gothic gallery. Next comes the modern black marble Hall of the Chronicles (decorated by Jose M. Sert) which commemorates the expedition and conquest of the Far East during the Middle Ages. This in turn leads into the even more modern chapel (1958–64). Other notable rooms include the Sala de Treball with its mural depicting the various guilds and trades of the city, the Quixote Room with scenes celebrating the romantic hero's visit to the city, Sala de la Ciutat with the city's history visually presented on its walls and The Room of the Thirty with its 15th-century painted ceiling, arches and fluted chambers.

Major renovations were carried out to the City Hall for the 1929 exhibition and again between 1958 and 1960. A twelve-storey extension was built between 1958 and 1969 in nearby Sant Miquel Square with its façade overlaid with aluminium reliefs by Catalonia's leading modern sculptor Josep Subirachs.

The Jews of Catalonia

There is evidence of Jewish settlement in Barcelona and Girona before the 9th century and by the mid-12th century, the Jewish communities in these two cities along with those in Lleida and Tortosa, had established their legal rights with Count Ramón Berenguer IV and became known collectively as aljama ('the community').

From the 11th century onwards outbreaks of intolerance periodically flared up, fanned by the Catholic church. Records document attacks on the Call in Girona in 1276, 1278, 1285, 1331, 1348, 1391, 1413 and 1418 when Jewish tombs, goods and homes would be attacked as well as the people themselves. In the 13th century the church instituted the restrictive laws of the Consilia on the Jews and the priests in Girona Cathedral inaugurated the custom of casting stones on the Jewish Quarter from the Cathedral tower at Easter.

Despite this constant persecution medieval Catalan Jewry managed an extraordinary flowering of its culture between the 12th and 14th centuries: ethical treatises, poetry, Talmudic interpetations, philosophical and scientific meditations and even studies of the Black Death were published (the works of over one hundred Jewish writers from this period have survived). Early count-kings often gave over the administration of their treasury to Jews and Jews were also prominent in the practice of medicine.

Throughout the 13th and early 14th centuries the Jewish community was swollen by those escaping persecution in Central Europe to a point where the 10,000 to 12,000 Jews living in the province constituted between four and seven per cent of the population. By the mid-14th century more than 20 autonomous aljamas existed in Catalonia with their own synagogues and rabbi, bakery, butchery, cemetery and miqwe (ritual bath).

The horrors of the Black Death and the concomitant economic slide in the second half of the 14th century found a convenient scapegoat in the Jewish community. By encouraging the notion that Jews were responsible for the plague, the Church was able to legitimise its persecution of the aljamas. 1391 saw the worst outbreaks of violence when the communities were made to choose death or apostasy. Most chose martyrdom. The Jewish community in Barcelona vanished and those in other Catalan towns were decimated. The Disputation of Tortosa discredited the doctrinal base of Judaism in 1414 and in 1492 Ferdinand and Isabella issued the final edict for the expulsion of Jews from Spain.

The Industrial Revolution of the 19th century saw Jews returning from Russia, Turkey and other eastern lands. Fugitives from the two world wars added to the influx and in 1918 the Israelite Community was established in Barcelona. Following Franco's victory many however were forced to leave once more as the witchhunt against 'The Jewish, masonic, Marxist conspiracy' got into its stride. Many of the 5000 Jews now living in Catalonia are recent immigrants from South America fleeing other dictatorships and other persecutions.

To the north of the Plaça Sant Miquel, off the C. del Call, is a cluster of antique shops that mark the centre of the old Jewish Quarter, **El Call**. The Catalans have traditionally prided themselves on their tolerant treatment of their Jewish community during the centuries of European persecution. This 'tolerance' was first shown in the 13th century when the district was ghettoised; in the 14th century they blamed the plague on the Jews and the ensuing riots resulted in 300 deaths (see 'The Jews of Catalonia' p. 47). Finally, in the 15th century, Queen Isabella of Castille banished the Jewish community altogether. The stones from the Jewish homes are now embedded in the Generalitat. On C. del Marlet one stone remains with the Hebrew inscription, 'Sacred foundation of Rabbi Samuel Hassareri, of everlasting life. Year 692.'

Back in the Plaça Sant Jaume, notice the tiled *salida* (exit) sign, on the street corner, a monument to the city's old one-way equitation system. It was in this square, where crowds gather on Sunday evenings to dance the *sardana*, that the Roman streets Cardo and Decumano intersected and both the Forum and the Market stood.

Leaving Plaça Sant Jaume via the main 14th-century façade of the City Hall, proceed down the C. Hercules to the Gothic church of **Sants Just i Pastor**, parish church to the kings until the 15th century and arguably the oldest in Barcelona (though at least two others claim this distinction). As early as the 10th century it was granted the unique Catalonian privilege of validating sacramental testaments. Turning left after the church up C. Lledó will lead you into the C. Llibretaria. On the right is the oldest shop in Barcelona, the Subira Cereria wax shop which dates back to 1760. Turning instead left and right again up C. Veguer, takes you to the 14th century stately **Clariana-Padellàs** mansion. In its **Museu d'Historia de la Ciutat** (open 3.30pm–8pm, on Mondays, 9am–8pm, on Tuesdays–Saturdays, 9am–1.30pm on Sundays and holidays) are works of art and maps showing the city's evolution up to the 19th century. In the basement Roman remains can be viewed. Amazingly the building was removed to its present location stone by stone from the Carrer de Mercaders.

The Palau del Rei

You have now reached the heart of the old quarter, the Italian patio of **Plaça del Rei**, the courtyard of the Great Royal Palace (once the residence of the Counts of Barcelona and Kings of Aragón–Catalonia) which in the summer months provides a dramatic setting for open air theatre and concerts.

The Palace stands at the far end of the square. Its most notable features are the 16th-century **Mirador** (Observatory) and the 13th-century **Palau Reial Major** which contains the most beautiful **Salo del Tinell**, a vast rectangular hall 17m wide and 35m long, supported by six huge arches. It was here that Ferdinand and Isabella received Christopher Columbus upon his return from the New World. On the right of the square is the Palatine **Santa Agata Chapel** (the 14th-century Royal Gothic Chapel) and on the left, the 16th-century Renaissance **Palau del Lloctinent**. The latter was the palace of the Viceroys of Catalonia and contains the **l'Arxiu de la Corono d'Arage**

(Archives of the Aragón Crown), one of the most important collections of medieval documents in the world.

Exiting from the square and turning twice right, you enter gardens adjoining the Royal Palace that were planted by King Peter the Ceremonious. The **Museu Frederic Marès** has two sections: sculpture from pre-Roman times to the present and the far more interesting 'sentimental museum' with its collection of everyday objects from the 15th century to the beginning of the 20th. Some of the delightful oddities here are fans, pipes, cigarette papers and stamps. The museum is open 9am–2pm and 4–7pm on Tuesdays–Saturdays, and mornings only on Sundays and holidays. On the wall, as you leave the museum, you will see the coat of arms of the Inquisition, before arriving at the head of the Carrer dels Comtes.

Skirting the **Pia Almoina**, where 100 of the city's neediest were daily fed, you arrive back in the Plaça de al Seu where you may view the Cathedral façade once more. Seventy metres up, surmounting the cathedral, is St Helen (mother of Constantine) tenaciously grasping the true cross of Jesus for which she spent her life searching.

Tour 4
The Waterfront and Barris Santa Maria, Born and Sant Pere

Although the waterfront has changed a good deal over the past couple of years, the districts surrounding it have remained mostly indifferent to the Olympic fever that has swept most of the city.

The Waterfront

Probably the best place to start this tour is 50m up at the top of the 19th-century **Monument a Colom** (Monument to Columbus) at the foot of the Rambla Santa Mònica where you can orientate yourself. Facing the sea on your right is the **Museu Maritim** (open 10am–1.30pm and 4–7pm on Tuesdays–Saturdays, mornings only on Sundays and holidays) housed in the **Drassanes** (Barcelona Royal Shipyards) that were begun by Peter the Great (Pere II, ruled 1276–1285) and completed at the end of the 14th century, the only surviving medieval shipyard in Europe. Inside, delicate columns and arches support vast naves where naval fleets and merchant vessels were constructed when Catalonia was a mighty seafaring nation. On display are models, navigational instruments, maps, drawings, figureheads and a full scale reproduction of the Royal Galleon on which Don Juan de Austria was victorious in the Battle of Lepanto.

The **Plaça Porta de la Pau**, in which the Columbus monument stands, is graced by the neo-classical façades and arcades of other grand old maritime buildings (including the **Duana** (Customs House) opposite the Royal shipyards). On the seafront, horse and carts can be hired for city tours or *golondrinas* (250pts for half an hour) for a tour of the harbour (the smaller boats further along are 50pts cheaper but you may have longer to wait as they don't leave until they're full). Next to the *golondrinas* there used to stand the second tribute to Columbus, a replica of his caravella, the **Santa Maria**, on which he sailed to 'discover' the New World. Unfortunately it was recently burnt by Catalan activists incensed by celebrations in his honour. Even when Columbus set off on his voyage of discovery he was pelted with eggs by Catalans. Perhaps they had a premonition of the city's demise as Spain turned its back on the Mediterranean to seek out new fortunes in the Americas (in which central government forbade Catalonia from participating for two centuries).

Skirting the harbour is a new pedestrian walkway (opened 1987) which must be close to 100m deep. With its seafood restaurants, modern sculptures, benches and palms, it is already vying with the Rambles for the nightly *passeig*. Between the dead

Mariscal's prawn at Gambrinus restaurant on the Moll de la Fusta.

fish bobbing on the water and the Pg de Colom which runs parallel to the walkway, are a number of raised fish restaurants overlooking the harbour.

The **Pg de Colom** itself has a number of imposing buildings such as the **Capitania General**. Behind the Capitania General is a warren of poor, narrow streets which conceal a number of tapas bars, cheaper restaurants and pensions. The late baroque **Mare de deu de la Merce** in Carrer de la Merce has a Renaissance door. Once inside, you are hounded by alms boxes asking for offerings 'for Purgatory' and 'for bread for the poor.' More often than not, visitors content themselves with a flick of the holy water and a hasty exit from this gloomy dungeon.

The basilica was initially founded in 1267 following a vision of the Virgin by Sant Pere Nolasc who was instructed to devote himself to securing the release of Christian captives from Barbary pirates and providing them with sanctuary. The monastic order folded in 1836 but the Virgin is still offered a song of thanks by Barcelona FC supporters after each victory. Outside, beneath the Gothic façade, they mix with more secular souls devoted to tapas crawls (each of the bars offers a different speciality).

Continuing along the C. Ample, once the city's most prestigious address accommodating visiting kings and nobility, you arrive at the city **Post Office** (with Noucentisme paintings in the lobby) and Plaça Antonio Lopez. You are now back at the waterfront with the Pg de Colom on your right and (at number 2) the 16th-century **Casa de Cervantes** where popular legend claims the Spanish genius lived during his sojourn in his favourite city (though there is no real evidence to substantiate this). On your left is the neo-classical 18th-century exterior and Gothic interior of **La Llotja**, the stock exchange (with the Pg Isabell II leading off to Ciutadella Park). The central patio and Gothic Salon de Contractions with its three fine 14th-century naves are the main attractions here. The Consolat de Mar was where the first legislation concerning Mediterranean commerce was issued in the Middle Ages.

Across the busy main road is the 7 Portes, one of the city's oldest, largest and most popular restaurants. Behind the restaurant is a bazaar selling Asian electrical equipment at bargain prices.

The Barris Santa Maria and Born

Turning your back once more on the sea, set off to explore the Barri de Santa Maria. A short way up Via Laietana, take a right down C. Agullers to the 14th-century **Santa Maria del Mar**, considered by some to be the finest example of Mediterranean Gothic architecture in existence.

The front entranceway to the church, alongside the Gothic fountain, is, more often than not, closed. Try the back entrance, though whether this will be open seems to be based on whim rather than official opening hours. On a wall to the right of the church, is a plaque commemorating The Martyrs of Catalonia who were executed here in 1714 during the War of Succession (in which Britain also participated, on the same losing side). It is for this reason the area has been called the home of the Catalan Independent Movement and to this day modern independentists still gather here to air their grievances.

The church was begun in 1329 at the centre of the new thriving merchant and seafaring communities. The beautiful stained glass windows, vast rose window and two bell towers are gently illuminated at night creating a magical effect that is surpassed only at evening mass by the marvellous acoustics and naked Catalan Gothic architecture found inside (the heavily ornate baroque innards were put to the fire during the Civil War). The central nave is twice as wide as each of the two side naves, the width is the same as the height and nothing disrupts the towering harmony of the octagonal columns supporting the main vault.

Looking down the Pg del Born from the Plaça Montcada, we see the enormous late-19th-century iron **Sala d'Exposicio** (Exhibition Hall) (also used for music festivals) that once housed Barcelona's wholesale food market and earlier, between the 13th and 17th centuries, staged jousting tournaments and festivals. Adjacent is the Pg Picasso where the Homage to Picasso was sculpted by Antoni Tàpies. The surrounding maze of medieval streets of the **Barri del Born** with their Gothic porticoes deserves half an hour's aimless wandering. A good watering hole is the Bar Rodrigo, next to the church.

To the left of the Plaça Montcada is **C. Montcada**, the most stunning of the medieval alleyways. An Arabic poet once said the three sweetest sounds in the world were the voice of the beloved, the splash of water and the chink of gold. In this street, the gold was provided by the merchants who chose to build their palaces here between the 13th and 17th centuries; water courses through their Moorish courtyards sustained riotous green jungles; and the voice of the beloved is found in the canvasses of Picasso whose museum was inaugurated in 1963 in another beautiful mansion, the 13th-century Palau Berenguer d'Aguilar.

The **Museu Picasso** now spans three *palaus* (the third one opened in 1987). It has perhaps the most comprehensive collection of the master's early period (1896–1917) spanning the years he lived in the city or was still returning to it. 'The Harlequin' may be the most famous canvas from this period but carnival posters, menus for Els Quartre Gats and a social security poster are just some of the unusual items on show. His later period is represented by more than fifty variations on his theme Las Meninas which he executed in 1957 and donated in 1968. In all, Picasso donated more than 900 of his works; other donations have come from Jaume Sabartès, Picasso's lifelong friend and secretary, and Jacqueline Picasso.

It has often been said that Picasso (1881–1973), learnt to paint as a young man in Barcelona and without doubt the museum he bequeathed to the Catalan people is one of the three most important in Spain. The 20th century's most celebrated Spanish artist lived in Barcelona from the age of 14 until he finally left to live in Paris in 1904. He made regular returns to see friends and his mother but his opposition to Franco turned him into a permanent exile after 1934.

The museum is open on Tuesdays–Sundays 10am–8pm. Both the museum and the street have been declared national monuments. Opposite is the most beautiful of the *palaus* containing the **Museu Téxtil i d'Indumentària** (Clothing and Textile Museum) (open 9am–2pm and 4.30–7pm on Tuesdays–Saturdays and 9am–2pm on Sundays and holidays).

The Barri Sant Pere

If your legs are up to it you might continue northwards to the **Barri San Pere**, snaking your way up past the **Mercat de Santa Catalina** to the Carrer de Sant Pere més Alt. Here we find Domènech i Montaner's stunning **Palau de la Música Catalana** (1905–08); (tel: 268 1000), home of the Orfeó Català choir. The pioneering use of sheet iron, statues representing popular song by Miquel Blay and the tiled façade with its red brick pointed arcades are easily outdone by the riotous fantasy inside. Innovative glass walls, inverted cupolas, Pre-Raphaelite girls radiating around the central ceiling illumination, Art Nouveau floral motifs and stained glass create one of the high points of the city's life-celebratory Modernism. The building was restored to its former splendour in 1988.

Opposite, in the Carrer Verdaguer i Callís, people have pre-show cocktails in the champaneria, the Cava del Palau. There's also a *bodega*, a *crêperie* and a very good restaurant, Sopeta Una, serving Catalan cuisine at moderate cost.

Across the way from the Music Hall is the gaudy old **Molino Textil** (Textile Mill), in Plaça de Lluis Millet which has a display of silk samples. A short way up the Via Laietania is another interesting building by A. Sagnier, the man who built the church at Tibidabo. At the time of writing it has just been sold by the Laietania Bank to the Generalitat but its future use has not yet been decided.

At the eastern end of the Carrer de Sant Pere més Alt is the 10th-century chapel, **Sant Pere de les Puelles** which probably is the oldest church in the city and signals the end of this tour. If you would prefer to go on to the next tour rather than heading homewards, then continuing along the C. de Sant Pere will lead you onto the Ciutadella Park, the start of Tour 5.

Tour 5
Ciutadella Park and the Barceloneta

The **Ciutadella** takes its name from the old military fortifications built by Felipe V (involving the demolition of 1162 houses in the Ribera district without any financial compensation to owners) after the House of Bourbon's victory in the War of Succession over Archduke Charles of Austria. The fort was built with the express purpose of keeping an eye on the troublesome Barceloneta area after the Catalan resistance of 1714. Nemesis had her day when the French stormed and destroyed most of it in 1808 leaving only the chapel, Governor's Palace and Arsenal (the seat of parliament). The rest of Ciutadella was created by Fontsere for the Universal Exhibition of 1888.

The Ciutadella park

Approaching the park by Vilaseca's preposterous *mudejar*-style **Arc de Triomf** and adjoining gardens, Pg Lluis Companys, you pass Sagnier's Modernist **Palau de Justica** (Palace of Justice) (with paintings by Sert inside) on the left before entering the park through equally ostenatious main gates flanked by Vallmitjana's statues representing Commerce and Industry. On the right is the famous Café (Pg de Picasso) which Domènech i Montaner built for the Exhibition using double thick unclad brick walls, simple geometric shapes, sheet iron, and Gothic decoration. The building was subsequently converted into an arts and crafts centre known as **Castell dels Tres Dragons** and now houses the **Museu de Zoologia** (entomology, malacology, vertebrates). Next door is the **Museu de Geologia** (minerals, paleontology, petrology and geoplanetology). Both are open 9am–2pm on Tuesdays–Saturdays (nearest underground Arc de Triomf).

Next you pass the **Umbracle**, a tropical arboretum covered partially by wooden lathes supported by wrought iron pillars and partially by the firmament. At the end of this passage at the intersection we turn left in the direction of the zoo. Having passed the statue of General Prim we branch left to the baroque **Arsenal** (Plaça De Los Armas; 1716–1727) which houses the **Museu d'Art Modern** with its fine collection of leading Modernist and Noucentista art (Rusiñol, Casas, Nonel, Sunyer, Noguès, Blay, Arnau etc). The museum is open 9am–7.30pm on Tuesdays–Saturdays. The building, once shared will soon be taken over wholly by the Parlament de Catalunya, a body of 135 deputies to which the Generalitat is responsible. The museum will then be removed to the Palau Nacional at Montjuïc.

In front of the Arsenal is a pond with a rather lovely statue by Llimona, called simply 'Desolation', surrounded by water lilies. The pond separates the arsenal from the chapel and high school. Beyond the pond we arrive at a boating lake and the grandiose **Monumental Cascade** (Gaudí as a student sculpted the rocks). The statue, La Dama del Paraigua (Woman with Umbrella) shielded herself from the spray with an umbrella in the lake here and had become another important symbol of Barcelona; for some inexplicable reason, they've now moved the statue inside the zoo's gardens.

The **Barcelona Zoo** (open daily 9.30am–7pm in the summer, 10am–5pm in the winter) is located in the park. It contains some 7000 animals including killer whales. There's a small farm (where children can mingle with the animals). The zoo's biggest draws are the dolphins and 'Snowflake', the only albino gorilla in captivity. Bikes (including tandems) can be rented in the park and boats can be hired on the boating lake.

Leaving the park along the Av. Marquès Argentera, we pass the RENFE **Estació de França** and one of the city's liveliest and largest restaurants, the 7 Portes.

Llimona's statue 'Desolation' in front of the Arsenal.

The Barceloneta

Arriving back at the commercial port, we turn left and enter the **Barceloneta**, the atmospheric Mediterranean fishermen's district with the best fish restaurants in Spain. The very orderly street grid allowed lookouts in the Citadel military fortifications to keep an ever-watchful eye on the district. The narrow streets criss-crossed by washing lines offer a sea-port atmosphere very different from the sombre Gothic Quarter and fashionable, fizzy Eixample.

55

The Carrer Almirall Cervera has a number of good value restaurants and leads from the harbour to the pleasure beach across the promontory. It is here, as the land strip thins, that the most famous of Barcelona's seafood restaurants jutted into the warm sands. These restaurants, really no more than extensive shacks but with magical names like Cal Pinxo and Can Costa, drew film stars, politicians and factory workers alike; unfortunately in the Olympic clean-up those directly on the beach were closed or moved. However there are still enough around to satisfy even the most gargantuan appetite.

Following a *zarzuela* (seafood stew) or seafood salad you could share with the whole restaurant you may choose to continue on to the next tour at Montjuïc via the cable car from the Pg Nacional no more than a couple of hundred yards away. There is a danger of losing your lunch but it's a wonderful experience with a superb view over the congested city to the foothills of the Collcerola Mountains.

It has been said of Barcelona in the past that, unlike Tarragona, it turns its back on the sea. The recent developments, together with the stripping back of the industrial scars along the coast northwards at Poble Nou to accommodate an Olympic village population of 15,000, make this less true than in the past. The city planners have realised any city blessed with such a sea front must make a feature of it. Barcelona has rediscovered its maritime past and once again looks outward over the Mediterranean.

Tour 6
Montjuïc

The tour of Montjuïc commences at the point overlooking the harbour where the cable car deposits its passengers from the Barceloneta.

The Montanya de Montjuïc was known as Mount Juniper during Roman Times. Since that time is has been inhabited by a Jewish community, by gypsies; and most recently dedicated to the Greeks with the arrival of the Olympics in 1992.

Beside the cable car is the café terrace of the Restaurant L'Ast, one of several miradors overlooking the city, the industrial port and the harbour. Behind it are sculpted gardens with cacti, palms, almonds, orange trees and rhododendrons. Above the gardens is the **Castel de Montjuïc**, a less than inspiring fort that houses the **Museu Militar** (open on Tuesdays–Saturdays 10am–2pm and 4–8pm and 10am–2pm and 4–8pm on Sundays and holidays) with its extensive arms collection. The fort does not evoke fond memories for Barcelonans for it was converted into a prison when the Nationalists gained victory in the Civil War. Lluís Companys, President of the Generalitat, was executed here in 1940.

Most of the attractions still standing on the Mountain of The Jews (Montjuïc) were built for the 1929 World Trade Fair and the best way to see them is on foot. First, descend the aptly named Avinguda Miramar ('view of the sea') past the **Parc d'Atraccions de Montjuïc** with its enormous slides, ferris wheel and other rides made doubly exhilarating by their location overhanging the city. A ride on the ferris wheel at night (as at Tibidabo) is an unforgettable experience. From 24 June to 11 September the park opens 6pm—midnight on Tuesdays–Saturdays and midday–midnight on Sundays and holidays. In winter it opens only from midday to 8pm on Saturdays, Sundays and holidays.

On the right the Poble-Sec outdoor summer pool which, out of season, used to lie ignored with its rusting waters unrippled like the ruins of a Roman amphitheatre, has been replaced by a magnificent new Olympic pool. Two more cafés appear, one self-service with a terrace overlooking the city and the other serving reasonably priced food. Here you can pick up the téléférique to the funfair (first stop) or fort (second stop). The nearby funicular will take those who have already visited the sights at the southern end of the mountain back down to street level.

However this tour continues through gardens and woodland to the city's loveliest new building, the **Fundació Joan Miró** (open 11am–7pm on Tuesdays–Saturdays and 10.30am–2.30pm on Sundays and holidays). Functional, simple, sublimely Mediterranean and flooded by light, the museum was designed by Josep Lluis Sert, a lifelong friend of Miró. There's a permanent exhibition of Miró's lithographs, canvases and sculptures downstairs and the upper gallery is set aside for temporary exhibitions of contemporary artists. Miró, unlike Picasso, continued to spend most of his time in Catalonia after the Republican defeat in the Civil War and remained perhaps even more rooted in its culture than Dalí (who supported the Nationalists).

Next you come to the Greek, Roman, early Christian and Visigothic exhibits in the **Museu Arqueològic** (open 9.30am–1pm and 4pm–7pm on Tuesdays–Saturdays, 10am–2pm on Sundays and holidays) with nautical motifs grafted onto its sun-bleached walls. Nearby is the **Museu Etnològic** (open 9am–8.30pm on Tuesdays–Saturdays, 9am–2pm on Sundays and holidays, 3pm–7.30pm on Mondays) with a large collection of artifacts from Asia and Africa, as well as American objects predating Columbus' discovery. Between the two museums is the **Mercat de les Flors**, a large performance pavilion that once was Barcelona's most important flower market. The theatre, with its fresco by Barcelo, offers mainstream theatre but also has a large performance space that has built up an enviable reputation for fringe productions. The seating however is notoriously uncomfortable.

At the **Teatre Grec** where a summer-long open-air festival of music and theatre is held, fork right. Around you is a pungent bouquet of heat, pine and dust, and above you to the left is the main **Olympic Stadium** and the delightful **Jardi Joan Maragall**. Eventually we arrive at the much maligned **Gran Palau Nacional** built for the 1929 Exhibition on two floors and surmounted by four domes. The building contains three important museums, the most notable being the **Museu d'Art de Catalunya** containing 35 rooms and housing the world's most important collection of Romanesque frescoes. The museum is open 9.30am–2pm on Tuesdays–Sundays.

The major paintings in the Romanesque section of the gallery come from the naves of chapels in the Pyrenees (though some come from as far south as Tortosa) and date

The Gran Palau Nacional built for the 1929 Exhibition contains one of the world's most important collections of Romanesque art.

from the 10th and 11th centuries. The paintings were discovered only at the turn of the century, buried under deep encrusted layers of subsequent religious paintings which had helped to preserve the egg- and vegetable-based paint of the originals. One most informative section outlines the laborious and sensitive process that was used to first unveil the paintings and then remove them for transportation.

The paintings are characterised by a naïve flatness, adorned with geometric and animal decoration (each animal symbolising a different human quality). The most famous and best preserved is the 11th-century Pantocrator removed from Sant Climent de Taüll (see Tour 14 – the Pyrenees) depicting God sitting high above the world, the Virgin and His Apostles. Christian instruction was provided for the illiterate congregation in frescoes along the chapel walls depicting the delights hell had in store for lax members. It must have been a close thing, though, choosing between the horrors of hell and the gruesome martyrdoms that awaited Christians (one martyrdom shows a saw going through one unfortunate, another having nails hammered into his face and two being boiled alive).

Other early objects include crude icons of the Virgin and Christ (known as Majesties and showing a far greater dignity than later gaudy representations). There's also a stone commemorating the great Modernist Puig i Cadafalch who was instrumental in establishing the museum.

The second major section of the Palau houses the Gothic Museum spanning 14th- and 15h-century art in the peninsula. The final section houses 16th- to 18th-century art with contributions from the Spanish, Italian and Flemish schools. The baroque section continues the progression from flat Romanesque to Gothic and onto greater colour, depth of field and elaboration. The ceramics section is particularly enchanting with a large number of decorative kitchen tiles, votaries and larger pieces depicting the 18th-century bourgeoisie partaking in 'Chocolatada' (afternoon hot chocolate drink) or dancing the *sardana* whilst black servants attend them.

Exiting from the Palau, flights of steps lead down through the Avda Maria Cristina and thus to the fountains and the **Plaça Espanya**. At night during the summer, the balcony outside the Palau offers the best view of the colourful synchronised light and water show below. The three floors of machinery that were installed underground for the 1929 Exhibition still operate the fountain, requiring a charge of one million volts to operate everything simultaneously. It is therefore understandable that the show is restricted to three hours nightly during the summer and to weekends only out of season (8pm–11pm, with musical accompaniment 9pm–10pm in winter and 10pm–11pm in summer (these times can change so check on arrival with the tourist office). The synchronised music was added to the music and light only in 1982.

Poble Espanyol can be reached on foot (facing the Palau from the fountain it's a ten-minute walk up the hill to the right) or by the free London double decker bus that ferries visitors to and from the village from the Plaça Espanya.

The busy Plaça Major in Poble Espanyol.

The village was erected for the 1929 World Trade Fair in just one year and was not expected to last much longer than that despite the enormous expense it took to erect buildings that were faithful replicas of every region of Spain. Somehow it limped on over the decades and in 1987 drains and electricity were installed and its eight squares, three patios, gardens, Romanesque monastery, Mudejar tower, 18 streets, cafés, workshops and homes were completely refurbished.

Entering through the Puerta de Avila, you will find the information centre and wall map showing the village's layout (there's also a theatre in the village that screens an audio-visual show, 'Barcelona Experience' with headphone translation into various languages including English). Passing under the Sangüesa Arcade you enter the Plaça Major. The square is lined with cafés, The Museum of Popular Arts and a reproduction of Valderroble's Teruel Town Hall (decorated inside by Durancamps).

In the whitewashed Cordoba cobbled alleyways you'll be able to stop off at an Andalucian restaurant and in Segovia you will be able to visit a musical instrument shop. The main square hosts a number of concerts to which the insomniac Barcelonans are increasingly drawn at night. The village opens daily at 9am and stays open into the early hours of the following morning; admission however is between 9am and 5pm.

When I visited, the Gypsy Kings were booming out of a whitewashed retaurant in a narrow Andalucian cobbled alleyway which gave way to the Catalan Quarter. One of the most popular areas is the Font de Prades where the best terrace cafés and restaurants are located. Fortunately meals and drinks do not cost the vast amount you might expect.

From the Poble Espanyol free buses ferry visitors back to the Plaça d'Espanya where this tour ends.

Tour 7
The Sagrada Família and the Hospital de Sant Pau

The Sagrada Família cathedral, whose towers dominate the city's skyline, can be reached by taking a metro to the station of the same name. So far it has taken one hundred years to complete just one-fifth of the city's new cathedral – the cost has

Two Gaudís in one: the Sagrada Família seen from the roof of La Pedrera.

61

been enormous and the controversy intense. This has only added to a notoriety that may well assist the Sagrada Família to eclipse The Alhambra as Spain's best known building in the 21st century.

The cathedral that is not yet a church, that has known existence only as a building site, already has the delicious melancholy of a ruin. Its permanent state of undress however leaves us in little doubt that Gaudí was right in saying that the true test of the architect has always been the church. Looking at the Sagrada Família, we can but marvel at both the egotism and the technical brilliance of Gaudí and even more at the craneless early church builders who inspired him to heave stone heavenward in celebration of the perfection of God's Creation.

Gaudí was brought onto the project in 1883, one year after Villar y Lozano completed the cathedral's conventional neo-Gothic apse and partially completed crypt. Gaudí's brief was to celebrate the largely ignored role of St Joseph in the birth of Christianity. He immediately made his own designs with three façades depicting the Passion and the Glory of Christ. Each façade would have four bell towers, the twelve representing the apostles. Towering above the central nave, would be Christ's tower – the largest at 170m. Immediately below it would be another for the Virgin and, descending, four more for the Evangelists. Of these projected eighteen towers, eight have been completed. No one is foolhardy enough to put a completion date on the project but you do get an idea of what it will look like, if ever completed, inside the museum where a full model has been erected. Only the apse, the Nativity façade and one of the bell towers were built before Gaudí's death in 1926.

In recent years the Passion façade has been sculpted by Catalonia's most famous living sculptor, Subirachs. Its angular simplicity has split popular opinion both as to its success and as to its loyalty to Gaudí's vision.

The **Museum** (open from September to March daily 9am–7pm, from April to June 9am–8pm, and from July to August 9am–9pm) charts, in black and white photographs, sketches and original models, Gaudí's life as well as the history of the project. In the museum they've even recreated the primitive, ramshackle studio which Gaudí rarely left during the latter part of his life. Unfortunately the real one was burnt down during the Civil War (when all his plans literally went up in smoke). Work re-started on the project in 1952 on the basis of the few drawings and models salvaged and copies of the originals saved from the fire by Bonet, Gaudí's collaborator on the project.

At the corner of the Nativity façade, take a look up the stairwell of the eternally spiralling staircase and you'll get some idea of the height, technical brilliance and symmetry of each of the Tarragon Cathedral-inspired Gothic towers. If you manage to catch a rare day when the lift is working and make it to the top and look down you'll know just how Hitchcock's swirling whirlpools feel in the opening credits of *Vertigo*. This conch-like spiralling in plants, trees and shells was the pre-Deluvian dominant image to which Gaudí retured in his primitive vision of all life spiralling upwards towards God.

The Sagrada Família is essentially neo-Gothic and its influence, apart from the high altar in Tarragona cathedral, are local crafts and Islamic architecture. The Nativity façade, representing the life of Christ, attempts, as early Christian churches did, to renew and extend the faith of an illiterate congregation (there was also a more

Details from the Nativity façade on the Sagrada Família.

hard-nosed reason for completing the Nativity façade first – Gaudí believed that it would inspire money to come pouring in to support the rest of his project). The façade graphically chronicles major biblical events: Christ's early career as a carpenter and his later confrontation with the merchants in the temple, the Virgin on the Donkey and her later Coronation; the killing of the innocents (dramatically brought to life with a mother throwing herself between her baby and a soldier who grasps a real sword ready for the execution). Throughout, there is an easy movement between architecture and nature. The columns, in the form of palm trees, represent Faith, Hope and Charity and animals, flowers and leaves constantly interweave to provide a natural mosaic. So far 30 different species of plant have been identified in Gaudí's faithful, tireless representation.

The main façade will be the Gloria façade which has not yet even been started. The Japanese have funded the bells and their own sculptor, Sotoo, has been working on the project (Gaudí is as famous in Japan as he is in Catalonia).

Behind the cathedral is a school built by the master in 1909 to educate (and of course Christianise) the children of the poor. It still operates as a nursery. This superficially humble building is revolutionary in design, containing no internal supporting walls and thus providing a spontaneous flexible space that is perfect for nursery education. One only wonders why more public buildings have not adopted this architectural innovation.

The Hospital de Sant Pau

From the cathedral, the Av. de Gaudí, with its iron street lamps by Pere Falques, leads to another very important Modernist structure, Montaner's **Hospital de Sant Pau**. The complex was designed in 1902 but the execution was lengthy with the master's son, Pere Domenech i Roura directing work from 1912 to 1930. Again simplicity is the keynote with unclad stone embellished with colourful mosaics. Inside, the Islamic influence is strongly evident in the ceiling and there is a magnificent wide staircase. Underground passages link the surrounding medical specialist buildings.

Tour 8
Nou Camp, Pedralbes and Tibidabo

Nou Camp

Futbol Club Barcelona' Nou Camp stadium is located in the Sarrìa district just off the Diagonal, surrounded by a posse of metro stations (Maria Cristina, Palau Reial, Collblanc and Badal). For a football fan, a trip to Nou Camp is the equivalent of a pilgrimage to the Vatican for those of another faith. For a British fan, its sumptuousness, size and friendliness belong to another planet and its trophy room would have even Kenny Dalglish green with envy.

The stadium, built in 1957 by Francesc Mijans, provides seats for virtually all its 120,000 capacity crowd. It is arguably still the most advanced in the world and its training sessions regularly draw larger crowds than top English first division local derbies.

The emphasis at Barcelona FC is very much on the family. The club operates teams at all levels and in all sports from volleyball to roller-skating. Its museum (open 10am–1pm and 4–6pm on Mondays–Fridays, 10am–1pm on Saturdays, Sundays and holidays, but closed on Mondays from Oct to March and on Sundays between April and September (tel. 330 94 11 to confirm)) charts the teams' histories and triumphs. It also has an exhibition of arts connected with the club and runs a multiscreen audio visual show. When I visited, 'fans' matchday' was building to a crescendo with a Barça victory in the late afternoon which had even those philistines who do not love the art rèaching for their hankies.

Barcelona's idiosyncratic sense of style became a rare commodity during Franco's lean years (known colloquially as 'the years of white bread') but there were always those irrepressible souls who continued to do things their way. One of Barcelona FC's greatest heroes, Ramallets, who kept goal in the late 1950s in their best ever side wore all black, kept a comb in his back pocket and a mirror tacked to the inside goal post. When he smoothed his locks after making a save, the women supporters, who gathered faithfully behind his goal each match, went wild. A friend Patrick Buckley, who grew up in Sitges, swears that through his childhood his 'Ramallets' boy's goalkeeping outfit never left his body.

It was the genderlessness of Barcelona FC's support and even more, the classlessness rather than style that most impressed Gary Lineker during his sojourn with the club. Unlike in Britain, the match is discussed in factory and board room (there is no rugby or cricket to distinguish class) and it is this universality, Lineker claims, that accounts for its lack of violent following. Of course the club does have a few hooligans and they do not hide behind euphemisms. 'The Mad Boys' are independentists who attempt to make racist xenophobia respectable by couching it in nationalistic terms, thus providing a political context for their hooliganism. The club's famous slogan is 'More than a Club' and under Franco it was. For 40 years the match provided the only forum in which Barcelona could chant 'Barcelona' – and mean Catalonia – and sing traditional songs. The stadium replaced government and political parties and was the one place Barcelonans could safely use their own language. The club is as important a symbol of the Catalan nation as Montserrat.

Pedralbes

Walking northwards up the Avda Joan XXIII leads you across the busy Diagonal to the **Palau Reial de Pedralbes** (National Palace of Pedralbes) at no. 686. The palace was given to King Alfonso XIII by the Güell family (Gaudí's main patron) in the 1920s and was subsequently used by other royalty and heads of state visiting the city. During the final stages of the Civil War it briefly became Negrin's headquarters. It now houses the **Museu de Ceràmica** (open Tuesdays–Sundays 9am–2pm, tel. 203 7501) and another museum devoted to coaches and carriages that opens 10am–1pm and 4pm–6pm on Tuesdays–Fridays and 10am–1pm at weekends.

The tour now moves into the Av. de Pedralbes (a continuation of the Av. Juan XXIII), the main artery of the fashionable, wealthy Pedralbes district at the foot of Tibidabo.

At No. 7 is another very early Gaudí work, **Finca Güell** (1887). The stables and riding school are now given over to the School of Architecture who devote themselves to studies of Gaudí and whose archives and library boast Spain's most comprehensive coverage of Modernism. Although it is no longer open to the public, still Gaudí pilgrims are drawn to stare at the master's extraordinary wrought Dragon Gate entrance to the estate. You can also see the roof and outer wall of the stables where the world's leading Gaudí expert, Señor Bassegoda, works.

On C. Bajada del Monastir at the northern head of the Av. de Pedralbes is the enchanting 14th-century **Monestir de Santa Maria de Pedralbes**, another fine example of Catalan Gothic, that was founded by Elisenda de Montcada, fourth wife of Jaume II (ruled 1291–1327). The church is open daily but the triple-tiered cloister with its Renaissance well can be visited only on Sundays between 12 noon and 2pm. The murals by Bassa (also 14th-century) in St Michael's chapel, stained glass, alabaster royal mausoleum and examples of religious art, ceramics and Catalan furniture from the 14th to the 18th centuries make the effort of getting to this outpost, now inhabited by Clarice nuns, well worthwhile.

Tibidabo

Tibidabo (523m) is Barcelona's second mountain mirador, located in the Collcerola range which protects the city from the cold north winds. Its name comes from the

Gospel of St Mathew where the Devil makes Christ the offer 'Haec omnia *tibi dabo* si cadens adoraberis me' ('All this I give to you if you fall down and worship me'). The mountain mirador can be reached by taking a metro to Av. de Tibidabo. On the corner with Carrer Balmes is the **Rotonda** built in 1906 by Adolf Ruiz Casamitjana and initially intended to open as a hotel. It is now known as the Hospital Sant Gervasi. This is where you can catch the delightful Tranvía Blau (little blue tram) which trundles up the steep ascent past some of the city's finest palatial residences. The tram stops at the top of the Avinguda where you may enjoy a spectacular view over the city from the mirador. You could do worse than stop here for lunch at La Venta (one of the city's most famous restaurants) or maybe, if your budget or appetite is more limited, just have a beer at the Mirablau (which at night transforms itself into a 1960s and salsa club) whose open window offers an even better panoramic view over the city. If you want to wait for a cheaper lunch, a better value option is provided at the top of the Tibidabo funicular at La Masia Restaurant (the celebrated Catalan sandwich, *pa amb tomàquet i pernil* is heavenly here).

For those driving themselves up to Tibidabo or taking a cab, take the Av. de Vallvidrera to see how an attractive old village can be buried when it's chosen as a summer resort.

A lift can be taken to the top of the church of **El Sagrado Corazón** (The Sacred Heart), whose boys' choir, though less famous than that at Montserrat, is still haunting to listen to at evening mass. The views from the top are truly spectacular. In front lay the city, the port and even Majorca (though you need a clear day for this, as indeed you do to see the Pyrenees breaking through the mists to your left). Behind us are the jagged teeth of Monsterrat, Catalonia's holiest mountain.

Christ looks longingly at the fairground from the top of Tibidabo's Sagrada Corazón.

Tibidabo is an incongruous mix of the secular and the sacred with its modern church, snack bars, amusement arcades, ferris wheel, pizza huts, gardens, hotel and Museu dels Autòmates (Mechanical Doll Museum) (open October–mid-March 11am–9pm weekends and holidays; mid-March–September open at these hours daily). Overshadowed by the ugly Barcelona TV aerial. Beside the church is the **Amusement Park** (open 4.30pm–12.30am on weekdays and 11am–8pm at weekends (tel. 211 79 42 to confirm times)), **Fabra Observatory** and **Gabinet de Fisica Experimental Mentora Alsina** (Alsina Mentora Experimental Physics Museum) (admits only pre-arranged visits). The best time to visit Tibidabo is late afternoon or dusk and the best viewpoint the ferris wheel, if you have the nerve, or the top of the church if you prefer something more substantial than air under your feet.

Barcelona: Practical Information

Note: Full lists of tourist offices – in Catalonia and abroad – are given under Further Information at the back of the book.

Transport

Useful phone numbers in Barcelona

Patronat Municipal de Turisme de Barcelona HQ, Pg de Gràcia 35, tel. 215 44 77.
Town Hall 24-hour information service 010
Airport flight information tel. 325 49 00 or 370 10 11.
Iberia tel. 301 39 93.
British Airways tel. 487 21 12.
City traffic information tel. 325 03 00.
Public transport information tel. 412 00 00.
Train information tel. 490 02 02 or 205 15 15.
Port of Barcelona tel. 317 42 62.
Motorway information tel. 204 22 47.
Telegrammes tel. 322 20 00.
International telephone information: European countries 008; other countries 005.
Generalitat tel. 402 46 00.
Information for young budget-conscious visitors – Centre d'Informació i Assessorament per a Joves, Avinyo, 7 Pral., 08002 Barcelona, tel. 301 12 21.
TIVE (National Tourist and Students and Young People's Exchange Office) tel. 302 06 82.
Lost and Found Office tel. 301 39 23.
Main Post Office tel. 318 38 31 or 302 75 63.
Medical Information Service (round the clock information on urgent medical attention, chemists open etc) tel. 218 18 00 or 415 00 66.
Emergencies tel. 310 50 50.
Municipal police tel. 337 53 53 (emergencies 092).
Radio-Taxi tel. 330 08 04 or 300 38 11.
Weather Information tel. 094.
Professional Association of Tourist Guides tel. 345 42 21.
Barcelona Guide Bureau tel. 268 24 22.

Getting there

Some London tour operators offering Barcelona packages include Mundi Color (tel. 071 834 3492) and Travelscene (tel. 081 427 4445). Iberia (130 Regent St., London W1R 5RG, tel. 071 437 5622) offers an 'Amigo Saver Discount' whereby a second traveller can receive a 50 per cent discount flying from Gatwick or Manchester and 25 per cent out of Heathrow. It also offers good discounts on Atesa car hire.

Students under 26 might like to check out London Student Travel's air prices or its option of a 36-hour return boat/train trip with unlimited stopovers over two months (tel. 071 730 3402).

By car the most direct route is from the French B9 highway onto the A17 motorway at Perthus – La Junquera frontier. The capital is 150km away.

Remember motorways in Spain demand tolls roughly equivalent to the price of the petrol you're consuming.

GETTING FROM THE AIRPORT TO THE CITY

El Prat de Llobregat airport is 9km from the city. Trains to Central Station go every 30 minutes (6.30am–22.30pm), take about 20 minutes and cost 175pts in 1992. A taxi from the airport to town cost around 1900pts in 1992.

Getting around the city

The city is compact and the best way of getting about is on foot. Driving in Barcelona is confusing until you've mastered the alternating one-way streets (between Paral-lel and the Ramblas you could disappear for weeks) and parking is a nightmare. Leaving a car in the street courts the risk of break-ins and official car parks can be as expensive as staying in some hotels (the cheapest car park I found cost the equivalent of £6 a day). **Taxis**, by the time they have negotiated the one way systems, can eat up more than loose change (the meter was starting ticking at 250pts at the tail-end of 1991). Taxi fares are subject to innumerable supplements (entering or leaving airport 150pts, 55pts railway station, 40pts for some items of baggage, 40pts for dogs and so on).

The major tourist information offices are at Barcelona Sants central station, Plaça Paisos Catalans (tel. 490 91 71; hours 8am–8pm daily) and at Gran Via Corts Catalanes 658 (tel. 301 74 43; Mon–Fri 9am–7pm, Sat 9am–2pm). The former offers literature and maps on Barcelona, the latter focuses on the whole province as does the one at the airport international arrivals vestibule (tel. 325 58 29; open Mon–Sat 9.30am–8pm, Sun 9.30am–3pm). Every day from 22 June–15 Sept, between 9am and 9 pm, a roving information service

operates in the Pg. de Gràcia, Rambles and Barri Gòtic. Look out for the red jackets and 'i' (information) badges.

BUS AND METRO

Bus information and routes are displayed at bus stops. All night buses either start or make a stop in the Plaça de Catalunya. The easy to negotiate, ridiculously cheap **Metro** operates from 5am to 11pm (and to 1am on Fridays and Saturdays, midnight on Sundays and holidays). A straightforward bus or metro single ride cost 75pts at the time of writing. The best deal is the ten-trip bus, tube, blue tram and funicular ticket. Ask for 'Una tageta T1 por favor' (*oona takheta tay oona por favor*). It cost 450pts at the end of 1991.

Between 22 June and 15 September a **tourist bus**, Bus 100, stops at all the major sights. The ticket is purchased on board: a full day ticket was expected to be 900pts in 1992 and half-day (commencing 2pm) around 550pts. These buses leave every half hour and can be joined and left as many times as you wish. Red Jackets (cassaques roges) will be on board to answer questions and announce stops (a free booklet to the sights is also provided) but there is no running commentary.

HIRING BIKES AND CARS

Bikes can be hired from Bicitram, Avda

Marquès de l'Argentera, 15 (metro Barceloneta). The city has four special signposted tours for bikers. **Motorcycles** (and cars) can be hired from Vanguard, Londres 31 (tel. 439 38 80). For **car hire**, Atesa has always proved reliable and economical in my experience and they operate a nationwide service. Cars can be picked up at the airport on arrival. *Atesa* Balmes 141, Barcelona 08008, tel. 237 81 40 (airport tel. 302 28 32). *Avis* Casanova 209, Barc 08021, tel. 209 95 33 (airport 379 40 26).

Europcar Consell de Cent 363, Barc 08009, tel. 317 58 76 (airport 317 69 80). *Hertz* Tuset 10, Entol 3a esc D, Barc 08006, tel. 237 37 37 (airport 241 13 81). *Geoffrey Davis* Viladomat 214, Barc 08029, tel. 439 84 03. *Ital* Travessera de Gràcia 71, Barc 08006, tel. 201 21 99. *Regente Car* Aragó 382, Barc 08009, tel. 245 24 02. *Totcar* Av. Josep Tarradellas 93, Barc 08029, tel. 321 37 54.

CAR REPAIRS

car/cycle make	Address	tel.
Alfa Romeo	Prats de Molló, 2-4	205 54 44
Austin Rover	P. Sant Gervasi, 46-48	418 49 50
Autobianchi	Gran Via C.C., 747	245 06 99
BMW	Buigas, 21-23	204 55 52
BMW (bikes)	Alcolea, 145	330 79 54
Citroën	P. Maragall, 365-369	420 04 04
Fiat/Lancia	Balmes, 212	237 97 04
Ford	Mandri, 15	211 00 00
Jaguar	Floridablanca, 133	423 08 82
Mercedes Benz	Urgell, 233	230 86 00
Nissan	Paris, 58-60	239 27 82
Opel	Pl. Tetuan, 19	245 08 55
Peugeot-Talbot	Capitán Arenas, 68	203 32 40
Porsche-SAAB	Tenor Viñas, 8	230 28 07
Range-Rover	P. R. Elisenda Montcada, 13	204 83 52
Renault	Av. Meridiana, 85-87	232 01 12
Seat/Audi/Volkswagen	Gran Via C.C., 90	332 11 00
Volvo	Urgell, 259	430 77 68
Derbi	Av. Meridiana, 156	231 33 60
Ducati	Mestre Nicolau, 12	200 45 40
Honda	Balmes, 120	215 15 17
Kawasaki	Provença, 207	253 48 36
Morini	Diputació, 154	254 87 90

71

CAR REPAIRS – CONT.

car/cycle make	Address	tel.
Suzuki-Puch	Mallorca, 495-497	256 20 01
Yamaha	Muntaner, 416	201 82 88

24-hour repair services are offered by the following:
Detroit, Biscaia 326, tel. 351 12 03 (workshop and 24 hour towing-in service)
Grúas Garcia, Nou Pins 24, tel. 350 75 35 (24 hour towing-in service)
ADA, Londres, 12, tel. 322 44 54 (workshop and 24 hour towing-in service) (members only)

Guided tours

Julià Tours, Rda. Universitat 5, 08007 Barc (tel. 317 64 54 or 318 38 95) and Pullmantur, Gran Via CC 635, 08010 Barc (tel. 317 12 97 or 318 02 41) offer a number of city bus tours. Prices given are correct in 1992.

VISIT TO THE CITY IN THE MORNING
Daily, all year round, leaving at 9.30am and finishing at approximately 12.30pm.
Price: 2,850pts.
Itinerary: Through the main city thoroughfares, with visits to the Gothic Quarter, the Cathedral, the City Hall, Poble Epsanyol and a panoramic view from Montjuïc.

'GAUDÍ-PICASSO'
Daily, all year round, leaving at 3.30pm and finishing at approximately 6.30pm.
Price: 2,850pts.
Itinerary: Along Pg de Gràcia, with views of the Casas Batlló and Milá, visit to Parc Güell, to the Sagrada Família and the Picasso Museum.
Note: The Picasso Museum is closed on Mondays, therefore there is a visit instead to the top of Tibidabo (a panoramic view of the city and the sea from 500m above sea level).

'PANORAMA AND BULLS'
Every Sunday during the bull-fighting season (April to the beginning of October), and on weekdays when there is a bullfight. Departure an hour and a half before the start of the bullfight.

Prices: 6,765pts in the shade, 5,725pts in the sun.
Itinerary: A panoramic tour of the city and entrance to the bullfight.

'NIGHT-TIME PANORAMA AND FLAMENCO'
Daily all year round, except Sunday and holidays. Departure at 9.15pm.
Price: 5,225pts.
Itinerary: A tour of the streets of the city and a Flamenco show with free drink included. Return trip to the hotels.
Note: Reserve in advance.

'FLAMENCO NIGHT WITH DINNER'
Daily all year round, except Sunday and holidays.
Depature at 8.00pm.
Price: 8,750pts.
Itinerary: A tour of the streets of the city, restaurant dinner followed by a Flamenco show with Spanish dances and dancing. Return trip to hotels.
Note: Reserve in advance.

'GALA IN SCALA WITH DINNER'
Daily all year round, except Monday, Sunday and holidays.
Departure at 8.00pm.
Price: 9,295pts.
Itinerary: Dinner and show at the Scala Barcelona. Return trip to hotels. Note: Gentlemen are required to wear jackets and ties. Reserve in advance.

'GALA IN SCALA'
Daily all year round, except Monday, Sunday and holidays.

Departure at 9.15pm.
Price: 5,335pts.
Itinerary: Entrance to the Scala
  Barcelona show and return trip to
  hotels.

Note: Gentlemen are required to wear
jackets and ties. Reserve in advance.

Events and places of interest

Museums and Monuments

All state museums offer free admission to groups of students but permission has to be sought at least two weeks ahead from the Ministerio de Cultura, Museums Department, Plaza del Rey 1, Madrid. Sometimes International student cards will get you in free too. Nearly all museums in Catalonia are closed on Mondays.

There are eight museums in the Parc de Montjuïc (including the Museu d'Art de Catalunya), 11 in the old town (including the Picasso Museum), two in the Ciutadella Park, another eight in the northern sector around the Diagonal (including Tibidabo's Museum of Mechanical Figures), then there are numerous others scattered around the city (including the Gaudí Museum in Parc Güell, and the Footwear Museum).

It's a matter of taste but I'd say the two not to be missed are the Museu d'Art de Catalunya in the Palau Nacional, Parc de Montjuïc, 'one of the world's foremost collections of medieval art,' and the Picasso Museum, Carrer Montcada 15–17 (metro Jaume I) which straddles three *palaus* (mansions) including the most beautiful Palau Aguilar. Here a succession of rooms chronicle the century's greatest painter's work from an eight-year-old in Malaga throughout his long career. Opening times of Individual museums and places of interest are listed under the individual Barcelona tours.

Sardana dancing

Plaça Cathedral, Sundays at noon.
Plaça Sant Jaume, Sundays and holidays
  7pm (summer) and 6.30pm (winter).
Plaça Evissa, Sundays at noon.

Plaça Sant Felip Neri, the first Saturday
  of the month at 6pm.
Parc de l'Escorxador, Sundays at noon.
Parc de la Guineueta, Sundays at noon.

Bullfights

The Monumental Bull Ring, Gran Via CC 743 (tel. 245 58 04). Box office Muntaner 24 (tel. 253 38 21). The season runs from March to September and fights are usually at 5.30pm on Sundays.

Popular festivals

During *The Feast of the Three Kings*, on 1–6 January, stalls of toys and sweets appear all over Barcelona but the best are at Gran Via. Pages or royal postmen collect children's letters from the largest stores to deliver to the Kings. On the night of 5 January children leave a shoe out on their balcony (to be filled magically during the night with sweets) and a bucket of water and food for the Three Kings' camels. The Three Kings' Cavalcade arrives 'by sea from the

Orient' with their courtiers laden with presents to be met by the city's toffs and a multitude of excited children.

Carnaval usually falls between the 1 February and 7 March. The medieval Festival of Sant Eulàlia sees gegants (giants) wheeled out, dancers dancing and actors acting out the Spanish Inquisition.

The Festival of Sant Jordi (Saint George – the province's patron saint) is on 23 April. Originally the festival centred around jousting tournaments in El Born when roses would be presented to ladies. The jousting has gone but the exchanging of roses remains (a rose fair is celebrated in the courtyard of the Palace of the Generalitat). A book fair (instituted in 1923) has dovetailed with this celebration and the day marks friendships with the exchanging of books and roses.

Due partly to the numbers of Andalucians living in Barcelona, Semana Santa (Holy Week) is celebrated with some gusto here. The Gothic cathedral is the best place in the city to view it.

The Fira de Sant Ponc is celebrated on 11 May in the Carrer Hospital, Plaça Pedro and in Sants with trade fair exhibitions of natural products.

On the Eve of Sant Joan, 23 June, the feast of Sant Juan (as well as the summer solstice) is marked with the eating of the sweet or salted 'coca' cake with pine nuts or fruit. Bonfires of old furniture are lit and the biggest fiesta, the verbena, on Montjuïc, is accompanied by great firework displays. Traditional verbena dancing also goes on beside the bonfire at Sant Pere de Ribes.

At the end of June and through July numerous events are held during the Grec festival: theatre, concerts, film, dance etc. Details are available each year from Tourist Offices.

The Catalonian National Holiday – the Diada – on 11 September has more resonance in Barcelona than elsewhere as the day commemorates the city's final submission to Felip V of Spain in 1714 after a 13-month siege. This blackest day in Catalonia's long history, when her institutions of self-government were abolished, is marked by the flying of the Catalan Senyeres flag on every balcony.

The Feast of La Mercè during the week of 24 September celebrates the city's patron with music, theatre and general partying. El Ball de Gegants (giants' ball), fireworks and fireworks display are just some of the events taking place during the week.

Markets

The vast 19th-century riot of colour that is the Rambles' La Boqueria in Sant Josep (metro Liceu) is well worth visiting.

At the Flea Market, Els Encants, Plaça de les Glòries (metro Glòries), on Mondays, Wednesdays, Fridays and Saturdays between 8am and 7pm in the summer and 8.30am and 7pm in the winter, you can buy your garden furniture, second-hand clothes, birdcages, iron tubs, ornamental lights and antiques. I bought a clock and a lamp in 1967. On my last visit in late 1991 I bought a pair of imitation docksiders for the equivalent of £10.

There is an Antique Market (metro Jaume I) in the Plaça del Pi on Thursdays, 9am–8pm (except in August), and a Coin and book market in the Mercat de Sant Antoni, on Sundays, 10am–2pm. The Plaça Reial stamp and coin market is held on Sunday mornings, 10am–2pm. On the first Friday and Saturday of each month a food market is held in the Plaça de Pi.

In the Plaça del Roser an art market is held on the last Sunday of the month,

10am–3pm (except in July and August). There is a *painting display* in Plaça Sant Josep Oriol on Saturdays, 11am–8.30pm and on Sundays 11am–2.30pm (except in August). Note also the *Sagrada Família district painters' exhibition* in Plaça Sagrada Família, 10am–3pm on Saturdays, Sundays and holidays.

A *craftsmen's trade fair* is held in the gardens of Turó Parc, Av. Pau Casals on the first Sunday of each month, 10am–3pm (except in August and September). It includes ceramics, glass, iron work, enamels, lace edging and textiles.

Beaches

The beach at the far side of the Barceloneta is popular and some brave souls even swim in the sea here. Ten years ago, before the cleaning-up programme started they would almost certainly have ended up in hospital. It is the best equipped beach in Catalonia with bathrooms, showers, children's playgrounds and an information service. The beach is regularly cleaned. Officials daily check the chemical and

bacteriological purity of the water.

Most Barcelonans however, given the opportunity will head out of town either north up to the Costa Brava or to Castelldefels and Sitges on the Costa Daurada. Trains leave Sants station every 30 minutes for Sitges (40 minute journey). Make sure you get the 'semi-directo' train or all you may see of the beach is a blur as the train whizzes by.

Shops and services

Shopping and banks

Shops are generally open 9am–1pm and 4pm–8pm on Mondays–Saturdays; department stores stay open 10am–9pm without a break. The two major department stores are El Corte Inglés, Diagonal 617–619, and Galerias Preciados, Diagonal 471–473 but their most visited branches are respectively at Plaça Catalunya and Portal de l'Angel.
The Centre Permanent d'Artesania. Pg, de Gràcia 55 has three permanent craft exhibition halls where samples of the work of new Catalonian artisans are on continuous display.

Banks are open Mon–Fri 9am–2pm, Sat 9am–1pm. Banco de Vizcaya at RENFE train stations are open 8.15am–10pm (and even later in the summer) but closed on winter holidays between 2pm and 4pm) but the exchange commission is around 700pts. American Express is at 101 Pg de Gràcia and is open every day until 6pm.
Amex tel. 217 00 70.
Diners Club tel. 302 14 28.
Visa and Master Charge tel. 315 25 12.

Fashion shops

Clothes and accessories are extremely stylish but can be expensive unless you get away from the fashionable areas around Pg de Gràcia. Window shopping

here though is a must. Boulevard Rosa (metro Pg de Gràcia) opposite Gaudí's La Pedrera, is a pioneering shopping arcade opened in 1978; it extends through the whole block formed by four adjacent streets. Many of Barcelona's top designers (e.g. Lydia Delgado at Galon Glace) have their outlets in the 102 shops here. The arcade is open 10.30am–8.30pm on Mondays–Saturdays. Entrances: Pg de Gràcia 55, Aragó 259, Rambla Catalunya 66, Valencia 266.

Other fashionable designers such as Luis Fortes, Toni Miró and Ramón Ramis can be found in shops across the city. Miró is the hottest name at the moment and his shop Boutique Groc, Rambla Catalunya 100 (metro Catalunya) is worth a visit.

Most Barcelonans do their major clothes shopping during the August sales when prices are slashed by up to 60 per cent.

Very fashionable too is the Metronom gallery in the dockland (Barceloneta metro). There's also a young designers' gallery of ten shops. Galeries Ferrissa, in the Barri Gòtic Quarter (Portaferrissa 23). It is open 10am–2pm and 4.30pm–8.30pm on Mondays–Saturdays.

Vinçon, next door to La Pedrera on the Pg de Gràcia, is where style-vultures shop. Owned by Fernando Amat, it has serious furniture on the first floor, bar stools and objets d'art downstairs. Overpriced but great fun browsing.

Tipping

Even though service is included, in luxury establishments you should leave a 10 per cent tip, in fairly smart establishments, 100pts and loose change in others. In bars leave 40pts per drink or 20pts in tavernas. Taxi drivers are happy with small change (30pts on 500 is fine).

Telephones

Telephones work on the same system as British phones. With older boxes, deposit 5, 25 or 100pts coins before someone answers; with the newer boxes deposit the coins before you dial. Reverse charge calls cannot be made from public phone boxes. From private call boxes dial 005 for international reverse charges or 009 for reverse charge calls within Spain. Phone rates are about double what they are in the UK so reverse charging is a good idea. To dial direct, dial 07 and wait for a continuous tone before dialling the country code. Directory enquiries is 003.

Electricity

In Catalonia, as in the rest of Spain, the electrical system operates on 220 volts but many hotels have 110–220 converter plugs available for guests to use. Plugs are mostly the two-pronged round variety.

Theatre, cinema, nightlife

The indispensable weekly guide is *Guia del Ocio*. More like *Pariscope* than *City Limits* or *Time Out*, it lists restaurants, clubs, live music, theatre and cinema with addresses and phone numbers.

Theatre/dance

Below are a few of the best-known names on the circuit at present. La Fura dels Baus (Vermin of the Sewer) who literally set London alight on their two visits to London in '85 and '86; *Sitges theatre group La Cubana, Els Comediants* who use Catalan popular theatre traditions in a modern context and Cesc Gelabert and Lydia Azzopardi dancers who scored successes at Edinburgh in 1984 and at the ICA's *Homage to Catalunya* in 1986.

The *Mercat de les Flors*, Lleida 59 (tel. 426 21 02) is worth a visit. It's an old flower market that has been converted into a performance space.

The *Gran Teatre Liceu* on the Rambles, booking at Santa Pau 1 Bis (tel. 318 92 77), is the second largest opera house in the world and must be visited if not to a concert at night, then at least on one of the morning guided tours.

Domènech i Montaner's Modernist *Palau de la Mùsica* is similarly essential viewing but there are no day-time tours here so you'll just have to book up for an evening performance and make what you can of the Catalan.

The Tourist Office provides a full list of theatres and you can check out what's on in the *Guia del Ocio*.

Cinema

See the *Guia del Ocio* for full listings. It has a 'Hit Parade de la Critica' where critics award 1–5 stars for current films. They also provide 15 different categories alongside the films from A (Adventure/Action) through to X (Porno).

Some of the city's cinemas put 'VO' (original version) in the listings and at their venues. This indicates the film uses subtitles so if it's originally an English speaking film, you're in luck. The following are three such cinemas:

Capsa, Pau Claris 134, tel. 215 73 93.
Casablanca, Pg Gràcia 115, tel. 218 43 45 (metro Diagonal).
Alexis, Rambla Catalunya 90, tel. 215 05 06 (metro Barcelona).

Centres showing English speaking films:
Filmoteca, Cine Aquitania, Av. Sarria 33.
Inst. Americà, Via Augusta 123, tel. 209 20 11.
Inst. Britànic, Amigó 83, tel. 209 63 88.

Clubs

Catalunya produces excellent red, white and sparkling wines. The latest boom palaces are the xampanyerias and the *Guia del Ocio* will tell you where your nearest one is.

Many of the trendy nightspots are either side of Travessera de Gràcia (Metro Gràcia) and entry costs between 350 and 1500pts (including first drink). Out in front it's still Otto Zutz, Lincoln 15 (metro Gràcia). Like a number of other clubs, it has what, for want of a better description, I'd call a 'precious

policy'. This involves advertising as members only (they've got 4000) and then allowing outsiders in at their discretion to make up the numbers. It all adds to the mystique, pomp, pose and trendy élitism. They were closed for a period in 1989 when illicit substances were found on the premises but they have since reopened. Close behind Otto Zutz in the trendy stakes are Si Si Si, Carrer Diagonal 442 (metro Diagonal), and KGB, Allegre de Dalt 55. Up and Down, Numancia 179, is for real members only. This was El Tel's hangout before he was booted out of Barcelona FC. *Pijos* (rich kids) groomed for the top, disco downstairs, whilst mum and dad who are already there, eat on top. The Metropol, Pg Mercader (a small road that joins Carrer València and Aragó – Metro Diagonal) is worth visiting. There's also the bar Universal on the corner of Marià Cubí and Sagues where hipsters from the world of photography and fashion pose on two floors. The Pg del Born is also worth a visit around 11pm. Here, a number of music bars rub shoulders. Studio 54, Paral-lel 64 (metro Poble Sec or Paral-lel) is also a popular disco and, set in an old theatre, is large enough to host many of the city's international concerts.

Another club worth a visit is the Harlem Jazz Club, Comtessa de Sobradiel 8, where live jazz bands usually start playing around 9pm. There are also a number of weirdo places such as Bodega Bohemia, Carrer Lancaster 2 (metro Liceu), where the original 1920s acts still perform in all seriousness and Molino, Vila i Vilà 99 (metro Poble Sec) (one of the oldest music halls in Europe) with its more kitsch Catalan floor show. At the end of the evening people go for a last drink to the Café de L'Opera (metro Liceu) on the Rambles.

Eating out

Catalan cuisine is sufficient reason alone to persuade you to devote a few more days to the city building up the waistline, instead of dieting for an appearance on one of her three costas. Barcelonans lunch around 2pm, take their evening meal around 10 and get to their clubs no earlier than midnight. You certainly need plenty of staying power for a holiday here. Fortunately you don't need a correspondingly large bank balance as the city offers such good value. Some restaurants, like La Venta, offer panoramic views over the city and others, like Can Majo, offer the bustling atmosphere of the Barceloneta, the purpose-built 18th-century fisherman's quarter. In good restaurants a meal will cost around £16 per head, in the very best around £50, and you can get a quick, cheap meal for as little as £4. If your budget favours the latter then ask for the *menu del día* (menu for the day) as it invariably represents the best value. Try El España (Carrer Montcada), El Rodri (Carrer Argenteria), or El Self-Naturista (Carrer Santa Anna). There are also the *tapas* bars with their trays of delicious snacks (mushrooms, meatballs etc) mostly priced at about 100–180pts a plate. Here you can also pick up a bocadillo (roll/sandwich) or *pa am b tomaquet* – the delicious tomato smeared garlic bread. At the cafés on the Rambla you pay for the sunshine (it's worth it). But take any sidestreet off towards the Barri Gòtic and you'll find a small square where the teeming streetlife is thrown in for free. Virtually every bar serves food of some description from full menus to *tapas* and *bocadillos*.

Restaurants

Prices are for a three-course meal without wine. C = cheap (under 3000pts; B = moderate (3000–6000pts), A = expensive (over 6000pts).

Reno, Tuset 27 (tel. 200 91 29). Closed Saturday. Hours: 1–4pm, 8.30pm–1am. A. Reno's is the classic Barcelona restaurant offering French and Catalan cuisine. The manager-owner José Julía has retained his father's great traditional Catalan dishes such as *hígado fresco de oca en terrina* (fresh goose liver terrine), and *solomilla al tuétano con trufas* (fillet steak in bone marrow with truffles) and added his own inventions such as *lenguado con ostras Alexandra* (sole with oysters), *pato asado con higos a la miel y vinagre de Jerez* (roast duck with honied figs and sherry vinegar). Everything is made on the premises and Reno boasts an extensive wine list stocking more than 400 different local, national and foreign vintners. The 'Menu Reno', from which six of the restaurant's dishes are selected, is a good introduction at around 7000pts.

Vía Véneto, Ganduxer 10 (tel. 200 72 44). Closed Saturday pm and Sunday. Hours: 1.15pm–4pm, 8.45pm–11.30pm. A. The Art-Nouveau style Vía Véneto mixes national Spanish dishes with bourgeois Catalan cuisine. Pleasant and luxurious with excellent service. Particularly good soufflés – try *soufflé de rodaballo* (turbot soufflé) – and the humble *botifarra* (sausage). Extensive wine list.

Eldorado Petit Restaurant, Carrer Dolors Monserdá 51 (tel. 204 55 06). Closed Sundays. Hours: 1.30pm–4pm, 9pm–12pm. A. Garden. Excellent Catalan nouvelle cuisine with French and Italian influences (e.g. *lasagne de salmón*). Good use of duck and goose and fish dishes (try the *suquet* seafood stews). Extensive wine cellar. The home made ice-creams and sorbets are legendary. Very fashionable and perhaps marginally cheaper than the two above.

FISH RESTAURANTS IN THE BARCELONETA

The Barceloneta has a host of good fish restaurants despite the recent closure of those directly on the beach. Try the following.

Can Majó, Carrer d'Almirante Aixada 23 (tel. 310 14 55). Closed Mondays.

Hours: 1.30pm–4pm, 9pm–11.30pm. B. Located in a rather seedy street leading down to the beach, inside it is awash with typically seafaring decor. Try the *suquet* (fish stew), *zarzuela* (mixed fish cooked in its own juices in a clay pot) or one of the rice dishes.

Amaya, Rambla Santa Mònica 20–24 (tel. 302 61 38). Open daily. Hours: 1pm–7pm, 8pm–12.30pm. B. Amaya is a good place for lunch (particularly on Sunday) or for an early evening meal (later it tends to attract the city's streetwalkers). Though a Basque restaurant (with fine Basque wines – try the white Chacoli de Zarauz) it also serves Catalan dishes. Try the fish soup (*sopa de pescado*), spinach dishes (*espinacas*) and Gerona duck with prunes (*pato amb prunes*). Home-made desserts.

7 Portes, Pg d'Isabell II, 14 (tel. 319 30 33). Located between the Parc de la Ciutadella and the Barceloneta. Open daily throughout the year non-stop 1pm–1am. B. Very popular, large (99 staff and 1000 diners), elegant and enchanting. Opened in 1836. The first building in Barcelona to have running water, first in Spain to be photographed and to have a gas light sign outside it; designated as of national architectural interest. Specialities: *paella pareillada* (shells and bones removed from traditional ingredients), *vic or vilafranca botifarra* (sausage), and rice dishes – a different one for each day of the week. Try *anchoas 7 Portes con pan de coca con tomate* (anchovies served with 'coca' bread spread with tomato) (890pts) to start or the *espinacas con pasas y piñones a la Catalana* (spinach steamed with sultanas and pine kernels) (590pts). The *fricandó con moixarnos* (veal stew with wild mushrooms) (1240pts) is just one of the splendid options on the vast main-course menu.

La Cuineta, Carrer Paradís 4 (tel. 315 01 11). Closed Mondays.

Hours: 1pm–4pm, 8pm–12pm. B. An excellent Catalan restaurant in the heart of the Barri Gòtic. Head downstairs to the barrel-vaulted cellar, furnished with antiques, for the best atmosphere. The only irritant is the taped American music. The *bacalla* (salt fish) is highly thought of and the *anchoas de la escala* (anchovies with tomato smeared peasant bread) (850pts) excellent. Try one of the traditional Catalan dishes for the main course: *pato con peras* (duck with pears) (2,800pts) or *conejo al romesco* (rabbit in romesco sauce) (1,950pts).

Egipte, Jerusalem 3 (tel. 317 74 80). Closed Sunday. Hours: 1.30pm–4pm, 8pm–11.30pm. C. Egipte is still good value despite its popularity. You'll find it tucked behind the Rambla's Boquerìa market (where there's also another good, economical restaurant, La Garduña, Morera 17 (tel. 302 42 23) – menu del día 750pts with a menu in seven languages). Very busy when the Opera House empties. It has a large menu with a number of Catalan specialities, larger salads and mountainous desserts (skip another course but not the dessert whatever you do!). Cosmopolitan clientele, lively, fun. Try to get there before nine and get a table on the balcony overlooking the main restaurant area (leading into endless labyrinthine small rooms at the rear and upstairs). Try *cadbells de tudela amb deessa verda* (baby lettuce with green dressing) (595pts), *Llangostis a la plancha* (grilled crayfish) (1350pts) and *pollastre farat amb prunes* (chicken stuffed with prunes) (945pts).

Agut, Gignàs 16 (tel. 315 17 09). Closed Sunday nights, Monday and the month of July. Hours: 1.30pm–4pm, 8.30pm–11pm. B/C. This restaurant has been in the business for 60 years, is very Catalan and very popular. 1930s style, intimate, whitewashed, woodpanelled and hung with original canvasses from the period. Good value and excellent food. Agut's *menu recomendado para hoy* (recommended menu of the day) is very good value at 2100pts for three courses with a glass of wine (I had *salmó fumat* (smoked salmon) followed by *pollastre amb gambes* (chicken with prawn main course). The *sopas de galets amb mondonguilles* (shell pasta with meatballs and bacon in a light broth) is very good, as is the *sopas de pescadores* (fish soup).

Viejo Pop, Gran Vía 635 (tel. 302 75 62). Hours: 8am–1am. Closed Sunday. The menu del día was 750pts at start of 1992. Cheap. Located opposite the Ritz. Informal, youngish crowd, simple and good value: pizzas, sandwiches and *platos combinados*, e.g. *merluza a la plancha con ensalada de atum y calamares a la romano* (grilled merluza with salad, tuna fish and calamares with romano sauce). You can sit at the bar on stools or at the tables at the rear. Friendly service.

TAPAS BARS

These are to be found everywhere. Each small dish (meatballs, mushrooms, shellfish etc.) usually costs between 100 and 200pts. *Tapas* can be viewed on trays at the bar and pointed at so lack of Catalan need not deter you. You can usually pick up a *bocadillo* (roll/sandwich) if you're squeamish – the best sandwich in the whole world is *pà amb tomaquet* – bread smeared with tomato and garlic. The Reina Cristina and the hole-in-the-wall bars along the Carrer de la Mercé offer atmosphere and possibly the best *tapas* in town. Worth visiting in particular are the following:

Hortalón, Carrer dels Banys Nous (just 100m from the Rambla). The Hortalón is for those who actually enjoy snacking in a blackened cellar. Hams, sausages and strings of garlic hang from bare beams, the floor is a sea of sawdust and the bottles on the wall sit covered in nicotine tar several feet deep. Good *tapas* and full of bohemian atmosphere.

Verdamia, Carrer de la Fustería (opposite the main post office at the waterfront behind Via Laietana) is again the real thing replete with sawdust on the floor, formica tables and a lunchtime babble of animated families and workers. A wide range of tapas. Very popular. Lots of atmosphere. As with Hortalón, not a touristy bar; full of locals.

Pinoccio, immediately on your right as you enter the Rambla's Boqueria market, is good for bar-stool tapas (or breakfast) as you simultaneously feast on the teeming market life.

Gran Colmado, Carrer de Consell de Cent 318, in the heart of the Barri Gòtic is also a good tapas lunch stop.

Cristal City, Carrer de Balmes 294. A comfortable bookshop/bar serving tapas.

Mundial Bar, Plaça Sant Agustí Vell 1. Particularly good for shellfish.

Xampanyet, Montcada (near Pg del Born and the Picasso Museum). A xampanyeria and tapas bar.

Cerveseria d'Or, Rambla Catalunya 44. A wide range of tapas and even larger range of beers.

XAMPANYERIAS

As Catalonia, and the Penedès region in particular, is the home of cava, or Spanish champagne, Barcelona is particularly well endowed with 'champagne bars' or xampanyerias. These offer glasses of cava (the brut is the best and most expensive) straight or in mixes. An average 75cl bottle will usually cost around 900pts; a quarter litre of standard Codorniu (by far the world's largest producer of 'champagne method' wines) will probably cost around 450pts. Here are a few xampanyerias for you to try:

Amarcord, 92 Pg de Gràcia (tel. 215 72 49), is a cocktail bar located in Gaudi's Pedrera building. Lively mid-afternoon.

Azulete, 281 Via Augusta (tel. 203 59 43), is very elegant with a fine terrace. In addition to the bar and restaurant, you can also buy charcuterie to take away.

La Xampanyeria, 236c de Provença, was the first cava bar to open and boasts a wide selection of local wines and cava.

The unnamed xampanyeria at 7 Reina Cristina must be the cheapest cava bar in town. It also serves delicious charcuterie and cheeses in sandwiches. No seats or stalls and mobbed between 2pm and 4pm.

Accommodation

Budget accommodation

Barcelona's cheapest accommodation is provided by its five Youth Hostels, most of which have cooking and washing facilities. Prices start from 350pts. The main one is Hostal de Joves, Pg Pujades 29 (tel. 300 31 04), close to Barcelona Terme-Franca train station (metro Arc de Triomf). Maximum stay here is 5 days.

The University lets out rooms in the summer at around 1000pts for bed and breakfast. Write to Universitat de Barcelona, 585 Gran Via, Barc. 108003 (tel. 318 42 66).

CAMPING

None in the city. The nearest are Badalona, Esplugues and Prat de Llobregat (all three around 7km away). Information from Tourist Information Office or Associacó de Campings de Barcelona, Gran Via 608 (tel. 412 5955).

Hotels

Most of the new accommodation, built for the Olympics, was at the hitherto very limited luxury end and there is still a dearth of mid-range accommodation. Prices are quoted per room rather than per person. Two people sharing a double can pay anything from 1300pts for a room with shared bathroom in a one-star budget hostel (these can be very basic) to 212,500pts (around £1150 per night!) for a luxury suite at the Ritz. A blue sign outside with 'P' or 'CH' indicates budget establishments – there are hundreds of these in the old city – Rambla, Carrer Portaferrisa, Pelai, Carme, Ferran, Hospital, Plaça Reial, Portal de l'Angel, Plaça Palau, Jaume 1 and Princesa are just some of the places to look. HR (hotel residence), HA (hotel apartment) and RA (residence apartment) outside a hotel indicate its facilities. This confusing classification is being phased out in favour of a simple 'hotel' or 'pension' classification. The new categorisation requires even one-star hotels to have bathrooms in every bedroom; one star pensions will have at least 15 per cent of rooms with bathrooms and two star establishments 25 per cent.

The Tourist Office won't book accommodation for you but will provide lists. If you don't want to do the leg-work yourself, Ultramar Express at train stations and airport will book for around 150pts fee per person. They also take 25 per cent of the accommodation cost – you pay the rest on arrival. The disadvantage with this system, apart from paying more, is that you don't get to see the room before you hand over your money. Apartments can be hired for a day, a week or for longer stays and are classified by 'keys': third class gets one 'key', luxury gets 'four' keys. The tourist office have a list of Real Estate agencies renting them out.

Three star establishments and lower, included below, do not have televisions in bedrooms. Unless otherwise stated, all establishments listed are central, open year round, have lifts, air conditioning, accept major credit cards and have en-suite bathrooms.

Add 13 per cent IVA (VAT) for five-star hotels and six per cent for others, plus four per cent sales tax. Prices quoted are per double room rather than per person. Single rooms rates are generally 60–70 per cent of the double room rate. C = cheap (under 10,000pts; B = moderate (10,000–20,000pts; A = expensive (more than 20,000pts).

Ritz (5-star deluxe), Gran Vía 668 (tel. 318 5200). A. A car park is expected to be completed in 1992. Historic building. 24-hour room service. Breakfast 2050pts. Dinner around 9000pts. The restaurant is open 1.30pm–4pm and 8.30pm–11pm. Opened in 1919. The least famous of the original four founded by César Ritz but still the city's most classically ostentatious (and snobbish) with grand salons, overweight rugs, marble floors and sparkling chandeliers. Sumptuous entrance hall and lobby where tea can be taken. Suites at the front overlooking the noisy Gran Vía are spacious and elegantly furnished; the back bedrooms however are small. The blue Diana Restaurant (tel. 318 52 00) replete with linen tablecloths, Venetian curtains and tinkling piano includes Catalan specialities amidst its predominantly French cuisine.
Gran Hotel Havana (5-star), Gran Vía 647 (tel. 412 1115). A. Parking spaces for 50 below ground. 24-hour room service. Breakfast 1,700pts. Average three-course meal 4,500pts. Restaurant hours: 1.30pm–3.30pm and 8.30pm–11.30pm. Opened in April 1991 (the façade dates from 1872), the most impressive of the new 5-star hotels. Excellent attentive service, handsome

and spacious rooms (employing a deep red African hardwood) that are the best soundproofed I came across (triple glazing). The most striking feature of this most elegant hotel is its kidney-shaped atrium topped by a glass cupola that creates an abundance of light throughout the building. An example showing that taste need not be sacrificed for modernity.
Avenida Palace (5-star), Gran Vía 605 (tel. 301 9600). A. 24-hour room service. Health club, sauna and gym. Breakfast 1275pts, dinner around 7000pts (fixed menu 4500pts). Open 1.30pm–3.30pm and 8.30pm–11pm. An old-world hotel dripping with chandeliers, gilt and character. Luxurious and very central. The standard rooms have personal safes. For the best views of the city and original fittings, ask for a room on the fourth floor upwards. The service here is very good. The Gran Vía is a terribly noisy street but the double glazing keeps out most of the noise.
Hotel Colon (4-star), Av. Catedral 7 (tel. 301 14 04). A/B. Historic building. Garage. 24-hour room service. Breakfast 700pts, lunch/dinner 4500pts. Open 1pm–3.30pm and 8pm–10.45pm. Marvellous location overlooking the 13th-century Gothic Cathedral. The bar is a very popular meeting place for Barcelonans and the hotel's location at the gateway to the Barri Gòtic, a stone's throw from the Rambla and Pg de Gràcia, compensate for the indifferent service and uninspiring food. Try to get a room on the sixth floor overlooking the cathedral: you get a deep terrace balcony thrown in for free.
Hotel Gran Vía (3-star), Gran Vía 642 (tel. 318 19 00). B. Central. Historic building. 24-hour room service. Breakfast 525pts. Dinner is not offered at the hotel. A privately owned, well maintained, handsome hotel with sweeping staircase and Doric columns

and a feeling of great spaciousness. The rooms are all the same: attractive, large, air conditioned, and good value.
Hotel Oriente (3-star), Rambla 45 (tel. 302 25 58). B. Historic building. Independent parking 100m away. Breakfast 750pts, dinner about 2200pts. Open 1pm–3pm and 8pm–10pm. Air-conditioning is expected to be installed in time for the Olympics. Glorious Modernist rotunda, glass-domed restaurant. Another institution; maybe a shade faded but still charming. It also has the advantage of being on the Rambla.
Hotel España (2-star hotel), Carrer Sant Pau 9–11 (tel. 318 17 58). B/C. (Prices include breakfast). Historic building. Car parking available nearby. A wonderful Art Nouveau (Modernist) building designed by Domènech i Montaner. The dining room is a living museum: sculpted woodwork, stained glass, ceramics, turn-of-the-century paintings and a chimney 4m high sculpted by Arnau. Large reception area, clean, spacious bedrooms. Owned by the same friendly family since the 50s. Ask for one of the rooms that have been recently refurbished (ten so far, another 25 of its 84 planned in 1992). Restaurant food fine but unexceptional. The room itself is the real feast. The menu del día is good value at 1200pts.
Hotel Principal (2-star hotel residencia), Junta de Comercio 8 (tel. 318 89 70). C. Breakfast 300pts, dinner 1,000pts. Restaurant open 1pm–3pm and 8pm–10pm. Adequate and central, just a minute from Domènech i Montaner's old Hospital and two minutes from the Rambla. The bedrooms can be a bit dingy but they are all air-conditioned. It is not too busy a street and the rear of the hotel is quiet by Barcelonan standards. The Catalan food is substantial, tasty and very good value.
Hotel Lloret (1-star hotel residencia), Rambla Canaletes 125 (tel. 317 33 66).

C. Prices here include local taxes and IVA. No restaurant but there are plenty downstairs on the Rambla. The air-conditioning cuts out most of the noise from the Rambla but this is a noisy street. Basically you choose a view of the streetlife (no supplement) or the comparative quiet of the rear. Rooms are clean and well maintained if a shade spartan. The air-conditioning operates through the peak summer months. Helpful staff.
Jardí (1-star hostel), San Jose Oriol 1 (tel. 301 59 00). C. Central, picturesque location. Breakfast 375pts. No restaurant. No lift. No air conditioning. The rooms are basic, some have the occasional damp patch but they are still spotlessly clean and offer good value. A particularly

picturesque location, overlooking two of the city's most attractive adjoining squares. There's no noisy traffic here but plenty of atmosphere. Breakfast overlooking the square (alternatively you may breakfast al fresco in the square or at the Bar del Pi, one of the Barcelona's finest, next door).
Roma (2-star hostel), Plaça Reial 11 (tel. 302 03 66). C. Historic building. Breakfast 250pts, no lunch or evening restaurant. Accepts only Eurocheques or cash. No air conditioning. The poky entrance and stairway are the Roma's worst features and sorely in need of a lick of paint. The rooms themselves are clean, spacious, light and airy. A great location particularly if you get a front room overlooking the Plaça Reial. Good value.

Moving on from Barcelona

TRAINS
(tel. 322 41 42 or 490 02 02 for information). There are special 'Blue Days' when rail travel is cheaper – check for discounts when purchasing tickets.

FERRIES
There are 12 to Mallorca and six to Ibiza and Menorca in the summer. The cost in 1991 was 4800pts for a seat only and 12,400pts for a cabin berth, but ask about discounts when purchasing tickets from any travel agent.

HITCH HIKING
For Tarragona, Zaragoza or Madrid the ideal point is the Diagonal, beyond the

end of Bus No. 7 route (metro Zona Universitària). For Castelldefels, Sitges and Vilanova try the Gran Via de les Corts Catalanes well beyond the Plaça d'Espanya (metro Espanya). For Girona and France wait at the Gran Via de les Corts Catalanes beyond the Plaça de Toros Monumental (metro Glòries).
   Viage Cómodo/Mitfahrzentrale, SA Carrer Provença 214.4.1a, tel. 253 22 07 and *Comparco*, Carrer Ribes 31.6.1a, tel. 246 69 08. are two organisations that provide hitch hikers with contacts and fixed, reasonable charges.

Part Two: The South

Tour 9
Montserrat and the Penedès Wine Belt

Montserrat

Catalonia may be Spain's most European province and its capital, Europe's most fashionable city but its interior might just as well be in the Urals for all the attention it receives. Whilst hordes annually flock to Barcelona and the Costa Daurada and even larger numbers to the Costa Brava, inland the vast tracts of sparsely populated agricultural land, medieval villages and fine ecclesiastical buildings, remain almost totally ignored.

The exception is the monastery of Montserrat, 50km from Barcelona. On Sundays and holidays, Montserrat receives almost as many visitors as Barcelona FC's Nou Camp Stadium. On the morning of Easter Sunday we had shared Barcelona with just a handful of others. As we drove up the Diagonal and onto the N340 (it would have been far more sensible to take the A2 autoroute to exit 25) we realised why; the whole city was on the same road out of town. We were stuck in a traffic jam for an hour and a half around Molins de Rei and impatiently took off on a side road. We got so lost at one point that we stopped and asked a family picnicking at the roadside for directions. The party promptly ended, picnic baskets were stashed and two cars crammed with an impressively complete extended family escorted us all the way to Esparreguera before putting me back on the right road.

At **Castellbisbal** abandoned warehouses gave the village the spectre of a ghost town. Suddenly free of the congestion, there were more cyclists than serious Sunday car trippers. One advantage of being lost was that the **Pont del Diable** at Martorell appeared suddenly and unexpectedly below us. Originally a Roman bridge at the

Peculiar rock formations overshadow the monastery at Montserrat.

hub of its important road network, it is understandable why something so beautiful was thought to be the work of the Devil. Legend has it that locals tired of the difficult crossing of the River Llobregat asked the Devil to build them a bridge in a night and in exchange they would offer him the soul of the first villager to cross the bridge the next day; the following day they craftily pushed a cat onto the bridge to keep their side of the bargain. The mostly modern town boasts three important museums devoted to Catalan, Valencian and Hispano-Moslem ceramics (to check opening times, ring the Town Hall, tel. 775 00 50). There's a 13th-century Romanesque chapel of St Joan and the remains of the similarly ancient monastery of Sant Genís de Rocafort.

When we reached **Esparreguera** the inhabitants were into the fourth hour of their passion play and the town was swarming. As we wanted to push on to Montserrat, we waved goodbye to my miniature caravanserai and, after a brief glimpse of the slender baroque belltower on the 16th-century parish church, headed north. On the far side of Olesa de Montserrat a cable car was taking pilgrims up to the monastery.

We had to leave the car clinging precariously to the cliff edge a mile and a half from the monastery at **MONTSERRAT**. If you are not driving, there are several alternative means of reaching the monastery. One option is to go on one of the numerous organised coach tours from Barcelona (contact the nearest Barcelona Tourist Office, see the list at the back of the book); or take a bus from Plaça Universitat 12 (Autocars Julià tel. 93 318 3895) or one of the Ferrocarrils de Catalunya trains from the Plaça d'Espanya. In the latter case take the Manresa line as far as Aeri de Montserrat and then the cable car to Montserrat (the first cable car leaves around 10am and the last down is around 6.45pm).

From the vineyards in the Penedès plain it is easy to appreciate the mystic awe in which the saw-tooth mountain is held, and the plethora of legends that attach themselves to it. Here Parsifal found the Holy Grail, St Peter left a statue of the Virgin carved by St Luke and Wagner found inspiration for his Opera, 'Parsifal'. The mountain is ten kilometres long and five wide and its highest peak, Sant Jeroni, is 1235m high. Apart from its religious significance (there are 13 hermitages here and a monastery has stood on the major site since the middle ages), the mountain has over 1500 different species of plant, over half the total registered for the whole of the province. The actual rock formation is as impressive as it is bizarre and it seems to take on the shape of a human spectre one moment, a forest of giant poplars the next, then a vast pipe organ and even the serrated teeth of a shark.

A visit here removes any doubt about the validity of Gaudí's extraordinary vision of organic form. Certainly one need look no further than Montserrat for the model for the roof of the Pedrera in Barcelona's Pg de Gràcia. But the mountain has impressed a good many others too. One of the Caribbean's prettiest islands was named after it by Columbus probably in honour of the former Montserrat hermit, Bernard Boll, who accompanied him on his peregrinations.

Montserrat is the soul of Catalonia and on 27 April and 8 September each year, the basilica's venerated Black Madonna (patroness of Catalonia) becomes the object of Spain's greatest pilgrimage. Apart from the Black Madonna, Montserrat is also home to the Escolaná – Europe's oldest boys' choir (founded in the 13th century) and most importantly of all, the Bendictine monks who first settled here in the 11th century. The monks were forced to leave the monastery (as happened throughout Spain) following the Secularization Laws in 1835 and the sanctuary, already sacked by Napoleon's army in 1811, fell into disrepair. The Madonna took up temporary residence in Esparreguera. Unlike the case in many other monasteries however, the monks managed to return after only nine years and restoration work immediately got under way.

Of the monastery, only the basilica and museum are open to visitors. The sanctuary of the Black Madonna is open daily 8am–10.30am, 12noon–1.30pm and 3pm–6.30pm. The museum is open daily 10.30am–2pm and 3pm–6pm. When we visited, the queue inside the Basilica coiled and coiled again as patient pilgrims, in total silence, awaited their turn to pass the monastery's most sacred icon, the diminutive Romanesque statue of the Black Madonna. Descending the stairs to the right of the throne of the Virgin one can sometimes visit a chapel, built between 1876 and 1884 by Villar y Carmona with the assistance of Gaudí who was just starting his career.

At one o'clock there was a surge of activity as more of the congregation elbowed its way into the church. It was the moment the Escolanía would sing. Unfortunately the Salve and Virolai (the hymn of Montserrat) by the world famous 50-strong boys' choir was over in a twinkling. Nevertheless the event had drawn sufficient numbers to underline the error the anarchists made indulging their penchant for burning churches during the Civil War. Montserrat escaped their catharsis by fire because it was felt that its unique cultural importance outweighed its religious influence. The monastery's continuing support of all things Catalan sees to it that it remains the most important and enduring symbol of Catalan identity.

The 7pm evensong was far less busy and a much better opportunity to savour the singularly beautiful Montserratine Salve when the boys' choir alternates with the monks. When planning your visit, bear in mind the Escolanía are not in Montserrat during July. Except when the choir is performing (1pm and 7pm), the church's interior mostly remains unlit and rather gloomy. One new, particularly compelling image is the concave head, hands and feet of Christ sculpted in wood by Subirachs, Catalonia's most acclaimed modern sculptor. Along the central aisle are votive lamps donated by different Catalan towns and overhead is a vast vaulted dome. Religious paintings adorn the walls of the sanctuary and the stone of the actual altar was taken from the mountain itself.

The **Museum** outside is housed in two buildings. The first, the old section (open 10.30am–2pm), is subdivided into a picture gallery (including canvasses by El Greco, Corregio and Caravaggio) and the Biblical Museum which houses a collection of artifacts belonging to the biblical lands (including an Egyptian room). A few steps away is the 'secció moderna' (open 3pm–5pm) that concentrates on the Barcelona school of painters. The bright modern building possesses an impressive array of the most significant Catalan painters of the past 150 years. The muted colours of Roma Ribera, where everything is seen as if through a haze, do not subdue the vitality of his Barcelona street life subjects ('Exiting from the Opera House Liceu' is a fine example). Santiago Rossiñol (1861–1931) has a large section chronicling his development from impressionist to realist and on to more classical studies. Ramon Casas' (1866–1932) gypsy portraits take up a third section of the museum.

Outside the basilica and museums, the more secular face of monasticism shows itself not averse to tempting the tourists with records, tapes, books, souvenirs, home-produced honeys and wines. A funicular ascends an almost sheer cliff face to another point of worship, the hermitage of Sant Joan. If you prefer not to risk the one-in-two ascent you may choose instead to refresh yourself in the moderately-priced restaurant which has a mirador overlooking the valley.

Before heading south to sample the vineyards of the Penedès, having got this far you may wish to continue north along the banks of the Riu Cardener through the mountain via a tunnel on the C1411 to Manresa, Cardona and Solsona.

Manresa (pop. 67,014) is the capital of Bages province. It is a mixture of old and new epitomised by its ancient 12th-century bridge, Pont Vell, and modern, busy Pere III boulevard. Located 68 kilometres from Barcelona at the confluence of the rivers Cardener and Llobregat, it is an important industrial and commercial centre. It boasts the attractive Agulla Park and a Gothic-Romanesque transitional collegiate church of Santa Maria, known as La Seu (the cathedral) that stands proudly on the Puig Cardener hill overlooking the town. La Santa Cova church and adjoining Jesuit house (where San Ignacio de Loyola supposedly wrote his famous Ejercicios) are worth visiting. The Palace of Justice is located in a 17th-century former palace and there's also an impressive 18th-century Town Hall. The town has a sprinkling of Modernist buildings including the casino. There are two musuems: La Seu and the City Museum. Major festivals take place on 21 February (Festes de la Misteriosa Luus – Festival of the Mysterious Light) and the last Sunday in August (Festa Major dels

Cossos Sants – Festival of the Holy Bodies). Check details and opening times with the Tourist Office in Plaça Major, tel. 93 872 53 78.

The imposing ochre-coloured castle of **Cardona** (pop. 6561) appears rising majestically from another hill 30kms further on. These formidable fortifications once guarded the nearby salt mines on which the Cardona family fortunes depended (the mountain of salt is still there and in fact has been mined since Christ's time). The maze of stone passageways and illuminated staircases create a delicious medieval atmosphere and the impressive buildings date from various periods between the 10th and 19th centuries. The castle houses the Parador Nacional Ducs de Cardona, a rather gloomy parador whose majestic setting is spoilt by poor food and service.

The Museum of Salt is worth a visit and if you happen to be in Cardona on the second Sunday in September you'll have the good fortune of witnessing the town's major festival, the Correbou when a bullfighter is placed in a large rolling wicker basket (La Cargolera) which the bull rolls around with its horns.

Solsona (pop. 6230), just 18km further up the C1410, is the capital of El Solsones comarque and the centre of the diocese. The town grew up round the 12th-century Romanesque cathedral of Santa Maria which houses the 13th-century statue of Santa Maria del Claustre. The major museums are the regional (which commences the comarca's evolution from pre-history through the Romanesque and Gothic flowering), the diocesan museum in the 13th-century Episcopal palace and the ethnological museum in the Town Hall. The medieval alleyways are a delight to stroll through and the town makes a good base for exploring some of the nearby sights: Olius, El Miracle, Port del Comte and Ribera Salada. The major festival (Festa Major de la Mare de Deu del Claustre) takes place on 8–9 September.

To continue the tour into the wine belt, return to Manresa and take the N141 east.

The Penedès Wine Belt

The tour now heads 46km south-westwards (take the N141 from Manresa) to **Cervera** (pop. 6444), an attractive medieval town that is the capital of La Segarra comarca. The city is cradled in a pass overlooking the river Onadara just 57km from Lleida. Despite its meagre population, Cervera was awarded the title of 'city' in 1702 by Philip V and granted a university (Catalonia's only one at the time as all the rest had been closed by Philip to punish the province for supporting his rival during the War of Succession). Its other important dates were 1359 when the Generalitat de Catalunya was formed by the Corts Catalanes and 1469 when the town was the setting for the marriage between Ferdinand of Aragón and Isabel of Castile.

Cervera's museum charts its history even further back with Iberian and Roman exhibits. The museum also contains paintings, 16th-century pottery and exhibits relating to the history of the university of Cervera. There is clear evidence of other cultural activity in the town too: the great Catalan sculptor Subirachs was commissioned to create a monument to the Catalan government (Generalitat) in 1982; there's a library, archives and a Cultural Centre (in the former 12th-century church of Els Hospitalers) as well as an 18th-century baroque town hall.

The city has good rail and road links. Its two most important churches are the

Gothic Santa Maria (note the older, Romanesque porch) which houses a 13th-century statue of the Virgin and the church of Sant Antoni with its similarly dated crucifix and icon of the Virgin. The city's major festivals take place on 6 February, (Festa Major del Santisim Misteri – Festival of the Holiest Mystery), 15 May (Sant Isidre's Fair in the neo-classical university grounds), 19 August (Festa de Sant Magi) and the last Sunday in September.

Turning eastwards, take the speedy N11 for 36km to **Igualada** (pop. 31,451), capital of l'Anoia comarca, and a noisy, sprawling town with important knitwear and leather industries. Like Tortosa it has a striking Modernist slaughterhouse and a number of equally impressive turn-of-the century private residences. These, together with the Renaissance Santa Maria church, Sant Agustí Convent, the 15th-century town walls and the medieval quarter, do their best to redeem Igualada; but its heart has long since been buried under the modern, ugly sprawl. Its major festival is on 24 August: bell ringing and fireworks mark the start of the festival at noon, and a parade of giants and dragons walk the streets during the afternoon.

From Igualada, leave the N11 and head due south for 34km across country on the 244 – a mountain switchback through the Penedès vineyards, Catalonia's most important wine-producing region. **Alt (Upper) Penedès**, enjoys on average 3000 hours of sunshine a year. Despite the dry climate, 60 per cent of the land is farmed. The region, roughly equidistant between Barcelona and Tarragona, was an important frontier between Christians and Moors during the Reconquest as is evident from the number of castles and fortifications that pepper the region. It is bordered to the north by Montserrat and to the south by a line of Cistercian monasteries. It is no coincidence that the never-ending vineyards should be cradled in a plain fringed by monastic retreats for it was the Cistercian monks who settled New Catalonia (and the Benedictines to the North) who cultivated the vines (see Box on p. 96).

Sant Sadurní d'Anoia (pop. 8591) (a 12km detour to the east from the 244) takes its name from the nearby river. Its medieval centre, just 44km from Barcelona, grew up around the parish of Sant Sadurní de Subirats and its main festivals are held on Ascension Day and on the second Sunday in September when, in the Fires i Festes de Sant Sadurní, there are fireworks, a ball, and a special Mass, as well as the spectacle of dwarves dancing with clubs.

Just over a hundred years ago when the town's main industry was craftwork, an insect pest known as phylloxera laid the vineyards to waste. Diseased vines were pulled up and new ones from America planted and grafted onto native ones. This experiment led to Josep Raventós at Codorniu producing the first bottle of cava (sparkling wine) using the 'champagne method' in 1872. The small town now produces 90 per cent of Spanish cava.

Hoardings at the roadside advertise the relative merits of Freixenet, Catasús and Castellblanch but I chose to visit Codorniu, the world's largest producer of sparkling wine, whose Modernist buildings have been designated one of Spain's national artistic monuments.

The idiosyncratic integration of art, politics and commercial life in Catalonia which achieved its most significant flowering at the turn-of-the-century has been diminished by some who translate Modernism as merely a Spanish version of Art

Nouveau. But as you tour southern Catalonia every other village will bear witness to the strength and vitality of Catalonian Modernism as it is exemplified un-selfconsciously in distilleries and workshops. Both the enormously wealthy wine barons and the local co-operatives (the first was established in La Conca de Barbera in 1894) struggling against extinction, commissioned artists instead of builders to create something other than utility in the workplace.

The **Codorniu** driveway leads past a row of cypresses guarding the cemetery up to the huge oak that is the symbol of the company. Alongside are the low-lying, understated Raventós cellars with a plaque that commemorates their opening on 15 September 1988. Opposite are the far more celebrated Codorniu gates with the older legend 1551 inscribed over them. The Codorniu and Raventós family histories are inextricably interwoven. In the mid 17th century, Codorniu, lacking the all-important male progeny, married his daughter into the Raventós family. The success of the company over the next 300 years was due to this new dynasty. But recently, following a family feud, Josep Maria Raventós left the fold and set up his own establishment across the road, whilst claiming at the same time the fabulous château that sits plum in the centre of the Codorniu complex. For the first time in 300 years, the Codorniu-Raventós 300-strong clan is split.

Puig i Cadafalch's château in the Codorniu complex.

Although Josep died in 1986 (from a heart attack while fishing in Iceland), his son Manel saw the project through and the family's new range of wines appeared in the shops for the first time at Christmas 1988 with the all-important oak logo prominently displayed.

The Codorniu complex was designed by Puig i Cadafalch, the third member (with

Gaudí and Domenech i Montaner) of the Catalan Modernist triumvirate, and has more in common with an art gallery than a factory. The building that now houses the reception area (which receives 160,000 guests annually), shop and cinema (which has a 12-minute introductory film in six languages) displays all the Modernist obsessions with unadorned brick, ceramic and glass; at the same time it acknowledges its Gothic debt in its interfacing parabolic arches which resemble a team of gymnasts constantly creating new harmonies through a succession of flips and somersaults. Even the lavatory could be turned into a gallery with its limpidity of light, stepped red brickwork and elegant single stone wash basin at the centre of the room. On the walls around the main building are original posters advertising the Codorniu wines designed by the likes of Utrillo, Casas, Tubilla and Junyent.

Both this original labelling hall and the Raventós chateau, also designed by Puig i Cadafalch, are set in tree-lined ornamental grounds with fountains, flower beds, ponds and old wine presses. Descending a staircase to the cellars you will be ferried in an open-top train past 120 million bottles of wine stored in the world's largest underground cellars (30km on five levels). You get some idea of the size of the operation when you consider that the three leading French champagne houses jointly do not approach Codorniu's size (interesting to note too that Moët Chandon recently bought vineyards in the region).

Turn-of-the-century commercial art is prominently displayed at the Codorniu plant.

The complex also has a fine museum housed in the cavernous old press house. The building's vast rear cantilevered glass roof undulates like waves and, like the reception area, is flooded with light. Linking the dome-roofed fermentation plant with the labelling plant is a covered walkway built only five years ago and designed

A game of chess in the wine cathedral at Codorniu.

to imitate the contours of the mountain behind it. Even the recently built modern presses do not compromise the artistic integrity and beauty of the place. Despite the fact the presses are used only two months every year there is no compromise with utility; instead the tiled domes grace the rolling countryside like Turkish cupolas over the Bosphoros.

For those wishing to extend their wine tour, a written request in advance to Codorniu (who bought the property in 1975) will allow a further visit to the smaller **Masia Bach** operation just 15km further north, situated alongside the small village of Sant Esteve Sesrovires en route to Martorell. *Masia* is Catalan for farmhouse but *masies* are much more than this. Often three or four homes for various family members and even a small chapel lie adjacent to the main building. This is the case with the Bach brothers' *masia*. The brothers initially built up a reputation through their distinctive Sauterne-like dessert wine, Masia Bach Extrissimo, but it is the crisp, fruity Extrissimo Seco that is now the fashionable tipple in the fish restaurants along the coast.

The 20th-century Florentine-style mansion is fronted by an elegant courtyard that is approached by an avenue lit by coach lamps. Inside the house is an inner courtyard fountain covered by a most beautiful stained glass roof. Below stairs are cellars that weave their way to the labelling and bottling plants behind the house.

Legend has it that the bachelor Bach brothers, who made their fortune selling uniforms to both sides during the First World War, didn't actually live here but merely entertained. This entertainment reputedly took two forms: the first set out to impress business contacts and the second indulged their own fantasies for the exotic and erotic. When one brother died in the Civil War, the second brother retired and the business was taken over.

If you do visit Masia Bach, then I would strongly recommend that you sample the typical rural Catalan cuisine at Can Parellada Masquefa, another nearby *masia* that has been converted into a farmhouse restaurant and hotel with swimming pool. When I visited, it was three in the afternoon and the homily on the facade's sundial did not exactly encourage a party mood: 'Good hours pass quickly but the sad ones last an eternity.' Inside, however, it was busy and noisy and the snails, *Esqueixada* (salted cod fish salad) and Catalan sausage with thick olive oil and garlic sauce were delicious as of course was the Masia Bach Special Reserva 1985.

Returning to the 244, a further half-hour drive due south will bring you to **Vilafranca del Penedès** (pop. 25,020), the capital of the Alt Penedès comarca. The modern outskirts were less than inspiring with their untidy industrial sprawl and scrummage of apartment blocks. Nevertheless I imagine that anyone living here 500 years ago would have willingly swapped both their Gothic homes and tax free status (vilafranca = free town) for a slice of the wealth the town now enjoys. The Rambla is not in Catalonia's first division despite the lines of mulberry trees. Of course even undistinguished towns have their features and in Vilafranca del Penedès the Medieval quarter certainly has charm. It centres around the 15th-century Basilica Santa Maria and 12th-century Royal Palace, which houses the Vilafranca Museum (important art collections, archeological and geological exhibits) as well as the most informative Museu del Vi (Wine Museum).

Apart from its wines, Vilafranca's other great contribution to Catalonia is in its rich folklore. Its *castellers* are thought to be the best in the province. The Fira del Gall (Fesitval of the Cockerel) on the last Sunday before Christmas is celebrated with some gusto as is its Festa Major which is held over the last few days of August and first few days of September. Its busy Saturday market is said to date back to the 12th century and boasts Catalonia's most important poultry market.

Just as Sant Sadurní is the capital of cava, Vilafranca is the capital of still wines. To give due attention to both, you may wish to make a visit to the Torres distillery (Bodega Torres, Dr Janer I, Vilafranca del Penedès, tel. 890 01 00) whose fame has been built on its Sangre de Toro or Bull's Blood, as well as on its brandies. It was here in 1904 that the present King Juan Carlos' grandfather, Alfonso XIII, dined in the largest wine vat before sending a letter back to his mother in Madrid by carrier pigeon telling her he was alive and well. Luckily the 500,000 litres of wine the vat holds had been removed before he got in. The vat is no longer there; it was destroyed by a stray bomb during the civil war (the townspeople turned out selflessly with every container they could muster to help the wine floods recede).

As with Codorniu, the complex is closed in August, also at weekends and on fiestas. Tours are on the hour, 9am–12 noon and 3pm–5pm and they last an hour.

A visit to the town's Wine Museum in front of the church of Santa Maria would be a fitting finish to your tour of the Wine Belt. In this, the old palace of King Peter III, is recorded the history of wine cultivation in the region starting with amphora pots dating back to the Greek settlements on the coast in the 4th century BC. The museum was founded in 1942 and has some delightful models of wine production through the ages. Its elegant porticoed rotunda flooded with light and its underground cellars are particularly deserving of your attention.

In September, just before the grape picking harvest, there are many festivals in the Alt Penedès. There's also 'Cava Week' in October and the Festa Major in Sant Sadurní in October. For those who have based themselves in Vilafranca or Sant Sadurní, I list a few nearby villages to which you may wish to make excursions.

From Sant Sadurní:
Sant Martí Sarroca. Romanesque church from the 12th century and ruined castle probably dating from the 9th century.
Gelida. Summer resort with funicular. Pre-Romanesque church of Sant Pere and remains of a castle.
Sant Quintí de Mediona. Caves and 22 springs which are collectively known as Les Deus. Remains of castle.

From Vilafranca:
Olèrdola. Graves dating back to the 9th Century, most of the human remains and artifacts of which are in Barcelona's archeological museum though Olerdola's own museum has some interesting artifacts. Ruins of castle with a wall dating from the 2nd century BC. 12th-century Romanesque church of Sant Miquel with 10th-century apse and adjoining 9th-century chapel.
Arbós on the N340 where there is a most extraordinary replica of Seville's Giralda.

The Cistercians in Catalonia

In 1098 a group of Benedictine monks wishing for a more rigorous religious order than was being practised by their brethren founded the monastery of Citeaux or Cistercium in Burgundy, where they tried to follow more closely the tenets of St Benedict. By the time the founder, St Bernard of Clairvaux, died in 1153, the Cistercians had 343 abbeys dotted through Europe.

The growth of the Cistercian movement in Catalonia during the mid 12th century coincided with the reconquest of lands in New Catalonia from the Moors. The presence of Moorish strongholds around Tarragona, Tortosa and Lleida explains why the Cistercian order, and military movements like the Knights Templar, are found chiefly in the south whilst northern Catalonia was settled by the Benedictine orders.

The Cistercians' desire for austerity and poverty led them to settle in isolated spots and devote themselves to simple labour, self-sufficiency and prayer. Unlike other orders, the monks worked the fields themselves with local conversi. Unlike the Benedictines they wore undyed habits,

earning themselves the soubriquet 'The White Monks'. Prayer was simplified, buildings plain and ornamentation minimal. More grandiose elements were added later as the order became wealthy and the renaissance spirit forged a more worldly outlook.

The first Cistercian monastery in Catalonia was established at Santes Creus in 1150 by monks from La Gran Selva. A year later Poblet was founded by Raymond Berenguer IV in another secluded, fertile valley near the Francolí River. Cistercian nuns were also established in the area by the same year but their most important convent, that of Vallbona de les Monges, was not established until 1175. These three Cistercian abbeys are recognised as being among the largest and loveliest in Europe. Whilst each has its own distinctive atmosphere, they share a common basic layout which saw all the important rooms and buildings – church, chapterhouse, refectory, dormitory, library, kitchen and calefactory (where monks and nuns warmed themselves in the cold winter months) – radiating from the cloister.

Tour 10
The Monastery Route and Lleida

Leaving the wine region behind, head first south, from Vilafranca del Penedès on autoroute A7 and then westwards on the A2 to Catalonia's celebrated triangle of Cistercian Monasteries centred around the medieval village of Montblanc. For those wishing to avoid motorways, the monasteries can be reached on winding secondary roads across the Penedès wine belt. However, the A2 provides splendid views of the countryside as it burrows through the valley between sierras.

After 18km on the A2 a signpost to the right points to the **Monestir de Santes Creus Aiguämurcia**, concealed in a leafy glade. The Cistercian community established themselves here in 1158 and dug themselves deeper into the region with impressive fortifications in the late 14th century making crucial contributions to the agricultural, cultural and spiritual life of the region. Monastic life was called to a halt in 1835 and, unlike in Poblet, the Order never returned. Santes Creus however remains a keen rival to its more celebrated cousin and certainly is blessed with the more impressive Mediterranean setting amongst white poplars and hazel trees alongside the Gaià river.

It is a light monastery boasting a superb cloister with lantern approached through a baroque gateway. Notable features of the rather sombre church are the rose window with 13th-century stained glass, and the three royal mausoleums (Pere II, Jaume II and Blanca d'Anjou) enclosed in early 14th-century Gothic pavilions with pinnacles, cresting and tracery. Behind the altar is a baroque retable by Josep Tremulles. The eight sided lantern was built in 1314.

Santes Creus has more of a village grafted on to it than Poblet. There's a Modernist wine co-operative designed by Gaudí's apprentice, Martinell, and a hotel across from the monastery (Hostal Grau). The major festivals are held on 17 and 28 (and 23 or 30) August and 12 September.

Back on the A2 the road starts to rise and the hills on either side become more densely forested. Electricity pylons take their quixotic strides across lands swathed in early evening mist. A further 22km on is the delightful medieval fortified town of **Montblanc** (pop. 5244). Once parked, walk across the ancient bridge up the Carrer Major past the old hospital Santa Magdalena (fine Renaissance cloister) until you reach the display board below the ramparts. Here the layout of the town is clearly shown. The 34 towers rise up out of virtually unbroken crenellated walls. The cobbled alleyway continues into the heart of the town past flower boxes and arched stone passageways.

The 14th-century Gothic church of Santa Maria has a baroque door and Romanesque belfry. The baroque facade shows the 12 apostles flanking Christ with a primitive representation of the Virgin above. Inside is an ancient organ built in 1607 and, beneath the vaults, numerous stained glass windows that do their best to dispel the gloom.

Festivals are celebrated here on 14 May and 8 September. In January the festa of Saint Antony, (known locally as Les Tres Colles – 'The Three Turns'), is a primitive fertility rite which commences with animals drawing specially decorated carts that are given three turns around a cross.

The Museu de la Conca de Barberà located in the 13th-century Casa Josa provides a comprehensive history of the comarca. There are also Modernist wine cellars by Gaudí's disciple, Cesar Martinell, which follow the typical red brick, warehouse-style model consisting of a large single room. On the main road (N240) just before the modern bridge is a new, international restaurant (Restaurant Molí) that offers a few Catalan dishes and a reasonable menu del día.

Two short excursions from Montblanc are worthy of a detour. One is to Modernist wine caves to the north in nearby **Rocafort de Queralt** and **La Conca de Barberà**, also designed by Martinell. The latter was in fact the first wine cooperative to be formed, in 1894, following the outbreak of phylloxera that destroyed virtually all the crops (other co-operatives soon followed at Espluga de Francolí and Poblet). Both these villages also boast castles and 18th-century baroque churches.

The second detour from Montblanc takes us south along the N240. Halfway to Valls the road starts to twist and turn and at L'Illa there are superb panoramic views.

Valls (pop. 18,857) itself is the capital of the Alt Camp comarca and has retained some medieval features, particularly around the old Jewish Quarter. It was the home of one of Catalonia's most important poets, Josep Maria de Sagarra. His 18th-century home can be found in one of the town's two main squares, the Plaça del Blat (the other is the arcaded Plaça de l'Oli, adjacent to the Town Hall). Valls is most celebrated for being the home of *castellers* – groups of men who have perfected the technique of standing on each others' shoulders in tiers reaching dizzy heights. This building of human pyramids dates back 200 years and is performed by the 'Xiquets de Valls', accompanied by *gralla* – rather primitive wind instruments. Major festivals are held on 24 June (Festa Major de Sant Joan – Feast of St John), 25 June (Mare de Deu del Lledó) and on the Sunday following 21 November (Fires i Festes de Santa Ursula).

From Valls you could continue on the N240 to Tarragona, just 19km away but to follow the route of this tour, return through Montblanc on the N240 Espluga de Francolí road. Just outside Montblanc, by the Citroën showroom, it is worth pulling off the road for the best view back over the fortified town.

L'Espluga de Francolí (pop. 3549) is just 6km west of Montblanc. As you enter the outskirts, on the right you will see the Museum of Rural Life with Pere Domènech's mural of the three Modernist wine cooperative buildings which can be found on the other side of town. Alongside the mural is a poem by Josep Maria de Sagarra extolling the dignified labour of those who work in the cooperative.

At night the illuminated Gothic church creates an eerie atmosphere. Facing it in the main square is a larger, newer church with a belltower that seems to celebrate each minute passed rather than each hour. The adjacent walkway has a plaque commemorating Josep Rendé who farmed the land and set up the village's wine cooperative. Winding up behind the churches is a warren of spotless medieval alleyways whose peeling plasterwork reveals the successive layers of history. Long wooden beams stretch across ceilings, coach lamps jut from walls and wrought grills wrap themselves round windows above large wooden arched doorways displaying distinctive door knockers. A less ancient feature are the black plastic rubbish bags suspended on hooks on walls, no doubt awaiting collection. At the summit a small playground overlooks the kitchen gardens in the valley. Beyond them are the Modernist wine cooperative buildings (far less impressive than the ones at Pinell de Brai) and skinny tottering chimneys of abandoned mills that were once the source of much of the town's wealth. Beneath your feet are the honeycomb caves that gave the town its name (*espluga* = cave).

The gathering of village elders outside the church in Espluga de Francolí.

My hotel, the Senglar, was simple though adequate and had an excellent Catalan restuarant which offered snails for appetizers followed by the local speciality, calcotada, young sweet onions cooked on an open fire and served with *salbitxada* (salt cod) sauce. The mess you make is unbelievable but it's worth it. The main course was rabbit in a thick sweet sauce. I tried the local fruity wine (vines of this region are known as the *vinyes del bosc* – the vines of the forest) before adjourning to the café-bar next door which was undoubtedly the liveliest place in town and inundated by Spanish families on a guided Medieval Tour of the area. Outside is a plaque commemorating the founding of the town by Ponç Hug de Cervera and the 900th anniversary of the expulsion of the Moors (1079). The town's main festival is held on the last Friday in July.

The road heads out of town into quiet vine-clad countryside past a hotel (with swimming pool and view overlooking the valley and monastery) at Les Masies towards the Serra de Roquerola whose forests are known as the Forest of Poblet. **Poblet** monastery, burial place of the kings of Catalonia and Aragón, is just 4km from L'Espulga de Francolí in a plain near the source of the River Francolí and roughly equidistant between Tarragona and Lleida. The area is heavily cultivated with vines, olives and almonds. The monastery mixes Romanesque with Gothic with Baroque and Renaissance features. The towers, crenellated walls and arrow fissures served to fortify the monastery and protect it from invaders. This mixture of the military with the ecclesiastical however did not protect it from the destruction that was wreaked on the monastery in the 17th and 18th centuries.

Count Ramón Berenguer IV of Barcelona donated land to Cistercian monks from

Poblet, built in 1151 and the resting place of the kings of Aragón.

the French Abbey at Fontfroide who founded the monastery in 1151 and lived there until 1835 when the monks were forced to leave as part of Mendizabal's *desamortización* (seizing of church property) when monastic lands were sold to pay the national debt. It is said locals took huge pleasure in the destruction of the sanctuary and other parts of the building as revenge for what they saw as years of privilege and corruption. The monks returned a hundred years later and commenced major restoration to the abbey. Thirty-five monks now live here, dedicated to prayer and simple labour.

Visits inside are in guided groups only (in Catalan, Castilian, English, German and French). Entrance is by way of the Porter's Lodge, a large semicircular arch built out of vast keystones. On the right is St George's Chapel bequeathed by King Alphonse the Magnanimous in thanks for his victory at Naples (1422). His coat of arms can be seen on the outer wall together with those of the Confederation of Catalonia and Aragón. It is the best example in Poblet of Gothic Ogival style. You enter the main square via the Golden Door (once gilded in 1564 following Philip II's visit). Inside the Main Square is the Romanesque chapel of St Catherine and traces of the hostelry and former administration blocks.

After viewing the church's Gothic façade, you pass through the Royal Door (a fine example of 14th Century military art) to visit the museum on the first floor which charts the history of the monastery – clearly English speakers are a minority group in Poblet; there are information boards it seems in every other language.

A recent striking addition is a 7m wrought dragon handrail (whose tail turns into a devil grabbing a serpent in one hand and a ball in the other) by Ramón Martin. This

The lantern, built on an earlier Moorish fountain, viewed from the 13th-century porchway of Poblet's Romanesque cloister.

separates the museum from the Abbot's Palace. The main cloister was begun in the 12th century and its simple Romanesque style is augmented with Gothic vaults. On the walls are the tombs of Catalan nobility as well as metal rings which used to hold chains to secure the holy books the monks were reading. Beneath our feet are the anonymous tombs of the monks. The portico has innumerable intricately carved capitals, usually of a floral motif (Cistercian orders, in a literal interpretation of the second Commandment, never represent human or animal form) each one different from its neighbour. The centre piece of the cloister is a lantern, probably built on an earlier Moorish fountain where the monks used to wash before going to the refectory. The passageway nearest the church is 12th-century Romanesque. Travelling clockwise you will next pass along the 13th-century arcade, and then the two from the 14th century (the stone had to be transported 50km from the next comarca, Les Garrigues, which might explain why the cloister took 200 years to complete).

The columns once rose up to the second floor where there was a second arcade with access directly from the dormitory.

The 13th-century kitchen is connected to the long refectory by a serving hatch. The refectory itself is supported by three sash arches and it is here that bible readings take place from the lectern built into the side wall. In the centre of the refectory is an octagonal stone fountain where ritual purification can take place before the meal, which the monks take in silence.

The austere calefactory was where the monks sought the warmth of a fire during the cold winter months. The ogival library houses the important manuscripts and books that managed to survive the fire of 1835. The Chapter Hall's perfect square is splayed with ribbed vaults that radiate from four sturdy columns. The purity of line and delicacy of the floral motifs on the capitals, the floor paved with past abbots' tombstones, the stepped wooden benches and arched windows, make it particularly memorable.

The ribbed wooden roof of the vast Dormitory, 87m long by 10m wide (the largest room in the monastery), is supported by 19 ogival arches. The large common sleeping space has been replaced by small individual rooms concealed from the public by a large partition bisecting the room.

The tower was restored in 1980 and is occasionally shown to 'special visitors', so it is up to you to convince the guide that you are one. Its bells still call the monks to prayer.

In the 14th century Poblet was named as the Royal Escorial and henceforth succeeding kings were laid to rest here. The added prestige saw a King's Palace and anterooms, King's Library and King's Tower quickly grafted on to the monastery.

Predictably enough, it is the interior of the church itself that really takes one's breath away. Here the monks gather four times a day for services (when visitors are not permitted). There are three naves, a transept, apse (with 16th-century alabaster altarpiece) and seven ambulatory chapels. The most unusual features are the two rows of 14th-century raised sarcophagi (only found in one other monastery, in Portugal) that contain the tombs of the Kings of Aragón.

Visiting hours are 10am–12.30pm and 3pm–6pm; tours start as soon as there are sufficient numbers and last about an hour.

Return to the speedy N240; the road winds gently north westwards through pretty wooded countryside until flattening into a plain. About half way to Lleida is **Les Borges Blanques** (pop. 5174) which is most famous for the olive oil it produces. Skirting its central square are gardens, an ancient oil press, cinema, a sprinkling of bars and the slowest restaurant in Europe. It is the capital of the Garrigues comarca (whose greatest claim to fame is the prehistoric – 5000-year-old – wall paintings at El Cogul). Borges' weekly Tuesday market dates back to 1338 and its main festival takes place on the first Sunday in September. The road continues alongside the Urgell Canal which irrigates the parched soil. You will be travelling through fields of olives and vine, occasional almond groves, copses of cypresses and water sprinklers all the way to Lleida.

Alternatively, from Poblet, you can return to Montblanc and take the C240 towards Tàrrega, branching off left to visit the convent at **Vallbona de les Monges**, the most important convent of Cistercian nuns in Catalonia. Unlike their male counterparts elsewhere, the sisters have enjoyed uninterrupted residence since its foundation in 1157. Again the setting, in a lush wooded valley, is typically Mediterranean. A square with monumental fountain, tombs and sarcophagi of 13th-century benefactors stand alongside the church and cloister. Two impressive doorways open onto it, the Romanesque Door of the Dead and the church doorway, above which is perhaps the first Catalan depiction of the Virgin accompanied by two incense-bearing angels. Tombs of various abbesses lie in the church and Jaume I's wife, Queen Violant of Hungary, and their daughter Sancha of Aragón, lie in the sanctuary. A polychrome stone statue of the Virgin by Guillem Seguer, originally part of the retable, stands on the high altar. Other notable features are the 15th-century sculptures of the Burial of Christ and the Gothic Corpus Christi Chapel. There are thirty nuns now living at Santa Maria de Vallbona and, like the other religious communities, they make a great contribution to the cultural and spiritual life of the region.

A short drive away is **Guimerà**, a perfectly preserved medieval village that few seem to visit despite its exquisite charm. The ruined castle (Gothic and Renaissance traces) and Gothic monastery of Vallsanta are notable but it is the village itself that will win hearts. The 'Restaurant Medieval' has built up a fine reputation serving dishes from the period (which means there are no chips – potatoes, along with America, hadn't been discovered yet).

From Guimerà, continue on the C240 to the medicinal springs at **Vallfogona de Riucorb** and thus to **Santa Coloma de Queralt** (pop. 2728) whose surrounding castles were the battlefields for the recapturing of Southern Catalonia from the Moors. Its 14th–16th-century Gothic Church of Santa Coloma has a notable 14th-century retable by Jordi de Déu. The medieval quarter has impressive portals and pretty arcaded streets and squares. From Santa Coloma, branch left on the C241 coming onto the N11 halfway between Igualada and Cervera; here you can either head eastwards through Esparreguera to Barcelona or turn westwards to continue this tour. If you choose the latter course you will quickly pass once more through Cervera (see page 89) and find yourself in **Tàrrega** (pop. 10,959), the capital of the comarca of Urgell, located 42km from Lleida. The ancient city is now an important commercial, agricultural and cultural centre with some fine municipal and ecclesiastical buildings, for example the 17th-century Town Hall and the 18th-century church of Santa Maria de l'Alba located near the arcaded Plaça Sant Antoni. The town has a regional archeological and ethnological museum and Monday weekly market. Its main festivals are on 13 May (Festa Major de les Santes Espines – Festival of the Holy Thorns) and the second Sunday in September when a street theatre comes to town.

Before putting your foot down to Lleida, those wishing to purchase ceramics may wish to make a 5km detour south: **Verdú** may not have Catalonia's largest ceramic industry but it does claim to produce the province's best pottery.

Lleida

LLEIDA is situated on the Riu Segre 157km west of Barcelona. The capital of inland Catalonia and the gateway to Aragón and central Spain, it was already a capital in Iberian times, was a municipium under the Roman Empire and subsequently the centre of a small Arab Kingdom. When it was reconquered by Ramón Berenguer IV in 1149 it became the seat of the bishopric; a hundred and fifty years later, it was home to the first Catalan university, the Estudis Generals, established in 1300.

The population of 107,954 has a reputation for being slow to open but, once prised, Leidatans are unlikely to close. This reputation for loyalty is complemented by a rather dour and hardy image (they need to be hardy with their merciless summers and cold winters). Occasionally, though, Leidatans do throw a party and the Festival of the Snail, which runs alongside the Cultural Fair, is without doubt their best one. A 25m feast of hams is laid out on the bank of the Segre inside which, somehow, snails are cooked.

Although Leidatans are proud of their city and their land, they seem surprised that anyone else should want to visit it. Indeed, having endured nine sieges (it has not shown great perspicacity in choosing the right side in wars), its treasure chest does look a little bare. To say there is not a lot happening at night is generous though somehow life in summer limps on till three or four in the morning. Lleida, nevertheless, is deserving of a day or two of your time and I, for one, greatly enjoyed its distinctive culture and cosmopolitan mix (migrant workers are drawn from the south and from northern Africa). There is an even greater pride here than elsewhere in Catalonia. After all, as Catalonia's first line of defence on its western flank, the city's history of resistance to invading armies makes it the most fiercely Catalan of all. It was here that Pompey and Caesar Augustus clashed and that the Moorish governor, Lope ibn-Muhammad killed Catalonia's founder, Wilfred the Hairy. Napoleon's brother paid it a lengthy visit and blew up the Suda as a farewell gift before departing for home. Most recently the city was razed during the Civil War.

There's a lot of money in Lleida (belying the begging you may encounter), most of it coming from cereal, olive oil, wine and fruit juice products. Many of its inhabitants, unlike most Catalans, prefer to eat out several times a week rather than entertain at home. Apart from this little indulgence however the people have a frugal reputation. Two local sayings point to their caution and frugality, 'Never buy something until you have three times as much in the bank'; 'Before saying yes, talk to

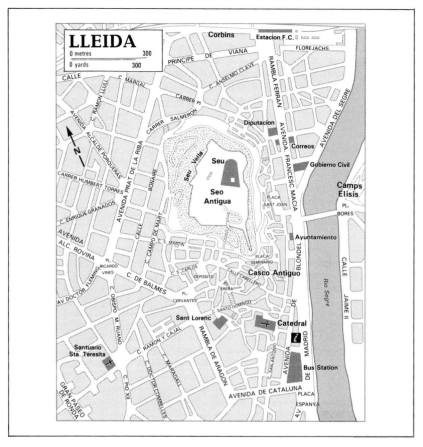

your pillow'. As one friend summed up, 'Leidatans like to keep their fortunes in the banks just in case'.

The outskirts are particularly ugly with industrial pipelines wriggling like maggots towards the town. Alongside the road are car-breakers yards, canning and cement factories and the other ugly stretch marks of unbridled industry. Fortunately, its greatest landmark, La Seu Vella cathedral, like a beacon on the hilltop draws one's eyes away from this wasteland. Just before you cross the Pont Vell there is a rather lovely park, immodestly named the **Camps Elisis** (Champs Elysées) whose gardens encircle fine Modernist buildings.

Crossing the bridge brings us to the Plaça d'Agelet i Garriga and the Tourist Information Office where literature can be picked up and tours arranged. Fronting the river are some of the city's finest municipal buildings gracing the length of the wide boulevard (Av. Madrid to the left and Av. del Segre to the right). Running off the square is the Av. de Francesc Macià which in turn leads into the Rambla de Ferràn, the town's administrative centre which also boasts a provincial palace and impressive Modernist railway station (completely renovated in 1988) replete with Turkish-looking cupolas. To the right of the station, on the streets heading back towards the river, is the daily market.

It is said that Lleida has the longest stretch of continuous shops of any street in Europe (the Carrer Major). More reasonable is the claim that the hill fort, on which the cathedral stands, has been inhabited for at least 4000 years. Situated on the Roca Sobirana are the remains of **La Suda**, or the Arabic Castle, which was converted into the King's Palace for Ramón Berenguer IV's marriage. The site is now dominated by the Seu Vella, the cathedral which was begun in 1203. The fortress offers a fine view over the *teulats* (tiled roofs) of the old square, the Canyeret, and beyond it the River Segre.

It must be said that apart from the magnificent cloister, the **Seu Vella**'s beleaguered state through sieges, vandalism and erosion (pollution), make it a far more impressive sight from a distance than it presents once you get inside. Indeed the night time illuminations are the most flattering, bestowing on it an imposing grandeur which daylight does not afford the crumbling edifice. Approached at night it is an awesome

La Seu Vella, built in the 13th century, dominates Lleida.

sight rising out of some childhood fairy tale to watch over the sleeping city. It was designated a national artistic-historic monument in 1918 and restoration work has been going on since 1949 but it's going to be an uphill struggle. Most of the damage was done after 1707, following the War of Succession, when Felipe V ordered it cease to be a place of worship and had it converted into a military barracks (the university was also closed and the city's other privileges revoked as punishment for the city's support of the Archduke Charles of Austria). The cloister was bricked in to serve as a dormitory. Gunpowder, stored in the first apse, has exploded on three separate occasions, the last time during this century. The high altar has disappeared, the 14th-century paintings depicting the life of the Virgin in the Presbytery are unrecognisable and the chapels skirting the edges are in a similarly poor state, and bare. Statues that have managed to survive are beheaded. The immensity of the building is marked by a feeling of nakedness rather than grandeur.

The ground plan follows the layout of a basilica with three naves, wide cross vault and five apses facing East. The octagonal dome of the central apse, brightly illuminated by its eight windows, is perhaps the most impressive feature inside, apart of course from the cloister which has with some justification been called the finest in Europe. Its individuality is in its location in the west wing of the cathedral (utilising the original Moorish courtyard) and more extraordinarily in its southern passageway whose great arches, intricately carved, line both sides of the walkway, providing an uninterrupted view out over the plain. The cloister, like the cathedral is vast. Light pours in on all sides and no two arches are the same. The portals start out Romanesque and journey through Catalan architectural history ending in the eastern wing on a late Gothic flourish. The capitals show the Cistercian influence (and Moorish before them) in the refusal to depict human form. There is an exception, if you look hard enough, located in the rose at the centre of the first corner arch on the third side depicting the Virgin with child.

Abandoned by the church when the bishop moved to the new cathedral towards the end of the 19th century, it is indicative of the central place it still holds in the people's hearts in that the new Plaça de la Sardana has been built below the Seu Vella and here important occasions are celebrated by a traditional wide circle dancing the *sardana*.

Exiting the fortress brings you to one of several markets (built on the old languages faculty). Alongside is the important 12th-century Romanesque church **Sant Martí** which houses a medieval museum. Unfortunately when I visited it was undergoing extensive renovation and all that seemed to be holding it together was an enormous sheet of plastic. Adjacent is the new Sant Martí's. Its four sets of metal wings, knitted together as a roof, look as if they've been trying to take off from the moment they were put on.

The Carrer de Jaume 1 el Conqueridor (a detour here down the Carrer de Sant Carles is recommended early evening, particularly on Fridays, when students gather for a few glasses of wine in the small dive bars that dot the street) leads into Plaça de Cervantes and thus into the wide Rambla d'Aragón. Standing on the far side of the road outside the university (it used to be a seminary) you can see the belfries of La Seu Vella, Sant Martí and the city's other important church, **Sant Llorenç**. The latter is situated across the street behind the Bishop's Palace and the Musuem of Medieval

Painting. Again it is transitional Romanesque-Gothic. Inside are the Gothic retables of Sant Llorenç, Santa Ursula, Sant Pere and Santa Llucia. Behind, church steps (Escales de St Llorenç) lead through the oldest and poorest district where the washing hangs from balconies, coach lamps jut from walls and the streets become a little less cared for. In Carrer La Palma there's a 'Brasseria' and the 'Assoc Pub' – popular with the over-thirties age group. *Assoc* is Arabic for cellar and this was where the city's grain used to be kept. We turn left in the square up the Carrer de les Monges and this eventually takes us out into the Carrer de Cavallers which by way of contrast was Lleida's wealthiest and most fashionable district a couple of hundred years back. It is still blessed with a number of fine mansions. One of these, an old convent, houses the **Museum of Modern Art**.

Where this street meets the Carrer Major there is another small chapel which marks the spot where the apostle St James once stopped to remove a thorn from his foot on the way to Santiago de Compostela. Apparently he was having a little difficulty so an angel with a lamp appeared and lent a hand and since that day, each year on the Eve of St James, children gather with lanterns and there is a procession of lights accompanied by the song 'Sant Jaume ve de Galicia' (Saint James comes from Galicia).

Turning right past a number of elegant shops brings you to the neo-classical **Catedral Nova** (18th-century) which houses some important Flemish tapestries. An artist was restoring the city's most famous statue when I visited. 'The Virgin of the Bruise' got its name when an overworked master craftsman delegated this commission to his apprentice. Unfortunately the master was so piqued at the beauty of his pupil's creation, he took a hammer to its head. I was assured that the bruise was not being painted out during polychromatic repairs. Opposite is the Gothic **Hospital de Santa Maria** (surmounted by 14th-century Virgin and Child) housing the Archeological Museum and the important archives of the Institut d'Estudis Ilerdenses (Lleida studies).

Retracing your steps along the Carrer Major, at the Plaça Sant Francesc, you will see another church and a Modernist apartment block by Morera (who designed most of Lleida's Modernist architecture). Walking through the square brings you to the riverfront (which was being landscaped when I visited). A few doors along, you arrive at the rear of the neo-classical Town Hall, La Paeria, a magnificent Romanesque 13th-century building. If you peer into the basement window you'll see where condemned prisoners were held before being deposited into the river with a boulder round their necks. Access to the town hall's museum (13th-century Romanesque façade) is back in the Carrer Major. Continuing along the front however, you arrive back at the Tourist Information Centre (again housed in a fine Modernist building) before turning left, past a statue of two unsung local heroes who fought the Romans, through the city gate, into the Carrer Major once more and thus into the **Plaça de Sant Joan**.

Local planners seem to have done their best to destroy what was once an elegant square here with an underground car park that threatens to pop completely back out of the ground at any moment. The lift, designed to ferry workers up the rock face to Seu Vella and over to the other side of town, has never worked. There's also a modern tower in the square that seems to have been covered with tiles rejected by the municipal swimming pool. Fortunately the café terrace, two hotels, delightful tiny old apothecary, and adjoining sweet shop, are putting up a spirited resistance to the onslaught. In the hot summer months water squirts up from the cracks between the paving stones, cooling things down.

I hope I don't sound too discouraging about Lleida because I actually liked it very much: its distinctive raw character and unselfconsciousness is hugely refreshing after some of the preciousness one meets in ancient cities in other parts of Europe.

Before you head south to follow Tour 10 along the banks of the mighty Ebre, a 14km detour north west on the N240 towards the border with Aragón to visit the Codorniu wine estate of **Raimat** is recommended. Below the Moorish castle (rebuilt in the 17th century), vineyards stretch as far as the eye can see.

The estate was transformed from a wilderness to a model vineyard by Don Manel Raventós Domènech at the beginning of the century. Like Puig i Cadafalch's Codorniu forerunner at Sant Sadurní d'Anoia, the winery is a Modernist architectural masterpiece. The *bodega* designed in 1922 by Joan Rubio i Bellver, a pupil of Gaudí, had an entranceway that was the first in Spain to be constructed of reinforced concrete and was built in such a way that water could run over the crow-stepped gable to keep the building cool in summer. The new *bodega*, all marble and glass mirror walls, was designed by Domingo Triay and opened only in 1988.

Tour 11
The Lands of the Ebre to Tortosa and the Delta

Looking at a map of this region, you know from the lack of motorways or even *carreteres nacionals* you are about to embark on untrodden tourist routes. From Lleida, sparsely populated undulating agricultural lowlands stretch southwards to Flix where a series of sierras rise up on either side of the great River Ebre which in turn leads down to Tortosa and on to the Delta d'Ebre marshlands.

Follow the sign 'all directions' out of Lleida, from which you will have a fine view back of the Seu Vella, and take the Albatàrrec N230 road south. As I proceeded, the ambience changed; city clothes were gradually replaced by blue dungarees, cars by tractors, combine harvesters and water trucks. The inhospitable earth yielded up a delicate beauty in the fields of almond blossom but the toll for the *pagesos* (land workers) who scratch a living from the almond and olive harvest is there for all to see in their weatherbeaten, lined faces.

Tottering brick chimneys and fields of yellow rape occasionally interrupt the march of the ubiquitous dusty olive. Clay-coloured villages appear, as if cloned from the same gene; a cluster of homes on a hillside surmounted by a church and some way off, a crumbling Moorish castle. On the outskirts, farm cooperative buildings indicate the mutual dependence of an industry that by necessity has had to be streamlined over the years to survive. In these villages children and young men are a rare commodity. The young have moved to kinder existences in the city (crop rotation on vast farmlands do not make for nine-to-five existences), perhaps exchanging callouses for ulcers.

As you turn left for **La Granadella**, barley and other cereal crops appear. The town has such a large baroque parish church that it is known as 'the cathedral of Les Garrigues' (the name of the comarca), and the ruins of an old castle. From Granadella, take the C233 to **Flix** where you will join the River Ebre for the first time on its journey from close to Santander on the Atlantic coast right across the Spanish heartland to the Mediterranean. Unfortunately to the right of the bridge spanning the river, a white industrial cancer clings to its bank and spreads up the hill. The river's breadth and power has been domesticated by a hydroelectric dam and its polluted waters are evidence of the lack of concern industry here has shown for the environment.

A ferry operates along the banks of the river at Flix but there has been no effort to make a feature of the river bank. The town squats on a hill above it resolutely ignoring its potential beauty. The medieval alleyways that abruptly end at the cliff face are neither as comfortable nor as interesting as those you will meet later and its main square, Plaça Espanya, is grubby and small. My advice would be that it is not worth stopping for the Gothic church and ruined castle. Do pause, though, at the petrol station at the top of the hill for a fine view back across the town and river. The town's major festival takes place at Easter.

It is unfortunate that this first encounter with the great green river should see it so humbled. Follow its progress along the C230 to the village of **Ascó** which is worth a look despite its two nearby nuclear power stations. On the hill two walls still stand from the Templars' castle. The Moorish archway in the Riu Morris leads through to the Carrer Hospital and into a rather lovely old quarter. For some reason the Moors remained here later than elsewhere and therefore their architectural influence is far more noticeable. Women seem to work shifts round the clock sweeping the alleys and attending their flower boxes ensuring Ascó remains a perfect example of the Ebre's Morisc (Moorish) villages. The town's festivals take place on 17 January and 29 September.

The hills start to build on both sides of the road (still the C230) as you follow the river through the deep valley, El Pas de L'Ase. On the far bank the railway line from Barcelona accompanies the road. The pretty village of Garcia comes next and here you leave the gorge and cross the lush green irrigated plain of Mora to **Mora la Nova** whose outskirts are a ribbon of garages descending to the river bank. Unfortunately the main throughfare passes through the heart of this commercial centre making it noisy and dirty.

Before turning right to take the N420 from Mora La Nova to Gandesa and the sierras that take you down to Tortosa, you might like to take a 20-minute detour in the opposite direction on the N420 to **Falset** (pop. 2657), capital of the comarca of Priorat and where the wines from the Terra Alta vineyards are traded. The old town walls are still visible and there is a medieval castle which served once as the residence of the counts of Prades. The town's major festivals take place on the third Sunday in January, 15 August and 7 September. Further north in the beautiful though tortuous Serra de Montsant (a favourite with hikers), the medieval village of **Cornudella** (pop. 980), perched on a rocky promontory on the edge of a sheer precipice, is worth a visit if it can be fitted into your itinerary (it can be reached on minor roads from Falset or by taking the 242, 26km east along the N240). There are a number of interesting chapels here, the Romanesque church of Santa Maria and an artificial lake on the Siurana River (the village of Siurana lies within the town's boundaries). The old quarter has been well restored and its surrounding precipices give the town a dramatic setting. The major festival takes place on 22 August. You might like also to visit the ruins of the oldest Carthusian monastery in Spain at Escaladei. Carnival comes to Cornudella in February.

Returning down the N420 through Mora La Nova, cross the concrete bridge into its twin town **Mora d'Ebre**, the capital of the Ribera D'Ebre comarca, still sheltering behind its ruined fortress (festival 1 May). Continue to **Corbera d'Ebre** (festival third Sunday in March), which sat right in the centre of the exchange of shelling by the Republican army based in Mora d'Ebre and the Nationalists in Gandesa. The town is still largely a ruin and war veterans gather here annually (including Americans from the Abraham Lincoln Brigade). The town's only other distinction is its convent whose outer walls plunge with the cliff face to the vines below. **Gandesa** (pop. 2831), the next town is the capital of another important wine-growing region, the Terra Alta. A number of concomitant traditional crafts, such as making goat skins into leather wine carafes, are still practised and a traditional barrel-making industry is also still flourishing. Gandesa corners 21 per cent of the present comarca's meagre population. It has been a commercial and agricultural centre back to the days when the Knights Templar of Miravet ruled the land.

It was near Gandesa that many British volunteers in the International Brigade lost their lives during the Civil War. In 1938 during the infamous Battle of the Ebro (the river's Castilian name) General Franco had his command post just a couple of miles to the north of the town (appropriately enough on the site of an Iberian necropolis). 60,000 men died here as the Republican advance faltered and was ground down over a dreadful four-month period. I'm afraid the town is generally dirty and dusty, but it does have its features. The town's best restaurant, the Hostel Piqué (with wine press and small garden displaying the vines of the region) is located on the approach to town as is Cesar Martinell's Modernist cooperative cellar (Cooperativa Agricola de Gandesa) with its brightly coloured turret surmounting simple red brickwork. At the rear, alongside the bus terminus, is a series of troughs with a huge corkscrew skewer passing through them that pulps the grapes. There is talk of the building becoming a museum. Across the street, down an alleyway is the Bodega Pedro Rovira. The wines from the region are fruity and notoriously potent (around 14 per cent).

The Plaça del Comerc, is distinguished only by a crumbling medieval terrace and by the plane trees that have been made to link hands round the square as if dancing a sardana. People were clearing up after the morning market when I visited (a Tuesday). Following the Carrer del Forn into the Carrer de Serrano i Sunyer will reveal some elegant *palaus* (mansions of the nobility). The 18th-century mansion at No. 12 was once the home of the barons of Purroi. I poked my nose through the doorway and saw inside the courtyard a wooden staircase and beams which showed that it had known better incarnations that its present one as a garage. Number 4 was the Casa Liori, again from the 18th century, with its coat of arms and similarly projecting wooden roof. On the corner of the street is a plaque commemorating a renowned biologist and monk who lived here. The road leads eventually to a Romanesque-Gothic church with intricate geometrical designs on its 13th-century doorway. Opposite is a medieval arcade whose wooden beams have been lent support by metal support joists. This in turn takes us into a delightful medieval alleyway past the Forn del Castel (castle bakery). The town's major festival is held on the first Sunday in September.

The town offers a number of excursions, including one to a 6th-century BC Iberian settlement. To the west, oak dominates the forest but in the southern Terra Alta, the pine rules. The area has been inhabited at least as far back as the Iron Age. When it was repopulated during the middle ages, Arabic names managed to survive.

From Gandesa travel southwards through a narrow pass on the C221. After 10km you may wish to visit Catalonia's best preserved Modernist cooperative buildings at **Brai**. A tiled mosaic running along the three connected buildings depicts a sublimely romantic story of the farm year by Xavier Nogués (1873–1941). When I was there a cart pulled by a tractor was being filled with almonds via the mechanised chute.

Apart from its wine and almonds, the town also has a healthy basket industry using the leaves of the dwarf fan palm which grows in abundance in the nearby hills. The town straddles a hillside which is reached by the Carrer del Gaudí, and its main festivals are on 17 January and 10 August. Interesting municipal buildings pepper the rather grand avenida out of town to Miravet. However, instead of travelling seawards, rejoin the tour along the N230.

Continue south on the N230 beside the Sanctuary de Fontcalda (a spa with its major festival on the first Sunday in May) whose gorge has been carved out by the river Canaleta, and Prat del Comte which rises naturally out of its surroundings like a rocky outcrop. At the latter we turn right onto a minor road to **Bot**. The ugly tenements on the outskirts conceal an attractive older centre radiating from the Plaça de l'Esglesia whose Town Hall clock face is the dominant feature among the splash of blue houses. The Candlemas festival takes place here on 2 February and there is a three-day summer festival around 15 August. At Bot, take the road which accompanies the railway to Horta de Sant Joan, 14km away.

This land you pass through is richly cultivated (olives, almonds and of course the

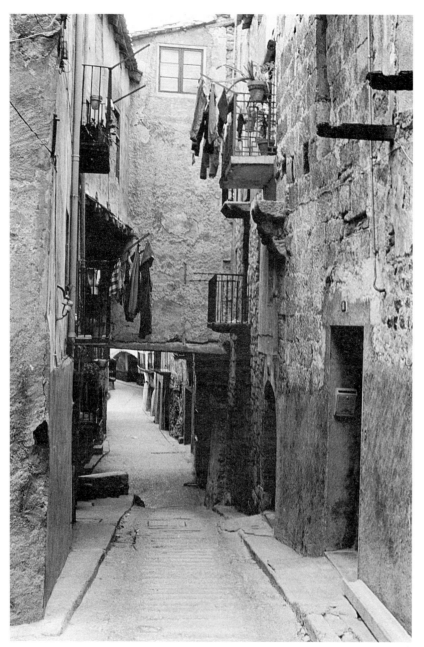

The medieval masterpiece of Horta de Sant Joan.

ubiquitous vine) and the climate healthy. There is little industry and the populations are concentrated in small villages. It is, as you might expect, extremely popular country for hiking. The perfectly preserved medieval town of **Horta de Sant Joan**, recaptured from the Moors by the Templars in 1197, with its wooden arcades and balconies overhanging narrow cobbled alleyways, is undoubtedly the highlight of this particular tour.

Approaching the town you can see a chapel and crucifix on the summit of a hill to the left, Santa Barbara, its approach impossibly steep and inaccessible. Below it is the Monastery of Sant Salvador d'Horta. In Horta, the church's buttresses along with the homes turn their backs resolutely to the hilltop shrine perhaps believing that anyone who got up there must have been in league with the devil. The unbroken terrace forms the town wall overhanging a valley filled with the heavy bouquets of blossom and pine.

At the centre of the small modern Plaça de Catalunya is a dugout which makes the absurd boast, 'Museu Municipal'. Inside are a few rusty gardening implements and the legend '1957'. If that's when it opened then I have little doubt that was the year it closed too. As you make your way up towards the church you will pass houses whose huge stone blocks lend their considerable powers of persuasion to tiles to remain fixed to roofs despite the attentions of the persistent winds that buffet these homes. The street that leads to the church passes through two inter-connecting squares, the Plaça de Sant Salvador d'Horta and Plaça de l'Esglesia. These are lined with a potpourri of mud-coloured and bare brick buildings alongside an elegant 18th-Century mansion and the parish church which has grass sprouting from its belfry. A commemorative plaque laments the town's war dead and beside it is another announcing the money raised between 1983 and 1987 for refurbishing the Town Hall.

The Carrer Baix has wooden balconies, slate and tin roofs, overhead galleries connecting houses on one side of the street to the other, cacti standing guard outside windows framed by Andalucian borders and Morisco archways leading off into further labyrinthine passageways. No wonder the town is said to have inspired Picasso's cubist period. The artist spent eight months here in 1898, supposedly living for part of that time in a cave. Miró followed and painted here in 1917. The town's major festivals are held on 25 April and 8 September.

From Horta take the road which loops back up to Prat del Comte and down to the river, which you then follow into **Tortosa** (pop. 31,445) and up the steep ascent to the fortifications encircling the Parador Castell de la Suda.

Tortosa

The River D'Ebre's banks have been washed with the blood of its people with disturbing regularity over the centuries but none has been harder to wash away than that spilt so freely during the Civil War. For more than a year the armies, divided by the river, fought their bloodiest battle. Today many families, brought back together only in mourning, are daily reminded of their losses by the huge commemorative metal sculpture that soars like a phoenix from the water. This ugly, militaristic,

Franco-inspired statue built from the only pillar that remained of the old bridge after the war, supposedly commemorates the war dead on both sides but fools no one as to its allegiance.

If you stay in **TORTOSA** and can't afford the parador then at least have a drink in the bar or better, splash out on a meal – the local dishes I tried here were the best I had in any of the paradors in Catalonia. Some of the Catalan delicacies on offer included fried frogs' legs and baby eels cooked in a heavy garlic sauce.

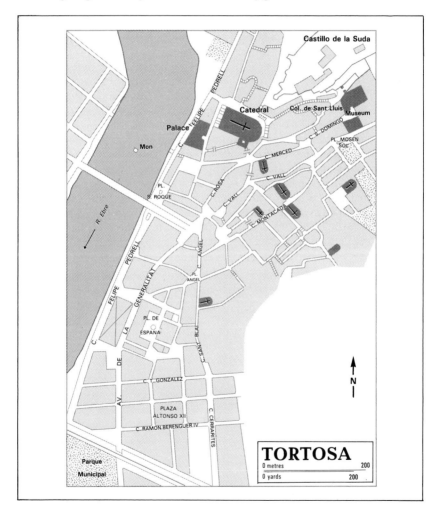

The parador is built at the centre of the old Moorish castle (the 10th-century well is still there). Before this incarnation it was a Roman acropolis and before that a prehistoric settlement. Roman pillars litter the grounds like breeze blocks on a building site. Though impressively grand inside, it is never ostentatious. Furniture is

115

solid and handsome rather than decorative and what the wooden balconies lack in hours of sunlight (they face the wrong way), they make up for in fine views along the river into the sierras. The castle mirador offers an uninterrupted view over the flying buttresses of the cathedral and the patchwork of tiled roofs that clatter down the hillside.

Opposite the cathedral is a large Modernist building running the length of the block. A glass gallery on the corner extends over all three floors and around the windows is floral pargeting. Beyond the cathedral's baroque façade, a flight of steps lead up to the main cloister. Entering under the archway, a small chapel opens on the right. Inside, when I visited, a number of youngsters were involved in restoration work on a tapestry of the last supper.

The cathedral cloister is neither as large or as light as Lleida's and certainly cannot compete with the beauty of Poblet's. Nevertheless its central fountain and two concealed sundials are deserving of attention as is the 6th-century gravestone of a young Jewish girl with its inscription in Hebrew, Latin and Greek.

For those souls for whom all cathedrals are more or less the same, the one at Tortosa is just another, and it is in fact pretty ordinary one despite the fact it's over 600 years old and was built on the site of a Roman temple and a mosque. It has three naves, a wooden retable of the Verge de l'Estrella, silver reliquaries from the 14th century and a chapel made out of jasper dedicated to the Verge de la Cinta. Poorly lit, cold and sparse, its most notable features are not from the Gothic period but from the anarchists' who during the civil war vandalised many church artefacts as well as firing the buildings. The defaced pulpit is a particularly good example of this period. To be fair, though, much of the vandalism in evidence here was done during

Tortosa cathedral overlooking the river Ebre.

the Peninsular War over 100 years earlier. A line of rather intimidating confessionals alternate with several small altars skirting the ambulatory.

Exiting the cathedral on the far side into Porta de Palau, you soon come upon the impressive Gothic Episcopal Palace and Palace of Oliver de Boteller (whose fortune was built as a salt dealer). Particularly impressive is the Modernist Escorxador Public (abattoir), a stone's throw away in the Plaça Escorxador down on the river bank. Built in 1908, the characteristic plain red stepped bricks are adorned with witty ceramic figures of goats and pigs. Continuing northwards out of town will take you into the old Jewish Quarter (head for the area around Plaça Platge – there's still a synagogue nearby).

Taking the opposite direction southwards past the river's commemorative plaque (put up on 5 April 1968) 'A los combatientes que hallaron gloria en la Batalla del Ebro,' ('To the soldiers who found glory in the Battle of the Ebro') you come to the Rambla Felipe Pedrell where the Armeria Descarrega shows the local passion for handguns, rifles and fishing equipment. Continuing under the bridge we come to the busy municipal market (1886) with its mountains of salt fish, flowers, strawberries, whole legs of ham, pastries and *tapas*. It is spotlessly clean, a riot of colour and definitely the liveliest place in town. The pastries, *tapas* and *bocadillos* make it a good place for breakfast or lunch. The El Parc restaurant, located in the beautiful park beyond the Plaça Alfonso XII (which incidentally is the centre of Tortosa's Modernista Eixample) is also a good place to eat. On the side of the restaurant, facing the road, is an old steam train (note too the fine Modernist building across the road which is now home to the insurance company, Mutual Cyclops) and on the park side a café terrace sitting in the centre of the wide palm lined avenue. The park also houses the

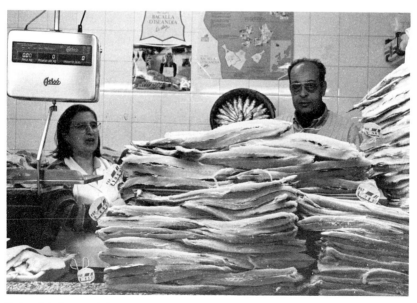

Tortosa's indoor market.

Market Exchange (La Llotja) where official prices of wheat were once fixed for the whole of the western Mediterranean.

Between the municipal market and the park is the Plaça d'Espanya where the Tourist Office is located. I walked through the Plaça de l'Angel and past the rather chilling C. de la Sang (road of blood) into the C. de l'Angel and the lovely C. de la Rosa. Here I admired the exquisite glass and marble façade of the Pharmacia Verges. Inside the panelled wooden ceiling was inlaid with tiles, the ancient oak cupboards and shelves held a plethora of fragile bottles and pharmaceutical products. Next door at No. 5, I pushed the huge wooden door ajar and found myself in a Moorish courtyard with water splashing in a fountain surrounded by a luxuriant jungle of plants. On the opposite side of the street was the Palau Despuig which houses an art school and library.

Brown-habited nuns appeared on every corner, either resident at one of the city's three convents or on pilgrimages. The Gothic Santa Clara Convent is worth a visit and the Renaissance style Convent of la Purissima even more deserving of your time. Whilst the rest of Tortosa's ecclesiastical architecture is characteristically on the grand scale, the latter, on the C. Montcada, is characterised by its delicacy and prettiness. The lightness of the vaulted celestrial blue ceiling and vibrancy of the stained glass is most striking after the gloom of the cathedral. Not surprisingly the Madonna takes pride of place on the high altar.

Nearby is the Municipal Archive and Museum and the 16th-century church of Sant Domenec which houses important medieval documents including Roman exhibits and the first legal document to be written in Catalan in 1272.

Medieval alleyways (ask for the C. del Castell) lead back up to the castle. The alleyways are narrow and plants cascade from balconies over which colourful straw blinds are airing. At moments I felt I was in the Casbah in Algiers and certainly of all Catalonia's cities, Tortosa had the most Moorish feel to it. It was an important Roman city 2000 years ago and then the capital of a Taifa kingdom. Its demise after the reconquest in 1148 by Ramón Berenguer, who made the castle his new home, was short-lived and it became a fabulously wealthy city again controlling all the salt and wheat commerce along the Mediterranean Occident. Now it has to be content with merely being the regional capital of the Baix Ebre comarca. The city is the furthest point inland navigable by large boats and the life of the river pervades the town no less than the sea does its big sister, Tarragona, further up the coast. The city's main festival is held in the first week of September and there is a swimming race down the Ebre to Amposta on 15 August.

A worthwhile detour from the city, particularly if you did not arrive from Lleida and thus have not visited the Terra Alta, is back up the eastern bank of the river into the Serra de Boix and the Serra de Cardo where locals exchange fishing rods for rifles and head into the hills on hunting trips.

The Delta de l'Ebre

The fertile river banks offer extensive orange groves and orchards of peach and apricot alongside smaller market gardens. Only the occasional whitewashed flaking rustic farmhouse replete with well, overhanging vines and barking dog breaks into the landscape of the fields. Just before the one-horse town of Tivenys (carnival ball in February) whose orchards spread down to the river's edge, you may like to pull off the road to view the swollen waters across the bank at the Xinys dam. The bottle-green Ebre has picked up speed here and is ready for its final spurt to the sea. As you climb higher up the valley, the hills fall away into cultivated valleys and the road twists and turns. In a valley a few miles beyond Rasquera (main festival at Easter) a chain-operated barge transports cars across to the western bank and thus into **Miravet**, cradled under a rocky outcrop surmounted by an extensive castle that is the finest example from the Moorish occupancy. Although, unlike some Moorish strongholds in the region, they didn't last beyond the mid 12th century, the Moorish flavour remains despite the Romanesque Church the Knights Templar promptly erected in its centre. The town's major festivals take place on the first Sunday in August (summer festival of St Domènec de Guzman) and on the Sunday closest to 12 October (Festa Major de la Mare de Deu de Grácia).

Alternatively, instead of taking the ferry crossing you could stay on the road a further 10km through Ginestar and on to Mora la Nova and loop across the river to its twin town, Mora d'Ebre. Either of these options would allow you then to take in the Gandesa and Horta de Sant Joan circuit and return to Tortosa on the western bank.

Travelling down the southern bank of the Ebre from Tortosa takes us away from the drama of the hills to the even rhythms of the flatlands. Tortosa's outskirts on either bank of the river provide some of the finest scenery in the whole area with Moorish wells and ingenious ancient irrigation systems. Beside the road are *masies* (farm-houses), avenues of broad-trunked plane trees, cypresses, tottering chimneys, orange groves and fields of poppies. The N230 to the south of the river leads to **Amposta** (pop. 14,449), the capital of the comarca of Montsia where the rice from the delta is traded. The town enjoys a view over the river as it stretches out towards the sea creating a rent in the land 300m broad. Unfortunately the Ebre is at risk from industry and the offshore oil rigs. Frequently dolphins and other large sea creatures get thrown up on the banks here, as they do at other points along the coast.

Boat racing between the town's two bridges seems popular (a race to Ampolla is held in June). Again tottering chimney stacks dot the outskirts and an occasional fine old building (such as the one at Plaça de la Pau) overlooks the river. The town has two interesting museums, archeological and ornithological, a market, *escorxador* and La Carrova Tower. The town's major festival is held between 14 and 22 August when bulls are chased through the streets. There is also another festival on 15 August.

The Tourist Office (tel. 977-70 39 53) has literature and information on the Delta de l'Ebre region, an extraordinary arrow head of land jutting into the Mediterranean and designated the most important aquatic environment in the Western Mediterranean after the Camargue. Some of the descriptions of this national park, Catalonia's largest area of wetlands, have evoked an antediluvian paradise of equilibrium and beauty. The landscape of the park is not, however, stunningly beautiful though it is bountiful, and touring the northern half veers closer to visual monotony than inspiration. Perhaps this explains the delta's reputation for mirages for the flatlands certainly create a mesmeric effect reminiscent of the Sahara. A thirsty V-shaped concrete canal carves its way through rice fields fringed with wild cabbages and flowers and, an occasional pond flanked by bamboo, reeds and rushes relieves the monotony.

Malaria and Barbary pirates saw to it that the population was kept down in the past. In the middle ages salt-mining, the trade in leeches and manufacture of soda supported the meagre population. It wasn't until the early 17th century that Cistercian monks from Benifassà attempted to grow rice; now the region accounts for 98 per cent of Catalonia's total output.

It is worth visiting the Eco Museum (just before you reach La Cava): this reduction of the delta with its miniature canals and ponds displays the region's flora and fauna in an outdoor natural habitat. There are noticeboards (which are very informative if you read Catalan) and a bird look-out post overlooking the egrets, periquets and ibis that have taken up residence by the pond. Next door a brick building houses the reptilian river life. The museum is open 10am–6pm (closed Sundays). The gaggle of town shops exhibit their local basketware, there are a couple of fishmongers, a sports stadium and surprisingly, a bike hire shop.

The **Isle of Buda** can be visited via a ferry from **Riomar**: you will find a sublimely indolent scene like something from a Catalan Laurie Lee reminiscence. From La Cava a transbordador raft will take you and your car across the Ebre to the southern sector of the park. The road leads out to the furthest tip of the delta where it meets the seemingly endless **Platja dels Eucaliptus**. Here I suddenly felt the atmosphere of the delta had overtaken me. Its beauty is not sudden nor dramatic but something that seeps and accumulates, finally flooding the consciousness.

From here take the road which loops back to **Sant Carles de la Ràpita** (pop. 9960) whose harbour you may find alive with the bustle of its afternoon fish auction and fleet of fishing boats. The town smells of salt and shellfish and displays no modesty in claiming to have 'the most important fishing harbour in Catalonia'. In fact it was the result of an 18th-century project by Charles III to found a great city port and its success is clear in the inflexible rectangular grids of its layout. The town is famed for its prawns and enjoys a very mild climate protected by the peaks of the Montsia range. Nowadays you're as likely to find oil men from the off-shore rigs in the bars as you are fishermen. The town's major festivals take place on 25 July and 8 September.

Tour 12
The Costa Daurada

Much of the littoral of the New Catalonia, recaptured from the Moors 800 years ago, is in dire need of reconquest from the speculators who, like their North African bedouin cousins, have covered the coast in canvas, in an attempt to corner the bottom end of the holiday market (70 per cent of Spain's camp sites are found in Catalonia). Their success has been so marked – even Sitges, in the peak season is totally besieged – that many residents leave in July and August and some are quitting altogether, convinced the downward spiral is irreversible.

Outside the peak season (July and August) though, the Costa Daurada (Golden Coast) still has much to offer. Unlike the tight pretty bays of the Costa Brava, it boasts gently banking sea floors and long straight stretches of fine sand that have earned the nickname 'baby beaches'. Another major difference between these coastal neighbours is in the tourists they attract. Costa Daurada, like the rest of Spain, may be inundated with foreign visitors in the peak season, but it remains fundamentally a destination for the Spanish (especially from Zaragoza and Madrid). One final significant difference is the fact that the Costa Daurada has a real coastal capital in Tarragona whereas inland, Girona appears totally indifferent to the effervescence of the Costa Brava.

One crucial feature that has spared the coast total disfigurement has been the railway line running through Barcelona down Spain's Mediterranean coast. This, along with the route nacional (whose restaurants offer excellent value menús del día) have proved to be important barriers to the developers and have mostly confined the concrete anonymity to a thin wedge overlooking the beaches. Sitges is therefore the only genuinely elegant seafront resort along the coast; the inhabitants of the other villages have preferred the safety of hillside defences, so that whilst many beach resorts are soulless places offering beach, disco, bars and little else, their elder sister villages, a mile or less inland, remain mostly untouched. Nowhere better typifies the janus-faced nature of Spain than New Catalonia. The cement scarred coast stares blindly out over the Mediterranean, brandishing fistfuls of pesetas, uncaring of its own ugliness. Inland however, the aristocratic good looks remain largely uncorrupted by the passing of time.

The Golden Coast stretches about 250km from the Delta de l'Ebre to Calella on the Maresme coast north of Barcelona. This tour continues from the south, heading northwards from the Delta de l'Ebre National Park.

L'Ampolla (pop. 1210), just to the north edge of the Delta on the N340, signals the start of the high rise holiday apartments that tend to dominate the coast before Tarragona. There has been little attempt by the developers to take into account landscape or local stone. Ampolla (main festival 24 June – Festa Major Sant Joan) has a pier and marina and a balcony runs round the rim of the town. There's also a cluster of fish restaurants (Ca'n, Pinana and Casa Llambrich) but a better recommendation for a lunch stop would be the Plaça Joan Miró on the harbour front at the next town up the N340 coast road, **L'Ametlla de Mar** (pop. 3750). It's an older town with palms, rusting anchors and brightly coloured fishing smacks. There is a small open fish market operated by the Confraria de Pescadors that sells fish freshly caught in the Gulf of St George. The Plaça del Canó also has some fine fish restaurants facing the old fortifications. Major festivals are on 2 February (Festa Major de la Candelera) and 29 June (Festa Major de Sant Pere Pescador – festival of St Peter the Fisherman).

Next up the coast is **L'Hospitalet de L'Infant** which is worth a detour only if you're desperate for a swim (it has a long beach of coarse sand and stone) or fancy a Sunday stroll along the beach front market which sells everything from kitchen utensils to *churros*. One mile south there is a nudist beach.

Miami Platja provides much of the same and you won't find a beach really worthy of the name until you reach **Cambrils** (pop. 11,211), where bars, take-away grilled chickens, discos, campsites and supermarkets are predominant. Older features include the 17th-century Church of Santa Maria, which faces the central, palm-lined Rambla Jaume Juan. There's also an arcaded square, 18th-century hermitage and Samá Park containing the palace of the Marquis of Marianao. Harbour restaurant terraces bubble with lunchtime conversation and visitors appear to be a notch or two wealthier than those so far encountered further south. The town has the distinction of possessing not one, but three highly thought of restaurants: the Can Gatell, Casa Gatell and Eugenia. The sandy beach is kept company by a never-ending succession of apartments, restaurants and hotels. Where land hasn't yet been built on, they're building on it. Major festivals in Cambrils are on 29 June (Festa Major Sant Pere – Festival of St Peter, with a boating competition and swimming across the harbour) and 8 December (Jocs Florals Infantils i Jovenils).

The only way of knowing that you've left Cambrils and entered the coastline's largest resort, **Salou**, is the sign over the road telling you. In rapid succession you pass 'The Railway – British Pub', a Wimpy and 'The Hideaway British Chippie'. Twenty years ago it was a small resort catering mostly for the inhabitants of nearby Reus. Its moment of history came earlier, in 1229, when Catalonia's King Jaume I the Conqueror set sail to seize Mallorca from the Moors. The 16th-century Torre Vella was built to protect the town from Turkish pirates.

Whilst very much catering to the British tourists who make up the bulk of the visitors, Salou is no Benidorm despite its permanent fairground and a population that swells to a quarter of a million in the peak season. True it has skyrise abominations that could do battle with the monstrosities of its southern cousin but these have wisely been corralled in one zone and the rest of the developments show a modicum of restraint keeping to a modest six storeys. The actual beach front stretches 13.5km and is mostly palm-fringed, attractive and surprisingly clean (though I should point out that I visited out of season). This stretch is a mixture of long straight beaches and small pine-clad creeks. The Pg de Jaume I El Conqeridor beach-front walkway is littered with modern sculptures (and a monument to King Jaume I), playgrounds and coloured fountains. The road then lifts and winds under overhanging palms creating a Riviera feel that is reinforced by restaurants bearing names such as St Tropez and

Cap Ferrat. The road twists for a further kilometre before running into the new resort of **La Pineda**. Salou's major festival is held on 15 August.

As you near the important port of Tarragona the gentle landscape of carob, vines, hazelnut and almond trees is replaced as an apocalyptic industrial skyline gets into its stride, with chemical factories belching into sky and sea (a nearby nuclear power station doesn't do much for the atmosphere either). Off-shore rigs such as Repsol's make their contribution to the pollution problem, determinedly ignoring their effects on monuments and beaches.

Tarragona

TARRAGONA is Catalonia's second city and undoubtedly its most Mediterranean one. Located roughly 100km from Tortosa, Lleida and Barcelona, its population (111,000) is double that of a generation ago and has now far outgrown its city walls.

The ancient Roman city of Tarraco was capital of half of Spain, its largest province and one of the richest seaports in the Roman Empire. Even earlier, in fact six hundred years before the birth of Christ, it was an important walled Iberian city named Cosse. It is hardly surprising therefore that Tarragona claims to be the most important archeological centre along the peninsula. Perhaps equally important for the modern visitor is its feeling of space with wide streets, abundant parkland, and its impressive sea view from the mirador skirting its southern boundary.

The **Plaça Imperial Terraco**, at the west end of the Rambla Nova, is a good place to start the tour as all the city's major road radiate from it. However, you may like to take a preliminary walk down Carrer Pere Martell which leads down to the fishing port, **El Serallo**, where the best and cheapest fish restaurants are located and a fresh fish market is held each afternoon when the fleet comes in. La Puda is recommended. Further along on the Pg de la Independencia is the **Paleo-Christian Museum** with its comprehensive collection of sarcophagi and mosaics from Spain's most important early Christian necropolis (3rd–4th centuries) which was unearthed along the banks of the River Francoli. It was here that Fruitós, the first Christian bishop to be martyred, and his deacons Auguri and Eulogi were buried along with two thousand others in the first centuries following Tarragona's conversion by St Paul.

Built in the 1850s and spanning 46m from one side to the other, the **Rambla Nova** runs for a kilometre before ending abruptly at the Balcón del Mediterraneon. On the right is a Modernist building built in 1910, and to the left the balcony leads us along the **Passeig de les Palmeres**. The 'Boulevard of the Palms' now manages only a single palm but nonetheless it remains the city dwellers' favourite promenading spot. The Balcony of the Mediterranean skirts the bluff for more than 200m round to the Rambla Vella. Here landscaped gardens fall away to a surprisingly complete **Roman Amphitheatre** (which hosts open-air theatre in the summer months) nestled just behind the sliver of man-made municipal beach. In the amphitheatre student volunteers are tirelessly piecing together the remains of a Romanesque church that was built on the site where Bishop Fruitós was martyred.

The Romans arrived in 3BC and stayed 700 years. Emperor Augustus himself lived in the **Praetorium** (now known as Pilate's Tower) a quarter of a century before the

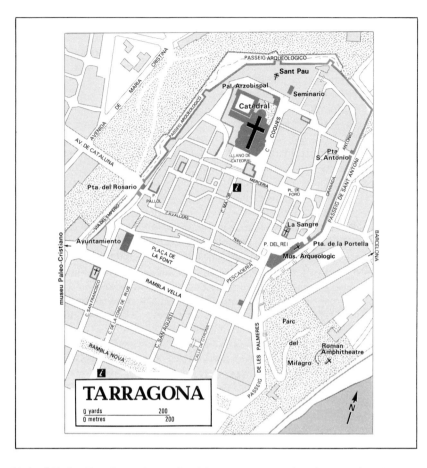

birth of Christ. Developers have a hard time in Tarragona for wherever they dig they find another historically important site and are required by law to stop. Some do. Others move the bulldozers in as fast as they can. As I passed one building site, I was shown a wall from the Roman Forum that had been uncovered the previous day whilst digging the foundations for a new pizza bar.

Continuing past the traffic island at the head of the Rambla Vella, you will come to a cluster of important sites and museums. Next to the Praetorium on the Plaça del Rei is the **Museu Nacional Arqueològic** which houses Catalonia's most important collection of Roman exhibits. Nearby are more important Roman and medieval antiquities in the **Museu d'Historia**. Retracing your steps to the Rambla Vella you come upon the recently excavated **Roman Circus** (it was discovered only recently when a cinema was demolished). A makeshift museum has opened displaying objects found so far.

A little further along the Rambla Vella, turn right into Carrer del Trinquet Nou and thus into the Plaça de la Font where the imposing **Town Hall** sits. Two thousand years

124

ago horses raced here for the amusement of 23,000 spectators. Now, in the month of September, the *castellers* gather to build their human pyramids.

Taking the pedestrianised Baixada de la Misericòrdia from the Plaça de la Font, climb the cobbled passageway through the oldest part of town, past the pastry and antique shops in the **Carrer Major**. The ancient, former Town Hall next to the Gothic arcades is well worth visiting with its medieval structures visible beneath 17th- and 18th-century later constructions. This very elegant street eventually leads into the **Plaça Santiago Rusiñol** where the city's transitional (i.e. Romanesque into Gothic) cathedral is located and a Sunday morning toys and antiques market is held. Some people still gather their drinking water from the fountain beside the medieval arcade here as it is better than that in the domestic supply. Local people were recently overjoyed to hear of plans to pump water to the city from the Ebre. That was until newspaper reports informed them that although it wasn't polluted, it was radioactive (from the two nuclear power stations at Ascò)!

In the adjoining Plaça de la Seu, which houses the **Cathedral of Saint Tecla**, a plaque dated 1911 commemorates the centenary of the billeting of Wellington's troops in the cathedral cloister and reminds one of the city's historical military and ecclesiastical duality. Apart from the Romans whose most infamous soldier, Pontius Pilate, was born here, the city has been levelled by the Visigoth King Eurico and Muslim invaders. Before the Civil War the city was known as the city of priests and soldiers because it had the most important archbishop in Spain (despite Toledo's more official representative) as well as a very heavy military presence.

The cathedral is another ecclesiastical triumph of Gothic architecture, its enormity (it is the largest in Catalonia) concealed by the warren of narrow streets that hem it in. Its façade was built from Roman stone and has a most lovely vast rose window. Unfortunately the figures of the apostles are badly disfigured. When I expressed sadness that so much had been destroyed by the Peninsula and Civil wars, my companion pointed to one figure and said 'We knocked that one's head off playing football here when I was a boy.' He went on, however, to say the cathedral did not suffer the vandalism prevalent elsewhere because 'it has a bigger place than religion in the people's heart.'

Its name, Saint Tecla, comes from the world's first martyred Christian and the city's patron saint, who was said to have accompanied Paul into the city. In the chapel of Saint Tecla a concealed tomb is opened annually on 23 September to show believers one of the martyr's arms. The martyrdom itself, as depicted in the cathedral, was particularly gruesome even by Roman standards.

The cathedral was built between the 12th and 15th centuries. Its height and sparseness are particularly resonant when filled with sounds of the 16th-century organ but to hear it you'll have to take a pew by 9am. The cathedral's high altar is a 15th-century alabaster work by the local artist Pere Juan depicting the life and martyrdom of Saint Tecla. It has been suggested, with very good reason, that it was this high altar that impressed the young Gaudí while he was studying here (he had grown up in nearby Reus) to such an extent that the towers of the Sagrada Família may have come straight from his unconscious memory.

In the Cathedral Museum is a large 15th-century tapestry, 'The Keys of the Pope', that came from the Vatican; there are several other impressive tapestries in this

Tarragona's cathedral square is dedicated to one of Catalonia's most important painters.

museum. On the right as you enter is The Funeral Tapestry from Poblet commemorating the death of the Duke of Cardona in the 17th century. Either side are more figurative 16th-century works; the first of Samson carrying two of his prison doors in Gaza and the second showing him tearing open the mouth of a lion. Opposite is one of the largest and most important early Renaissance tapestries, 'The Powers' celebrating the might of the army, church and land.

The Cathedral Cloister is one of the loveliest in Spain; its island of calm showing a distinct Arabic influence (it was built on an old mosque which in turn was built upon the Roman Temple of Jupiter). It is unusually large even by Catalonia's standards, 70m high and spanning 45m from wall to wall with 267 columns. The capitals occasionally depict animal form, a novelty after the Cistercian monasteries tour in the Conca de Barberà (see Tour 9). One particularly witty example depicts rats so contemptuous of a very old cat they carry him on a stretcher to his burial, only for the cat to pounce half way there, reminding observers that brains are preferable to brawn, stealth to strength.

Turning right outside the cathedral leads through the old whitewashed Jewish quarter, now filled with Andalucian migrants (it is claimed two-fifths of the city's population is migrant) and thus to Baixada del Roser where you will find more Roman ruins jutting out at the side of Romanesque arches below Gothic arches below a 16th-Century Dominican convent.

Nearby lie the city walls and **Pg Arqeológic** that again clearly display the successive layers of Tarragona's long and varied history. At the base are the vast stones of the aptly named Cyclopian period, that must have taken enormous strength to move and work. Immediately above them are the smaller, much more regular Roman blocks followed by Iberian and Etruscan contributions. Passing under the Town Gate ('del Roser'), one of six cyclopean entrances built in the megalithic base, you can either turn right to another of the city's archaeological museums or alternatively turn left along the **Via de l'Imperi Roma**. The latter, a Roman mosaic-paved walkway lined with cypresses, leads back into the modern town.

Carrer Mendes Nunes and Santa Agustina, off the Ramblas, are pedestrianised and the Carrer Unió is a popular shopping street. Another worthwhile visit (as always) is to the market. The bullring has six or seven bullfights a year and is unusual in being located within the city rather than a few miles outside. On even years it also plays host to *colles* (groups) of *castellers* from every corner of the province who build their monumental towers to great applause (the towers also walk from the Cathedral to the Town Hall annually on 24 September). The bullring can be visited during the daytime though opening hours seem to be dependent on whim alone. The handsome three-tiered stadium is one hundred years old and can hold 15,000 people. It is located near the Lower Forum on Carrer Lleida. The city's **Tourist Office** is on Carrer Fortuny.

From St John's Night on 24 June there is hardly a week in summer without some saint or historical event being celebrated. A particularly important day in the city's calendar is St Tecla's Day on 23 September; a flour battle takes place during the winter carnival and Holy Week processions are also memorable events in Tarragona.

Excursions from Tarragona

Four kilometres north-west of the city, alongside the Lleida road is a two-tier Roman aqueduct known as Pont de Diable, Devil's Bridge (it can also be seen from the Tarragona pay booth on the motorway). It spans more than 200m and originally ran for 32km, an eloquent testament to Roman engineering. Although it was probably built over many years during the first half of the 1st century AD, in medieval times it was thought to be the Devil's work executed in a single night.

Eight kilometres from town on a minor road leading from the N420 to Reus is a 4th-century paleo-Christian structure in Constantí that was built over an important Roman villa (a national artistic-historic monument) whose domed roof still has the traces of mosaics. Less worthy of a visit are the remains of the Tower of the Escipiones, 6km from town.

Nearby **Reus** (14km from Tarragona, pop. 85,000), on the borders of the vineyards of the Baix Camp, is worth a very brief detour. It claims to be the world capital of the dried fruit trade as well as the birthplace of Gaudí, Fortuny and General Prim but its commercial centre disguises a larger industrial reality. It may be where Gaudí grew up but the town and the Barri Gaudí council estate, designed by Ricard Bofill certainly don't pay the great man any compliments. The one exception to its distinct ugliness is its glorious main square with impressive buildings and terraced cafés surrounding a statue of General Prim. If you do visit, don't miss Domenèch i Montaner's wonderful Casa Navas and Institut Pere Mata.

The coast north of Tarragona

Leaving Tarragona behind, you quickly arrive at the least developed beach along the coast. For beach and nothing but beach you'd be hard pressed to beat the endless sands of **Platja Llarga** whose march is only interrupted by a couple of restaurants (the Meson del Mar is cheapest and best). **Tamarit** has a pleasant beach with a castle dramatically surmounting a rocky outcrop. There are a number of camp sites here with access to the long beach which is a mixture of sand and small stones. In fact from here on up there will be camp sites by the dozen backing onto beaches. Fortunately this, like the urbanization, is somewhat muffled by pine-clad hills.

Working your way back towards Barcelona we next come to **Altafulla**, a favourite of mine despite the fact that it only has a sliver of sand at either end of its pebble and rock beach. The line of fishermen's cottages along the front gives it a Bréton feel, disrupted only by a very Spanish *tapas* bar, El Niu, half way along with a smattering of tables overlooking the sea (and with the cleanest toilet I've found in Spain).

Crossing the route national takes you immediately into the old village which, in my opinion, is the finest of the coast's hillside inland villages with its castle, church, medieval alleyways and mansions (to call them houses would be demeaning) mostly dating from the 18th century. The streets are spotlessly clean and at night most beautiful when illuminated by coach lamps jutting from the walls. The Town Hall now stands where once the Forum did. Conservation orders protect everything within the three medieval gateways and it wasn't so long back that a river brought

Tamarit castle on the Costa Daurada.

pirates right the way up to the castle. One of the village's fiestas remembers other bad days when bodies were taken out of the gates for burning during the plague years. Twenty years ago another chilling reminder came when the church's garden wall came down during a flood and a mountain of human bones deluged the village.

The Marquès of Tamarit's daughter married one of Franco's grandsons here in the early 1980s and invited the whole village into the castle for cocktails. A fair number of foreigners have settled in Altafulla giving it a decidedly cosmopolitan lively atmosphere at night when imported restaurants and local bars open up. The Bar El Coral (which has a few self contained apartments) is the favourite watering hole. At weekends it is filled with the sounds of Spanish guitars and singing as Catalans and South Americans from Barcelona come to party with the owners Jill Rassmussen and John Arnold. For an earlier glass or two of local wine in the summer try Paco's Bar where you can get *churros* or *tapas* (out of season it opens only at weekends). Paco and his wife Rita make everybody welcome.

Continuing up the coast you come next to **Torredembarra** where you can turn off left to join the A7 motorway (Barcelona is 80km away) or to visit the old town with its 12th-century castle and restored 17th-century neo-Classical church. Turning off right however will lead you down to the beach, bars and discos such as Black Steps and Long Play. Fishermen's boats are pulled up on a fine long beach that, out of season, is sparsely populated. The Co-operativa Maritima (1895) is an interesting café and fine old building on the Carrer de la Industria.

Next along the coast road is the smaller, more appealing resort of **Creixell** with its limpid waters and long clean beach. Here the fishermen's houses have been restored and a few older style villas punctuate the glare of whitewashed breeze blocks. Most visitors tend to be Spanish and like Altafulla and Torredembarra, the resort has a fine old 'sister' village slightly inland with a 17th-century church and castle remains. The Bar el Celler is good for breakfast and coffees.

Continuing northwards along the N340 you will next pass the **Arc de Berà**, erected on the ancient Via Augusta (which linked Tarragona to Rome at the beginning of the 2nd Century AD) in memory of Lucio Licinio Sura, consul and imperial legate. The arch is situated 13km from Tarragona.

The next beach, **Coma-Ruga** has a similar mix of old and new apartments and villas. Again there is a pleasant beach front and superb beach.

From Coma-Ruga, continue up the coast road alongside another long beach to Sant Salvador (these beaches are supposedly the most iodised in Europe) and Calafell but before doing so, it is worth turning inland to the market town of **El Vendrell**, the capital of the Baix Penedès with a population of 11,262. The town has its origins in an old Roman villa and was mentioned in written records for the first time in 1037. It has a moderate sized commerical centre with one of its five original gates still standing. The hermitage of Sant Salvador is the town's oldest building. The Pardo gatehouse dates from the 16th century with an impressive Gothic-Renaissance façade. The museum of the poet and dramatist Angel Guimerà (1845–1924) and the public library are other notable buildings. The Archeological Museum is housed in a 17th-century building and contains pre-historic exhibits from the region. The town is better known for its human rather than stone architecture, the Vendrell *castellers* (Els Nens del Vendrell) being one of the most acclaimed in the province. A large market, which operates daily in different parts of the town, is considerably cheaper than its counterpart in Barcelona. The major market is held on Wednesdays. The town has a large, modernised pedestrianised centre and a modest rambla where you can sit, drink and observe. It has a good but pricy fish restaurant El Pi on one of its corners. Major festivals take place on 1 May, 15 August, 11 September; also worth noting are the Festa de la Bicicleta (Bicycle Festival) on the last Sunday in May, a *sardana* gathering (last Sunday in August), the Baix Penedès Marathon (last Sunday in September) and the Fires i Festes de Santa Teresa on the Sunday closest to 15 October.

Vendrell's maritime district takes you 3km back to the coast to **Sant Salvador** which continues to draw many locals for the nightly *paseo* (procession). Mostly frequented by Spaniards, it thankfully lacks the nightlife of some of its near neighbours. Most importantly this small, unassuming seaside resort, with its mix of older villas turning sand-colour with age and newer whitewashed ones, was home to the 20th century's most celebrated cellist, Pau Casals (1876–1973). Less known internationally perhaps than his playing, was his championing of human rights and his strong commitment to Catalan independence (he refused to speak anything but Catalan in public and never returned to his cherished home while Catalonia was ruled by Franco). His home has now been converted into a museum commemorating his life. Whilst listening to his recorded music, visitors can browse through letters, pictures, photographs and medals that chart his periods in Madrid, Paris and at home. The rooms are pretty much as they would have been when he lived here. In the garden (which has a balcony overlooking the splendid beach) is a bust of the maestro. The auditorium, which seats 400, hosts a number of concerts annually particularly during the Casals Festival in the high season.

Calafell (pop. 4597), between Calafell and the coast itself is, like Sitges, an old resort and has therefore escaped most, though not all, of the excesses of more recent developers. In the 18th century there was a single line of fishermen's cottages along the front. During the 19th century it expanded and in the early 20th century its waters were found to contain large quantities of iodine so Barcelona City Hall chose it for one of its children's camps. This provided a base for the 1960's transformation into a cosmopolitan tourist centre.

Although there is the usual warren of tat shops, the palm-fronted esplanade has been made into a pedestrianised walkway and its narrow streets are one-way. Inland, its old 'sister' village and Romanesque hermitage date back to the 1st century AD and remains unimpressed by the hullabaloo on the coast. Cats and doves seem more populous than people. The narrow cobbled alleyways lead up to the Ajuntament and the 16th-century 'Comunidor', built above the neo-classical 18th-century church with open sides all round to ward off storms and devils and bless the local people. The alley continues to twist and turn up to the medieval castle, Santa Creu de Calafell. It's worth braving the dogs, the castle's unpaid guards, just for the view back over the plain and along the coast. Circling the fortress are strange troglodyte dwellings dating back to the 15th century. The town's major festival is held on 16 July.

As already mentioned, little now interrupts the concrete march between Calafell and Cunit, though you may be tempted by the superb, long, sandy beaches fronted by bars which strangely would have us believe we are anywhere but Spain; Bar Aloha, Bar Dusseldorf, Bar-restaurant Milan, Bar Hawaii.

Cunit itself has only a sliver of its heart left in amongst all the transplants and the sliver stretches no more than 150m from the 18th-century Sant Cristofol church (built on the site of an earlier 12th-century Romanesque church whose apse is still visible) to the Hotel Diligencia in the Carrer Major where horse-drawn carriages used to deposit guests (a sign on the front door advises guests that entrance is via 'The bag door'). It's certainly no longer the quiet village I worked in one summer. The bar where I used to work on the Av. de la Font is now a pizzeria but thankfully the beach bar where we used to sit drinking rum baba for breakfast is still there. The major festival takes place on 10 July.

Cubelles, although the old village has castle ruins and a church with a graceful belfry, is not really worth a stop, so the next destination is the coast's other major market town, **Vilanova i la Geltrú**, capital of the comarca of Garraf and ancient Greco-Roman site of Darro. The town has a population of 45,000. Its wealth was built in the 18th century by returning *indianos* and *cubanos* who had made their fortunes in the Americas and returned to invest in the town. Vilanova i la Geltrú has a long and proud commercial, industrial, agricultural and maritime tradition. Its major features are its seafront promenade, the remains of the 13th-century Gothic castle of La Geltrú, the museums and the churches of Sant Antoni, Santa Maria de la Geltrú and De la Concepció.

The Rambla leading up to the parish church is a little run-down these days but still a pleasant place to read the paper and sip *horchata*. Running parallel to it is the pedestrianised Pg de les Cols with pastry shops, cafés, book and leatherware shops, and croissanteries. In a side street is a small disco that does not deal in euphemisms, 'The Pick-Up'. Farm produce continues to be brought to the municipal market as often by horse and cart as by van. The town's other industries include textiles, paper and cork. It is also an important fishing port and boasts three beaches linked by a sea-front promenade. The Pg Marítim has café terraces and fish restaurants (Can Col and Peixerot) overlooking the marina. The fish auction starts at the port around 8am.

The Museu Balaguer houses 16th-century paintings (including an El Greco), Egyptian archeology and Oriental art. The Casa de Santa Teresa has Spanish furniture from the 17th–19th centuries. Both museums are in the Av. Víctor Balaguer. Catalan and avant-garde art is displayed in the Castle la Geltrú museum (C. de la Torre). There's a Mariners' Museum at No.2 Almirall Cervera and a Museu Romantic on the Casa Papiol.

Sitges

SITGES is to Barcelona what Brighton is to London. It has been a resort since the 19th century and therefore has an unhurried dignity that the other resorts do not approach. The Garraf mountains protect it from the northern winds ensuring few really cold days, thus making it popular all-year round. The tourist season, however, is naturally weighted to the summer season and many of the town's hotels and restaurants wait until Semana Santa (Holy Week) before they open (they then remain open until October). The British have made up the majority of visitors since 1955.

Unlike the rest of the Costa Daurada (and the whole Spanish coast for that matter), Sitges is the exception to the rule 'speculation over legislation'. A good example of the far-sighted seriousness of their protective measures is the Villa Lolas, a Modernist house that had to be knocked down but was reproduced exactly five years ago. Nevertheless, as mentioned earlier, the resort has gone increasingly down-market. The Terramar is a good example of the slide from first-Class hotel to holiday apartments and the Calilpolis similarly has lost much of its quality despite recent refurbishment.

Fortunately most of the new developments are on the periphery of town; to the north is the new port, to the west an 'aquatic paradise' (one of the few in Catalonia that hasn't recorded a recent fatality). Barcelona is just 40km of cliff-hugging hairpin-bends cliffs north (a new motorway will connect it by 1993), and Montserrat around another 40km further north, and the wine growing capital, Alt Penedès, about 25km westwards.

Sitges is more than 2000 years old and those who have taken more than a two-week summer break here include Carthaginians, Romans, Visigoths, Moors and the Franks of Charlemagne. For a considerable time it has been an important centre for the arts. At the turn of this century it was 'the Mecca of Modernism' and today it still has a flourishing arts scene with a major contribution from British, Dutch and South American expatriates and particularly from the gay community who have made it their own Spanish capital.

There is an excellent, large daily food market and a small central market in the old part of town, dramatically located on a bluff (La Punta – The Point) overhanging the sea. Dominating La Punta is the bell-tower of the church (16th–18th centuries) of Sts Tecla and Bartolomeu, where a medieval castle once stood. There are numerous museums, undoubtedly the most interesting being the one that once served as the home of the region's most famous painter, Santiago Rusiñol (1861–1931). The most beautiful **Gothic Cau Ferrat Museum** (founded in 1933) with its arches, stained glass and intricately worked wooden ceiling, exhibits eccentric flourishes any morphine-addicted Modernist would be proud of. My own particular favourites amongst the weird and the wonderful were two votaries giving thanks to the Virgin, the first from a smuggler for five years of uninterrupted contraband trade and the second from a gambler for a seven of spades that broke a potentially ruinous poker run. Apart from Rusiñol collections of door knockers, window grills and glass objects, there is also an important art collection featuring amongst others Casas, El Greco and Picasso (who made several visits). There's even a 'Botticelli' – the Birth of Venus – executed by Rusiñol and then signed in the original's name.

In the small square, Racó de la Calma (Corner of Calm) outside the museum is some rather ill-looking marble on which are engraved the coats of arms of Sitges' nobility. Opposite the Cau Ferrat is the Gothic door of a Salamancan palace that provides access to the Maricel Museum (part of Sitges university). Unfortunately its collection of mosaics, ceramics, jewellery, iron-work and glass can be visited only in pre-arranged groups). At the centre of the square is a large bust of El Greco and adjoining the Cau Ferrat is yet another museum, the 14th-century Maricel de Mar (originally the town's hospital) with a local collection of sculpture, painting, gold, silver and iron-work.

The Cau Ferrat dramatically overhangs the sea on La Punta's promontory with beaches sweeping either side of it. Dropping down on the northern front is a tight bay where fashionable Barcelonans congregate at the Voramar Bar (there are also a number of delightful narrow medieval streets, D'en Bosch, Sant Joan and La Vall behind it) whilst to the south, steps lead down to an elegant palm-fronted promenade (Pg de la Ribera) which boasts exclusive clothes shops with designer labels Kenzo, Gaultier and Raquel Vega. It also has the town's best seafood restaurants and some of its finest turn-of-the-century Modernist buildings. The 3km long beach has sensibly been divided into a series of smaller beaches of powder sand. Rusiñol is credited with starting the fashion for nude bathing at Sitges and some of these beaches have been designated for his followers.

The Carrer Dos de Maig, more popularly known as Carrer del Pecat or 'street of sin' sounds more exciting than it is, though its noisy late bars come alive in the evening and don't sleep till dawn. Running across it at the top is the long pedestrianised Carrer Parelladas, again with bars (that even offer Guinness) and some fine restaurants as well as patisseries and old style cafés such as the Cafe Roy and Granja (good for coffee and cakes at 8am after an all-night binge!) with their marble tables and burntwood chairs. There are also a number of clothes shops (leather goods are manufactured in the town).

Ten years ago the mid-February/March Carnival was a small affair. Now 'it's like a revolution' someone told me. The fiesta is probably Spain's biggest and certainly its most colourful. Everybody works on their costumes during the year. Sunday and

133

Tuesday's *cercavila* are the main days when the floats roll and Rio comes to Sitges. There's also a vintage car rally during the week. Other notable festivals include the Festa Major between 23–27 August (commemorating the patron saint of the town, St Bartholomew, and signalling the start of the Penedès grape harvest), the international Science Fiction and Fantasy Cinema Festival in October, the drama Festival and the Feast of Corpus Christi in May/June when the town becomes a floral carpet. In fact the comarca of Garraf, of which Sitges is a part, has a very long festival tradition dating back to pre-Christian times and mythological giants, dragons, dwarfs, dogs and devils still feature prominently in the festivals.

Another museum, worthy of a visit, especially if you have youngsters in tow, is the **Romantic Provincial Museum** in the small 18th-century palace Casa Llopis on Carrer S. Guadenci. The museum has 320 dolls on show in the upper floor as well as an 1857 Parisian carriage and neo-classical furniture on the ground floor.

Leave the town on the C246 which, hugging a limestone corniche, winds, plummets and soars until it reaches Garraf. This resort is very much a case of beauty and the beast. On the one hand is the cement factory covering the countryside in fine grey-green dust like military camouflage and on the other are the pure lines of Güell Wine Vaults built by Berenguer and Gaudí at the end of the last century. The steeply arched roof, stepped belltower and pepperpot chimneys are a delight to the eye and help to erase the memory of the eyesore a few bends earlier.

Legend has it that Hannibal gave the mountain range its name El Garraf after one of his captains. The range runs 24km north to south and 28km east to west and its highest point is El Montau (660m). There are more than 200 caves concealed in the southern stretch alone but few have the stomach to visit them (the municipal Val de Joan dump is a considerable deterrent).

Coming out of the last bend there is a pretty bay, then more industrial spillage before domestic beach reasserts itself, spreading out for another 15km until you reach the old defences at **Castelldefels**, just a twenty minute drive from Barcelona. Designed originally as the capital's playground, the long sandy beach takes large numbers at the weekend from the Catalan capital. The only remnants of the old fortifications are the 12–15th century watchtowers on the outskirts of town. There's a municipal museum showing local archeology and paintings.

From the pine groves of Castelldefels the fine sandy beach runs through to El Prat airport past a succession of hotels, campsites and residences. 'The Marina' is the name bestowed on the richly fertile delta of the River Llobregat, profuse with pondlife. We are now on the borders of the capital.

The Costa Daurada, has fabulous beaches, marvellous touring country inland and the cities that mark its 100km limits, Barcelona and Tarragona are deserving of holidays in their own right. It does, of course, have its warts but it is a part of Spain that draws me back again and again.

The South: Practical Information

The Consorci de Promocio Turistica, Pg de Gracia 112, 08008 Barcelona (tel. 415 16 17), provides useful guides and literature on the region. A full list of Catalonian tourist offices is given under Further Information at the back of the book.

Useful telephone numbers

International telephone information:
9398
Telephone information within Spain:
003

LLEIDA
Rail travel information: (973) 23 7467

Taxis: 23 10 00/2720 20/24 00 34
Telegrams: 24 70 00

TARRAGONA
Rail travel information: (977) 23 36 43
Taxis: 23 60 64/21 56 56
Telegrams: 22 20 00

Restaurants and accommodation

Restaurant (R) prices: cheap = under 1500pts; moderate = 1500–2700pts; expensive = 2700–4000pts; very expensive = over 4000pts.
Accommodation (A) prices (per double room with bathroom, per night): cheap = under 3000pts; moderate = 3000–6000pts; expensive = 6000–18,000pts; very expensive = over 18,000pts.

ALTAFULLA
A. **Bar el Coral** (self-contained flats), C. Lleó, Altafulla (tel. 65 04 86). Cheap.
A. **Yola** (Hostel), Via Augusta 50 (tel. 65 02 83). Moderate.
R. **Faristol**, Sant Martí 5 (tel. 65 00 77). Traditional Catalan cuisine. Cheap.
R. **El Pozo**, C. Lleó (tel. 65 02 73)

owned by Janet from Sheffield who specialises in fondues. Moderate.
R. **Paco's Bar**, C. Sant Antoni. Tapas and churros. Moderate.
R. **El Parc** and **Els Pescadors** are two moderately priced fish restaurants on the beach.

L'AMETLLA DE MAR
A. **Hotel Bon Repòs**, Plaça de Catalunya 49 (tel. 45 60 25). Moderate.
R. **L'Alguer**, Trafalgar 21 (tel. 45 61 24). Traditional seafood cuisine. Cheap-moderate.

AMPOSTA
A. **Hostel Bajo Ebro** (1-star), Ctra N 340, km 170 (tel. 70 00 25). Cheap.
R. **El Rem Pitxuli**, Corsini 75 (tel. 70 10 90). Home cooking. Cheap.

LES BORGES BLANQUES
A. **Els Llacs** (pension), Plaça Terrall 4 (tel. 14 29 62). Moderate.

R. **Masia Garrigues** (tel. 14 01 62). Closed Mondays. Home cooking. Cheap.

CALAFELL
A. **Kursaal** (4-star), Av. Sant Joan de Déu 119 (tel. 69 23 00). Moderate-expensive.

A. **Hotel Canada**, (2-star), Mossén Jaume Soler 44 (tel. 69 15 00). Moderate.

A. **Papiol** (Hostel), Av. San Juan de Deu 56 (tel. 69 13 13). Moderate.

R. **Da Giorgio**, Angel Guimerà 4 (tel. 69 11 59). A genuine Italian restaurant as good as you'll find in Italy. Moderate.

R. **La Barca**, Av. de Sant Joan de Déu 79 (tel. 69 15 59). Seafood specialities. Moderate.

CAMBRILS
A. **Augustus** (3-star), Ctra Salou-Cambrils (tel. 38 11 54). Moderate.

A. **Tropicana** (2-star), Ctra Salou-Cambrils (tel. 36 01 12). Moderate.

R. **Joan Gatell** and **Can Gatell** both on Pg de Miramar 27 (tel. 36 01 06 and 36 00 57) are excellent, moderately priced fish restaurants.

CARDONA
A/R. **Parador Nacional Ducs de Cardona** (4-star). (tel. 869 12 75). Historic castle hotel. The restaurant is the best in town offering moderate-expensive Catalan cuisine. Expensive.

A. **Alberto** (Hostel), Abad 3 (tel. 869 10 20). Moderate.

CASTELLDEFELS
A. **Gran Hotel Rey Don Jaime** (4-star), Torre Barona s/n (tel. 665 13 00). Very expensive.

A. **El Tiburon** (Hostel), Carrer 11 N1 (tel. 665 24 79). Cheap-moderate.

R. **Las Botas**, Ctra C-246, km 19.5 (tel. 665 40 96). Good service and typical Catalan cuisine. Moderately priced.

CERVERA
A/R. **Canceller** (3-star), Pg Balmes 2 (tel. 53 13 50). Moderate.

CUNIT
A. **La Diligencia** (2-star), Major 4 (tel. 67 40 81). Moderate.

A. **Europa Los Hunos** (3-star), Riera 11 (tel. 67 43 78). Moderate.

R. **L'Avi Pau**, Av. Diagonal 20 (tel. 67 48 61). Fine Catalan cuisine with the emphasis on sea food. Moderate.

ESPARREGUERA
A/R. **Montserrat** (Hostel) Francesc Macià 130–133 (tel. 777 54 47). Moderate.

L'ESPLUGA DE FRANCOLI
A/R. **Hostal del Senglar**, Plaça Montserrat Canals s/n (tel. 87 01 21). Moderate accommodation prices and excellent value moderately priced regional cuisine.

GANDESA
A. **Piqué** (Hostel), Via Catalunya (tel. 42 00 68). Cheap.

GUIMERÀ
R. **Restaurant Medieval.** Moderately priced recipes from the Middle Ages (no potatoes!)

HORTA DE SANT JOAN
R. **Fonda Miralles**, Av. Generalitat 48 (tel. 43 51 14). Cheap.

IGUALADA
A. **Hotel America** (3-star), Ctra Madrid Francia, km 557 (tel. 803 10 00). Expensive.

A. **Canaletas** (Hostel). Ctra Madrid Francia, km 557 (tel. 803 27 50). Moderate.

El Jardin de Granja Pla, Rambla Sant Isidre 12 (tel. 803 18 64). Closed Sunday evenings and Mondays. Catalan cuisine. Moderate.

LLEIDA
A. **Contes d'Urgell II** (3-star), Av. de Barcelona 17, (tel. 20 23 00). Modern,

soulless, out of town on busy main road. Moderate.

A. **Residencia Principal**, Plaça Paeria 8 (tel. 23 08 00). In the heart of the old town. Comfortable. Moderate.

R. **La Huerta**, Av. de Tortosa 9 (tel. 24 24 13). Good value typical cuisine with local wines. Cheap-moderate.

R. **Forn del Nastasi**, Salmeró 10 (tel. 23 45 10). Closed Sunday evenings. Dominantly Lleidan cuisine. Local vegetables. Grill and wood-fired oven. Moderate.

MANRESA

A. **Pedro III** (3-star), Muralla Sant Francesc 49 (tel. 872 40 00). Moderate-expensive.

A. **Mundial** (Hostel), Carrer del Cos 11 (tel. 872 44 11). Cheap.

R. **La Cuina**, Alfonso XII 18 (tel. 872 89 69). Specialises in shellfish. Moderate.

MONTBLANC

A. **Coll de L'Illa** (2-star), Ctra Nacional 240, km 29 (tel. 86 09 07). Very expensive. Good, moderately priced restaurant serving local cuisine.

A. **Ducal** (Hostel), Diputació 11 (tel. 86 00 25). Moderate.

R. **Fonda Colom**, Ctra Civadria 5 (tel. 86 01 53). Lunchtimes only. Cheap Catalan cuisine.

MONTSERRAT

A. **Abad Cisneros** (3-star), Plaça de Montserrat (tel. 835 02 01). Moderate.

A. **El Monestir** (Hostel), Plaça Monestir (tel. 835 0201). Cheap-moderate.

POBLET

A. **Fonoll** (Hostel), Ramón Berenguer IV 2 (tel. 87 03 33). Cheap.

SALOU

A. **Salou Park** (4-star), Bruselles 31 (tel. 38 02 08). Expensive.

A. **Los Angeles** (2-star), Carrer Falset (Tel. 38 14 66). Moderate.

R. **Casa Soler**, verge del Carme

(tel. 38 04 63). Catalan cuisine. Moderate.

SANT CARLES DE LA RÀPITA

A. **Miami Park** (3-star), Av. Constitució 33–37 (tel. 74 03 51). Moderate.

A. **Hostal Casa Ramon**, Carrer Arsenal 14 (tel. 74 03 61). Moderate.

R. **Fernandel**, Ctra N340, km 163 (tel. 74 03 58). A highly respected popular restaurant overlooking the sea, haute cuisine and pastries are served with equal grace. Expensive.

R. **Miami Can Pons**, Av. Constitució 37 (tel. 74 03 51). Seafood and local dishes. Cheap-moderate.

SITGES

A. **Mediterraneo** (4-star), Av. Sofía 3 (tel. 894 51 34). Expensive.

A. **Hotel Los Pinos** (3-star), Pg Marítim (tel. 894 15 50). Moderate.

A. **Hotel Subur** (2-star), Pg Marítim (tel. 894 00 66). Overlooking beach, pleasant. Moderate.

A. **Mariangel** (Hostel), Parellades 78 (tel. 894 13 57). Cheap.

R. **Mare Nostrum**, Pg de la Ribera 60 (tel. 894 33 93). Excellent seafood restaurant. Moderate.

SOLSONA

A. **Gran Sol** (3-star), Ctra Manresa (tel. 480 975). Moderate.

R. **Sant Roc**, Plaça de Sant Roc 2 (tel. 480 827). Typical Catalan country cooking with local wines and cheeses. Moderate.

TARRAGONA

A. **Imperial Tarraco** (4-star), Rambla Vella 2 (tel. 23 30 40). The city's best hotel overlooking the Roman ruins and the Mediterranean. Expensive.

A. **Hotel Residencia,** Lauria (3-star), Rambla Nova 20 (tel. 23 67 12). Moderate.

A. **Catalonia** (Hostel), Apodeca 7 (tel. 21 10 08). Cheap.

R. **La Puda**, Moll dels Pescadors 25 (tel. 21 15 11). Good regional fish dishes. Moderate.

R. **Mesón del Mar**, Platja Llarga, Ctra de Barcelona (tel. 23 94 01). A very good fish restaurant. Moderate.

R. **Sol-Ric**, Via Augusta 227 (tel. 23 20 32). Expensive but quite simply the best restaurant in the city.

TÀRREGA

A. **Hotel España** (1-star), Plaça Rafal Casanova 3 (tel. 311 357). Expensive.

R. **Fengara**, Carrer del Mestre Güell 3 (tel. 311 159). Traditional Catalan cuisine. Moderate.

TORTOSA

A/R. **Parador Nacional Castell de al Suda** (4-star), Castell de la Suda, Tortosa, Tarragona (tel. 977 44 44 50). Expensive accommodation. Excellent, moderate-expensively priced Mediterranean and local cuisine.

A. **Hostal Siboni**, Carrer de l'Angel 6 (tel. 44 00 41). Cheap.

VALLS

A. **Masia Vallense** (Hostel), Ctra de Barcelona, km 8 (tel. 60 07 15). Cheap.

R. **Masia Bou**, Ctra Lleida, km 21,600 (tel. 60 04 27). Catalan specialities. Moderate.

VILAFRANCA DEL PENEDÈS

A. **Pedro II el Grande** (3-star), Plaça Exercit 2 (tel. 890 31 00). Moderate.

R. **Casa Joan**, Plaça de l'Estacío (tel. 890 31 71). Very good traditional cuisine. Moderate.

VILANOVA I LA GELTRÚ

A. **Hotel Cesar** (3-star), Isaac Peral 4 (tel. 815 11 25). Expensive.

A. **Costador** (Hostel), Pg Marítim 49 (tel. 815 55 42). Cheap.

R. **Peixerot**, Pg Marítim 56 (tel. 815 06 25). Very good seafood restaurant. Moderate.

Part Three:
The North

Tour 13
The Costa Brava

The Costa Brava has traditionally been known as 'The Gateway to Spain' and I had always treated it as such, hurtling through on the A17 autopiste in search of 'the real Spain' further south. I knew the Costa Daurada intimately, Costa Blanca well, the Costa del Sol as well as I wished to, but had presumed the Spanish coast closest to the rest of Europe must long since have been buried under the nasty developments that thrive on slim profit margins and mass traffic. I therefore couldn't have been more surprised to discover that the Costa Brava is the finest costa of them all, its diaphonous waters fringed by pine-clad coves, its nearby hinterland quite breathtaking and, in the distance, the snow-capped Pyrenees beckoning the adventurous. The Costa Brava has all the beach one could ever want. The fascinating city of Girona lies 40 minutes' drive away from St Feliu of Palafrugell and those staying further up the coast have stunning touring country in the Garrotxa volcanic park or indeed the Pyrenees. Medieval clifftop villages, Romanesque churches and one of Europe's great unsung cuisines await those adventurous souls willing to venture into the interior.

The Costa Brava was given its name 75 years ago by the poet and journalist Ferràn Agulló. Josep Plà, another Catalan writer, claimed it was the coast's distinctive ruggedness that created such individualism in the people and spawned its inordinate number of artists, singers, politicians and writers. Certainly the Pheonician, Greek and Roman inheritance has created a proud people confident of their origins and their futures. One of the most famous Catalan folksongs is a *sardana* called 'L'Empordà' in which a shepherd falls in love with a mermaid. It is such meetings between the hard pragmatism of the mountains and the romance of the coast that has forged its distinctive culture.

The coast stretches for 214km from Port Bou to Blanes through three comarques: Alt and Baix (Upper and Lower) Empordà and La Selva. L'Empordà is a land of gently

The pine-clad bays of the 'rugged coast'.

rolling hills that stretch from sandy beaches up to the Pyrenees whilst La Selva's Montseny and Les Guilleries mountains are covered in great forests of oak, cork, pine, beech and chestnut.

The Pyrenees themselves descend eastwards from their highest peak (Pic d'Aneto 3404m), finally plunging into the Mediterranean at Cap de Creus. Where the mountains take their dip, the 'Tramuntana' blows. They say the winds in winter can drive you crazy and that's why Dalí was the way he was, living in Port Lligat. In summer the gentle off-shore 'Garbí' cools the coast and in winter months the people seek the warmth of the hot thermal springs at Caldes de Malavella and Santa Coloma de Farners. The climate is typically Mediterranean with mild winters and hot summers.

Roads are good and boat trips operate out of virtually every resort (usually around £5 for two hours). There are nudist beaches at Cala Conca, Illa Roja, Salt de Ribes, Cala Estreta, Cala Bona, Cala Gamarús and Cala del Senyor Ramón. There are also naturist camping grounds at Montràs. The coast enjoys 2500 hours of sunshine a year which averages out at around seven hours a day warming the vivid pines, red soil, golden beaches and aquamarine waters.

140

Crémat is the favoured hootch made from dark and white rum, brandy, coffee and cinnamon, and served as a hot toddy. There are a number of good wines produced on the coast and food generally is reasonably priced considering that you are in tourist resorts. Shopping at the local market instead of the supermarket can halve your weekly food bill. Restaurants on the coast serve mostly fast foods though genuine Catalan cuisine can still be had if you look hard enough. Prices are still cheap compared with Northern Europe; a three course menú del día with salad and wine will usually cost little more than £6.

The Maresme coast north of Barcelona has little to detain the beach-lover, so take the A17 autopiste out of town and put your foot down until you slip off at Massanet de la Selva (just 30km south of Girona) and, gritting your teeth, make for the eyesores of Lloret de Mar and Blanes.

Blanes (pop. 20,178) has the remains of the palace of Cabrera, botanical gardens and the 16th-century Church of Santa Maria under the shadow of the high rise abominations. Pass through as quickly as possible unless you have unwisely booked a holiday here in which case, good luck. The fishing harbour and the fine beach should compensate somewhat for the modern ugliness. Sardana dancers gather here on the Tuesday after Easter.

Lloret de Mar (pop. 10,480) has the dubious distinction of possessing the highest concentration of hotels in Spain and now that some of the major British tour operators have pulled out of the resort, no doubt there will be less money about and things will become progressively more run-down. Buried somewhere under the apocalyptic skyscrapers are the shrine of La Mare de Déu de Gràcia, Lloret Castle (also known as the Castle of Sant Joan), the chapels of Santa Cristina and La Verge de les Alegries. Personally, I lacked the stamina to seek them out and fled. Its major festivals are held between 23 and 26 July and on 18 November.

Be reassured the worst is now over and things will improve as you travel up the coast. From Lloret a dramatic corniche winds it way through a succession of tiny bays until you reach **Tossa de Mar** (pop. 2969). Tossa's deep sandy beach and its 12th-century hill fortifications, enclosing the old town, Vila Vella, are certainly its best features. But its bustling centre, whose pretty narrow streets become a heaving mass in the early evening, is too cramped and trashy ('Sexometers', a Wimpy and a string of souvenir shops) to hold you long despite the only painting by Marc Chagall in Spain (it hangs proudly in the Museu de la Vila Vella and dates from a pre-tourist time when the artist called Tossa 'the blue paradise'). Major festivals are on 20 January and 29 June.

The corniche continues to twist, turn, and plummet through more delightful bays scarred by ugly new architecture until we leave the comarca of Selva behind and enter the Baix Empordà whose finely fretted coast will run almost to l'Escala. Along this, the Costa Brava's finest stretch, there is the added bonus of 53 listed Romanesque churches, several important monasteries and innumerable hilltop castles.

St Feliu de Gúixols (pop. 15,485) is much larger than Tossa though somehow less frantic with its palm-fringed promenade and apartment blocks that, unlike the uncontrolled monsters at Lloret, manage to restrain themselves to a modest five storeys. Perhaps the fact that the esplanade was built 150 years ago and that the front therefore already had life before tourism explains its sense of unhurried calm. The town itself grew out of a Benedictine Monastery that in turn was built upon an Iberian settlement. The Romanesque church with its 11th-century Mozarabic portico is all that's now left of the monastery. The main festival dates are 1–4 August.

La Platja d'Aro (pop. 2597) is the next major resort which mushroomed in the 1960s to its present ugly featurelessness. Here package holidaymakers and high rise abominations resume the scrummage alongside the superb 2km-long sandy beach. Unfortunately La Platja d'Aro has been turned into an oversized weekend disco for Gironins who have the good sense to keep such things outside their own city walls. Just outside town, set back from the road is a medieval castle and the four-star Park Hotel Sant Jorge. The major festival takes place on the second Sunday in September.

Sandy beaches continue to accompany you to **Palamós** (pop. 12,178). There are a few fine modernist buildings here, the 15th-century Gothic church of Santa Maria and the Cau Museum. Redbeard was said to have holidayed here and created more devastation than today's lager louts. The fishing catch is still auctioned off in La Llotja. Palamós boasts a fine, long, sweeping beach, busy port (it was once one of Catalonia's busiest commercial ports) and great children's playgrounds. Festival dates are 24–26 June.

It is not until we reach the cluster of bays that radiate round **Palafrugell** (pop. 15,030) that the Costa Brava really comes into its own. Pine-clad hills drop dramatically to small sandy beaches backed by a handful of restaurants, shops and hotels without ever a hint of a tower block. Palafrugell itself draws both locals and visitors to its excellent shopping centre particularly on Sundays when the local market is held. Flowers, snails, herbs, electrical equipment and a hundred different varieties of olives crowd the stalls. The Plaça Nova is a popular place to sit at the terraced cafés and stare and Piscolabis Café-Bar serve up *bocadillos* at the other end of the street. The 16th-century Church of Sant Martí, Modernist homes, an indoor market and attractive shopping streets draw visitors from the coast at night. Festivals are on 29 June, 20–22 July and 15 August.

Calella de Palafrugell (pop. 10,751) signals the start of a 10km stretch of tight pine-clad bays that are the prettiest resorts I've come across in Spain. Up on the hill is an 8-hectare botanic garden where a Russian ex-Colonel by the name of Woevowsky has nurtured 1200 different species of typical Mediterranean flora. The view across the bay to Calella and Llafranc is stunning. The promontory at Calella has a sprinkling of elegant terraced bars on the south Canyars side and whitewashed arcades and imposing villas set back from the promenade on the northern El Canadell beach. It still has the feel of a fishing village despite the influx of wealthy Barcelonans at the weekend. Calella is the most important location for the traditional singing of *havaneres*, South American sea shanties (lubricated by 'crémat' – hot rum and coffee toddy). The resort is linked to **Llafranc** (pop. 172), the next bay, by a 2km-long cliff-edge path which can have few rivals in Europe for an early morning or sunset stroll. The bars Bolero Tres Pins and Bar l'Espasa will provide both the aperitifs and the views. Across the bay above the perfect crescent of the beach is the Sant Sebastià lighthouse and 18th-century chapel which offers spectacular views and very good Catalan cuisine at moderate cost. Llafranc's delightful bay with its flotilla of colourful yachts bobbing in the marina is followed by the even smaller sheltered cove of **Tamariu** (named after the abundant tamarind trees). Good food, good hotels and fine sandy beaches that shelve steeply in the water characterise these bays and virtually every visitor I spoke to had been coming here for years.

For those lucky enough to be based along this stretch, **La Bisbal** (pop. 7362), one of the most important centres of Catalan pottery lies just a 20-minute drive along the C255, with Girona 20 minutes further. A sprinkling of Modernist homes, the 17th-century church of Santa Maria within the old walls and the 15th-century castle-palace of La Bisbal (recently restored) are La Bisbal's principal features apart from the pottery industry. A street market is held on Fridays. Festivals are on 15–18 August and 10–11 October.

A stone's throw from La Bisbal is the marvellously unselfconcious medieval village of **Peratallada** with its fortifications, watchtowers and castle still largely intact. A warren of cobbled alleyways lead into the arcaded main square. As in Pals many of the renovated old houses have become holiday homes of wealthy Barcelonans. The major festival here is on 6–7 August.

Nearby is **Ullastret** which boasts the remains of the most important Iberian city in Catalonia and its second most important archeological site after Empuries. The walls, dating back to 5BC, are vast and set in glorious countryside. In the Acropolis Museum is Greek earthenware found on the site, coins, agricultural tools and weapons from its various settlements. The town's old centre is dominated by the 11th-century Romanesque church of Sant Pere but the Gothic 14th-century La Llotja (exchange) is also worth a look. Festivals are held on 10–11 August.

Returning to Palafrugell, make your way north to **Begur** (pop. 2277) which is the nexus for the next cluster of bays. It is a handsome, ancient town with a Sunday market that is quieter than that at Palafrugell, an imposing hilltop castle, casino (where locals used to gather to play cards), wrought balconies and whitewashed houses. The Plaça de la Vila has terraced cafés, and a good snack bar, la Granja, next to a NatWest bank and the parish church. The town's festival is held on the third Sunday in September.

The first bay in Begur's necklace is **Aiguablava** (Blue Water) which has a stunning location and two of the coast's three best hotels set in dramatic isolation at either end of the fjordlike cala. Incarnadined sandstone, hardy Mediterranean pine clinging to its back, drops dramatically into the sea. Uncharacteristically, the small beach shelves gently and thus is popular with young families. From the monastic peace of the parador precariously jutting out over the high bluff, the mottled floor of the sea bed creates a shimmering mosaic through the limpid waters. Whilst the parador offers peace, the Hotel Aiguablava offers a livelier atmosphere, good value and in Xiquet Sabater – the lovable owner whose story one day no doubt will be re-told in Hollywood – the legend of the coast. The menu has some real Empordà specialities among the international dishes. Xiquet received the Gold medal for Tourism in 1982 from King Juan Carlos.

Sa Tuna (again a pretty bay cut deep into the valley but with a small pebble beach), **Aiguafreda** (another fine but small sandy beach) and **Sa Riera** (sandy beach but a slightly more modern resort reached by a dirt track from Aiguafreda) offer more of the same and the finely fretted coastline continues its mantra until you come upon the seemingly endless white sands of the **Platja de Pals**. From this point the coast will become gentler and more open as you pass through the Empordà flatlands, Cata-

Begur.

lonia's northern wheat basket, until the rugged steep pine forests reassert themselves at Cadaqués.

It is hard to believe that this stretch was virgin territory a couple of years ago; unfortunately the new developments and campsites springing up are predictably soulless. Urbanisation after urbanisation lead to where the River Ter flops breathlessly into the sea. A golf course and camp site run behind the magnificent deserted beach. In the distance at the end of the bay's long, gentle curve, you can see l'Estartit which you reach by turning inland to Pals.

Pals (pop. 1722) has won more 'Best preserved village' and 'Prettiest village' awards than Spaniards have had paella. It is a superbly preserved and reconstructed village best visited early in the morning before the coachloads of tourists arrive. Local historians will try to convince you that this, rather than Palos in Huelva province, was the starting point of Columbus' journey to America. Medieval tombs conceal themselves in walls of rough-hewn stone and bird cages hang from Gothic arches on the Carrer Major leading up to the Romanesque St Peter's. Behind the church is the

14th-century tower that remains from the El Pedró Castle first constructed in the 9th century. Beside it is the village's most impressive mansion belonging to a Barcelonan doctor who is largely responsible for the restoration of the town. Beyond the old fortifications is a mirador that looks out over the Ter as it winds through the marshlands of the Baix Empordà. The town's festival is on 4 August.

Four kilometres away at **Mas de Torrent** is an old farm hotel-restaurant that has built up a very good reputation (it is a member of the Relais-Châteaux). A little further due north you come to **Torroella de Montgrí** (pop. 17,257) watched over by a most imposing recently restored castle on top of a perfect mountain hemisphere (all materials had to be flown in by helicopter – there's no road and it's an hour's trek to the top). Torroella became a Royal town in the 13th century when the castle construction and town walls were started (The Torre de les Bruixes – Witches' Tower – is still one of the town's most notable features). There is the 14th-century Gothic Church of Sant Genís and other fine 15th–18th century buildings including the Casa Pastors on C. l'Eglesia and Major. The Museum (open 11am–2pm and 6pm–9pm on Wednesdays–Saturdays and Mondays, mornings only on Sundays, closed Tuesdays) contains ancient artefacts and records of the region. Also worth a visit are the old hospital and the fortifications of the Lords of Torroella. The Santa Catalina Tower is the only one of four original towers still standing on the road to Verges. The Tourist Office can suggest walking and cycling itineraries (bikes can be hired in town). Market day is Monday and there's an important international music festival in July and festa major on 25 August.

West of Torroella is **Verges** which comes alive on the night of Maundy Thursday when 'skeletons' perform the ancient 'Dansa de la Mort' ('Dance of Death'). Retracing your steps through Torroella, a short (4km) drive brings you back to the coast to **L'Estartit** (permanent resident population only 500 but this swells enormously in the season). The town, popular with British tour operators, is nothing to write home about but not objectionable either. The resort has a number of excellent beaches and a large marina. Bikes can be hired to tour the marshy flatlands of the Empordà. Festivals here are on 26 June, 16 July and 20 August.

Off-shore is Catalonia's only island, the **Medes** (frequent boat trips) once a pirates' sanctuary, later a military prison and now a protected marine park with some of the Western Mediterranean's most important flora and fauna reserves. A favourite haunt of scuba divers admiring the coral beds, the island has over 7000 pairs of resident silver gulls.

The comarca of Alt Empordà stretches from L'Escala up to the French border, across Figueres and well beyond. The old earldom took its name from the Greek colony at Empúries. Its main crops are olives and vines. Its first important resort is **L'Escala** (pop. 4048), renowned for its anchovies and its 17th-century Alfolí de la Sal (salt shed), whose best beaches (favoured by Gironins) lie to the north alongside the ancient ruins of **Empúries**, claimed to be the best preserved Greek settlement west of Italy. The Greco-Roman city covers 40 hectares and is the most visited archeological site in Catalonia. The earliest Greek settlement is just a few hundred yards further on at the small, walled village of **Sant Martí d'Empúries**, which at the time of its settlement was an island. There are a few cafés and restaurants with fine views across the bay. Fittingly, it is here that the 1992 Olympic flame first came ashore and when I

145

last visited there were feverish archeological digs going on attempting to make some major find to coincide with the event. There follows a succession of camp sites skirting the perfect crescent of the Bay of Roses as it gently arches northwards. The road crosses the River Fluvià at the pretty village of St Pere Pescador.

A little further on, we turn off the main road into the **Parc Natural Dels Aiguamolls de l'Empordà**. Here there are a number of observation posts for birdwatching (it is a very important migration site) and an information centre where you can obtain walking itineraries in English that lead through grazing land, deer enclosures, ricefields, lakes and lagoons to the migrating bird observation towers. Here you may glimpse squaccos, purple heron, hoopoe or kingfishers. There are daily guided visits in July and August. The rest of the year you have to phone ahead to make arrangements (972-25 03 22).

Roses (pop. 8131) has a substantial sandy beach and good fishing to compensate for its impersonal apartment blocks. Originally settled by the ancient islanders of Rhodes who established a colony here, Roses is claimed to be the oldest port in Catalonia. There is a smattering of Roman ruins, plus those of a 10th-century Benedictine abbey and 17th-century fort. Mature palms front the attractive promenade. The Costa Brava's most important fish market is held daily down at the harbour. There is a festival on 15 August.

Seven kilometres beyond Roses is the small bay of **Montjoi** which has the most renowned gourmet restaurant on the Costa Brava, Hacienda El Bulli where a meal will set you back 5000pts a head.

From Roses the steep ascent twists and turns past vineyards abandoned during the dreadful phylloxera decimation of the 19th century – many farmers emigrated to the United States and South America. The cork trees have recovered from a major fire five years back but the charred pines have not. From the top of the range there are views inland to Figueres and across to the Pyrenees as they plunge down into the Mediterranean. Starting the descent you will see El Port de la Selva and in the distance France, 20km further north.

Cadaqués (pop. 1547) is the arty St Tropez of the Costa Brava. In Cadaqués it is unlikely that you'll run into a Honolulu Fun Party or Pirates' Invasion organised by one of the major tour operators. This resort, thankfully, is for the independent traveller and remains a haven for artists despite the death of its most famous resident, Salvador Dalí. Nestled in the hills between two promontories, its pretty cobbled whitewashed alleyways clatter down the hillside to two small bays dotted with 18th-century and modernist homes, fishing boats and fashionable yachts. The elegant old casino, where fisherman gathered for drinks and to play cards, is still there, set back from the shingle and pebble beach. The wine cellars which were active until the phylloxera outbreak also serve as gathering places and meeting halls. The 16th-century church of Santa Maria has a baroque altarpiece by Jacint Morató and Pau Costa. The Perrot-Moore Museum of European Graphic Art is the town's most important museum.

Dalí's own residence, known as The House of Eggs, lies (abandoned at present) a few kilometres out of town in the tiny fishing village of Port Lligat. An island, once inhabited by hippies, now lies unpeopled off-shore. Calm waters and delightful cottages make the detour worthwhile despite the lack of sandy beach. The festivals

Cadaquès.

here are on 5–6 September and 18 December. At the time of writing the village was undergoing restoration.

At **El Port de la Selva** (pop. 725) the mountain range runs straight into the sea. A number of sandy beaches backed by restaurants and cafés skirt the bay offering those with the energy a chance to escape the crowds even in the height of summer. There is a festival on 6 August. Across the bay is the important 10th-century fortified Romanesque Benedictine Monastery of **Sant Pere de Rodes**, reachable by car up a small paved road or walkable in an hour and at present undergoing restoration.

A windy switchback leads round the promontory to the larger **El Port de Llançà** (pop. 3001) on the northern side of Cape Creus. The train from the border stops here, making it a popular location for French budget travellers who just want to dip their toes into the Mediterranean. Also popular with Spanish holidaymakers, El Port de Llançà has a substantial sandy beach and good fishing. Its most famous monument is the 300-year-old Liberty Tree, but there is also the 11th-century Chapel of Sant Silvestre de Valleta and d'el Terrer. There's a defence tower in the main square and the town also boasts 15th- and 17th-century gateways and the 18th-century parish church of Sant Vicenc. In 974 the town belonged to Sant Pere de Roda. The town's festival is on 22 January.

The final resort before the train terminus at the Port Bou border post, is the unfortunately named **Colera** (pop. 491) which has a delightful bay and a Romanesque monastery – Sant Quirze de Colera. Its festival is held on 29 September.

Tour 14
Inland Loop: Following the Rivers Fluvià and Ter; Girona

Once you have prised yourself away from the delightfully indolent upper Costa Brava, this inland tour will take you through some of Catalonia's most interesting and varied scenery. From Alt Empordà, you enter Catalonia's latest comarca, Pla de l'Estany (created only in 1988) and the Garrotxa Natural Volcanic Park. High up in the Pyrenees (2400m) is the source of the River Ter which will be your constant travelling companion for the next 200km, taking you to the trinity of important Romanesque monasteries at Camprodon, St Joan de les Abadesses and Ripoll before you leave the river's upper reaches to chart the river's course through a second incarnation as the source of power for Catalonia's industrial revolution, through the magnificent medieval city of Girona and then a final dash back to the Costa Brava at Platja de Pals where the river, and the tour, end.

The journey will take you through the heart of Old Catalonia where the Christian reconquest started and the first dawning of a distinctly Catalan identity was born in the plethora of Romanesque churches and monasteries. Away from the coast you will find the best of traditional rural Catalan cuisine with its idiosyncratic marriage of meats with sweet sauces: peaches with chicken, geese with pears, lobster with chocolate. Grilled meats, local sausages, hams and wild mushrooms will also be the order of the day and the waistline will be encouraged to spread further with the delicious almond cakes that are found everywhere. Pottery, wood carvings and religious figures are the local handicrafts to look out for.

Taking the fast C252 road inland from **El Port de Llançà**, you pass through the vineyards of the Empordà and, a few kilometres before Figueres, take the secondary road into the capital of the Empordà wine growing region, **Perelada** (pop. 1238). The town happens to possess the most ostentatious of Catalonia's three casinos, located in the perfectly restored castle-palace of the counts of Peralada. Medieval elements including two large towers sit comfortably within the overall 18th-century château adaptations. The casino has a highly thought of restaurant as well as important paintings and tapestries of the Flemish School.

Opposite the casino is the Co-operativa Bar, a popular, no-nonsense economical restaurant offering local dishes such as *mongetes amb botifarra* (sausages and white beans). They also sell wines of the region such as the local cava (champagne method) and slightly sparkling Blanc Pescador – a crisp, very slightly sparkling wine. The town museum claims the largest private library in Spain, has an impressive art collection and a comprehensive display of the region's wine production. The museum can be visited only between July and September and guided tours (not in English) take place on the hour between 10am and 12 noon, and 4pm and 6pm. The wine caves are located beneath the 16th-century Carmelite convent which connects to the castle casino by a raised passageway over the road. The town's main square is skirted by Gothic arcades on three of its sides and has a fountain at its centre. Its major festival is on 11 November. It also hosts an important classical music festival in the summer.

Continue on the minor road through corn fields to **Vilabertràn** with its exquisite 10–12th-century Romanesque belfry towering over the old Benedictine abbey. The Gothic Chapel of the Rocabertís, 12th-century cloister, restored Romanesque chapter house and Chapel of Sant Ferriol are the most notable buildings. The town hosts an important music festival at the end of August following its *festa major* on the 15th.

Follow signs now to FIGUERES (pop. 30,532), the capital of the Empordà comarca, which is just 3km further on and only 37km from the border with France. Even more than Port Lligat, Figueres belongs to Dalí. The town was his birthplace and where he died and has the only museum in Europe dedicated solely to the work of Spain's greatest eccentric (the only other Dalí Museum is the Morse Collection in Cleveland USA).

The **Theatre Museum Dalí** first opened its doors in 1974 and continues to do so from 9am through to 8pm during the summer months and from 11am to 4.45pm during the rest of the year. It is the second most visited museum in Spain and since Dalí's death (when visitors doubled overnight), it is now threatening to overtake even Madrid's mighty El Prado. No one can miss the Museum, with its enormous eggs balancing on the roof and bread rolls running down the walls – and no one should miss it either for it will make you smile, if not laugh out loud, more than any other museum you are likely to visit. The menagerie of surrealism is, appropriately enough for someone whose work is so participative, located in a 19th-century theatre.

Dalí's museum and last resting place. Behind it is the church in which his funeral was held.

Dalí's sense of fun is often overlooked by those delving deep into the symbolism of his surrealist dreamscape but it is this quality, together with his business acumen (many of the exhibits don't work without the lubrication of 5pt and 25pt coins) that comes through just as much as his technical skill.

The old Dalí favourites such as Gala's Cadillac which rains on the inside, and Mae West's living room, still draw the biggest crowds, but there are visual tricks round every corner. Gala, of course, is omnipresent either in person in the innumerable sculptures and portraits of her, or impersonally through her cadillac, her boat and the hundreds of other Gala objects on which Dalí lavished his art. Sadly Dalí was not granted his wish to be buried in the graveyard alongside his great love and his tomb lies under the museum floor. Commerce rather than sentiment governs art once the artist is out of the way and the museum owners are planning a lavish underground crypt in the museum.

Make sure you visit the first two floors even if you skip the collection on the third by his lifetime friend, Pitxot. If you can avoid the peak season, do: there are 4–5,000 visitors a day here in August.

Dalí insisted that no catalogue be sold in the museum as he felt it would pre-empt the interactive dynamic with his audience, but outside is the Libreria Surrealista which appears to be doing very nicely out of the Dalí industry. Opposite the museum is the Church of St Peter where Dalí was baptised and where his funeral was held. The Carrer de Sant Pere leads to the tree lined Rambla where Dalí drank with friends at the Bar Astoria. In the Rambla, no doubt much appreciated by Dalí, is the Museum of Toys, a private collection which claims to be the only one of its kind in Spain with over 3000 specimens.

Figueres' restaurants have good reputations and are heavily patronised by the French at the weekends. Good examples are the Hotel Duràn and the Ampurdan (both offering meals at around £15 a head). The town's major festival is on 3 May.

From Figueres, take the C260 inland, turning left at the Cabanelles crossroad, to **Banyoles** (a 29km drive). The town has a population of 12,378 and is the capital of the province's Pla de l'Estany comarca. Banyoles has a long manufacturing tradition and is home to one of Spain's most fashionable espadrille factories, Castañer, whose designs are copied through Europe. But it is its natural lake, virtually the only one of its kind in Catalonia, that draws visitors and is the reason it was selected for the 1992 Olympic rowing competitions.

Subterranean springs formed the lake millions of years ago and its peculiar suspended sediment gives rise to all kinds of legends of weird creatures lurking in the murky depths. Lake cruises or rowing boat hire can be arranged from the lakeside café where a sign claims that in its fish tank is a 60-year old, 15kg carp that answers to the name of Ramona and has a penchant for peanuts.

In September (usually the second Sunday) there is an annual 2km swim across the lake. The full 8km perimeter is not all accessible. On the far side is the very tranquil church of Santa Maria de Porqueres, popular for marriage nuptials. Doves have requisitioned the Romanesque *oculus* (eye) above the door, their nests obscuring the hole that should filter light into the church. The oriental influence of the carvings surrounding the door make its origins even more intriguing. Cypresses stand guard in the adjacent cemetery.

A tour of the town should start at the Monestir de Sant Esteve around which the town grew. The monastery was founded in 815 by Benedictine monks who accompanied Charlemagne on his crusade. The monks have gone but the church remains worthy of a vist. Its most valuable exhibit is the 14th-century Gothic altarpiece.

Proceeding down the Carrer Nou, you pass the recently restored Gothic Esglesia de Santa Maria dels Turers on your right before taking the second turning right (C. de Sant Martirià) to the **Museu Darder d'Historia Natural** at number 2 Plaça dels Estudis. I leave it to you to decide whether Dalí's musuem in Figueres or Darder's (it should be dada) in Banyoles is the most surreal. The five rooms the museum spans have human skins splayed on walls like hunting trophies, stuffed pygmies, double-headed sheep and bottled foetuses. One of the founders of the Barcelona zoo, Fransesc Darder i Llimona (1852–1918), first came to Banyoles to recuperate at the lakeside after being savaged by a lion in Africa. He started up a veterinary practice and soon sidelined in artificial human eyes and embalming. His 'new scientific method' for 'Embalsamamiento Humano' claimed to preserve dead loved ones in beatific states they never achieved in life. The method involved pumping what looks like cement into the intestines for 'as little as 500 pesetas'. If the museum is closed, knock at No. 10 across the street and the elderly curator will usually shuffle across, open up and leave you to get on with it.

Next, retrace your steps down C. de Sant Martirià and continue on into the Vila Nova where you quickly arrive at the 14th-century Gothic **Plaça Major**. This fine porticoed square with its copious plane trees has a weekly market on Wednesday mornings that has been operating since 1086.

Leaving the square by the C. Hospital, pass the Llotja del Tint (dye market) on your right before arriving at The **Museu Arqueològic Comarcal de Banyoles** (Plaça de la Font 11). Although the museum cannot compete with Darder's morbid exoticism, it does its best to compensate with archeological treasures such as a Neanderthal jawbone found near the lake in 1887 and estimated to be around 100,000 years old. The museum is housed in the 14th-century Pia Almoina (alms house) and has an impressive collection of phrehistoric exhibits, paleontological remains and stamps. The museum is open 10am–1pm and 4.30pm–8pm in July and August and 10am– 1pm and 4pm–6pm during the rest of the year. Major festivals are held on 15 August and 24–26 October.

From Banyoles, you could travel due west on the C150 directly into the Garrotxa Natural Volcanic Park through Sant Pau to Olot but this tour takes a more circuitous route northwards via **Besalú** (pop. 2087), a magnificent medieval fortified town perched high above the River Fluvià.

To really appreciate Besalú's superb location, I recommend you park just before entering the town and proceed to the Pont Vell toll on foot. Across the waters you will see St Peter's dominating the skyline and below it, the terraced café, La Curia Reial, which seems to attract most of the tourists. To its right, partially concealed by willows, lies the Miqwé, the only Jewish Baths in Spain to have survived from the 13th century (in fact there are only two others in the whole of Europe); it was discovered only in 1964. Steps descend to the simple vaulted baths in which women ceremonially bathed following childbirth or menstruation. Above the miqwé are the remains of the synagogue wall built into the medieval walls.

On entering the Plaça de la Llibertat, look immediately to your right and you will see one of the finest Romanesque private dwellings in the whole of Catalonia tottering precariously over the cobbled street (C. Comte Tallaferro). Again Gothic arcades line three sides of the square, one side of which houses the Tourist Information Office where you can pick up the keys to the Miqwé or St Peter's if they are locked (which is likely).

Plaça St Pere is where the Tuesday weekly market is held and where the eponymous church is located. A resident told me that when a travelling cinema first used to set up in the square locals called it 'The Fear Machine' because of its flickering images and beams of light. Fear of the machine, encouraged by the priest's accusations of possession, rekindled animistic souls that were gullible enough to pay for church services in St Peter's to exorcise their demons.

Apart from the 11th-century church, it's also worth visiting the ivy-clad Romanesque mansion Casa dels Cornellà across in the far right-hand corner of the square. Graceful arches and an elegant stone stairway lead from the ground floor where animals were kept (and provided the home's under-floor heating) up to the living quarters. As you enter the house you'll see *festajadors* or 'flirting benches' beside a window grill where chaperoned girls were allowed to speak to suitors.

Nearby is the 12th-century Romanesque **L'Esglesia de Sant Vicens** where exorcisms, I'm told, were carried out not very many years ago. The lower part of the church is unequivocally Romanesque but the slightly pointed vaults and the stained

Besalú.

glass rose window are of a later date. There's a good restaurant opposite the church, the Can Quei which offers an excellent value menú del día for 800pts. From the church, the Carrer Major leads back to main square, the tourist office and the mirador overlooking the Fluvià. The town's main festival is held on 24 September.

Leaving Besalú, at the junction with the Banyoles–Olot road, is another highly recommended restaurant. The earth grows increasingly dark as you proceed towards

Olot, the volcanic ash undersoil providing a fertile bed for the cereal crops, particularly corn, that are grown in the region. Half way to Olot a road leads off to the pretty village of **Montagut** where river excursions upstream can be arranged. The Sadernas Farm campsite provides a good base for walking in the valley and surrounding hills.

A little further along the C260 is the extraordinary spectre of **Castellfollit de la Roca**, a slate-grey town built on a precipitous outcrop held up by prismatic columns of basalt formed as a result of the pincer-like erosion by the rivers Fluvià and Turonell. The modern town is less compelling and is inclined to encourage you to stick to the road as it sweeps up through it and out the other side. This would be a shame, however, for the old town, particularly the church of St Salvador perched on the cliff edge, has a special charm and is worthy of half an hour of your time.

Continuing through the valley you may catch sight of the Witches' Peak if it's not shrouded in cloud. It was here that the Sisterhood supposedly gathered to work their magic and wreak revenge on troublesome neighbours. We are now inside the **Garrotxa Natural Volcanic Park** and grass-covered craters become increasingly visible. The volcanic zone, designated natural parkland only in 1982, is unique in Europe. Its finest views are offered at la Mare de Deu del Mont, El Puig de Bassegoda, La Fageda d'en Jordà and la Font de la Moixina in Olot. There are some 30 Strombolian volcanic cones, a few explosive craters and more than twenty basaltic lava flows in the park. The exceptionally moist climate provides a rich and varied plant life. Almost 75 per cent of the park is woodland (predominantly oak, beech and, along the riverbanks, alder) with the other 25 per cent used to cultivate fodder plants for grazing. Short-toed eagles and peregrine falcons have been known to put in an appearance and wild boar is on the increase. Horse-and-cart tours have a number of pick-up points in the park and offer various itineraries to the Fageda d'en Jordà beech forest, Can Xel, La Moixina and Santa Margarida. (Information from Joan Masoliver, tel. 972/6932 10).

A steep descent leads to the modern sprawl of **Olot** (436m), at the centre of the park. Olot is a typicall noisy Catalan town that offers compensation for its modern ugliness in a number of fine shopping streets, numerous art galleries and monuments. The town was wiped out by volcanic eruptions between 1427 and 1428.

Olot's main industries are pork sausages, textiles, ratafia (a lethal drink), chocolate and, more interestingly, the export of religious images to South America. I was told most orders emanating from Latin America specify detachable 'Madonna-Christs' so that buyers can separate the Virgin from her offspring if she doesn't answer their prayers. Other more specialist images are ordered for voodoo sessions. The religious workshops are an overspill from the 200-year-old Fine Arts School whose landscape artists are famed throughout the province and considered to embody particular Catalan naturalistic qualities born from the volcanic park's lush vegetation shrouded in its early morning mists. The school was founded by Joaquim Vayreda and Josep Berga in the mid 19th century and in 1934 the Catalan government gave it the official seal of approval as the Escola Superior de Paisatge (college of landscape artists).

The **Museu Comarcal de la Garotxa** opened only in 1987. Housed in an 18th-century hospice, the museum has an interesting collection of *gegants* – the enormous puppets that are wheeled out at every festival opportunity. The Olot painters

The 'gegants' of Olot.

(particularly the 19th-century brothers Joaquim and Maria Vayreda i Vila) are well represented and one of Casas' most famous canvases, La Càrrega, which depicts the dramatic clash between the Guardia Civil and striking workers in Barcelona at the turn of the century, is displayed prominently. Of all the rooms and exhibits in this excellent museum, it was the work of the sculptors Miquel Blay and Josep Clarà that really impressed me in their uncomplicated pursuit of beauty.

The weekly market is held on Mondays on one side of the main promenade whilst on the other side men from the surrounding villages huddle together wheeling and dealing livestock or playing chess at the Café Sport. You'll notice the houses in town are mostly recently painted – an ingenious town council policy reduces the rates of those who do so. At No. 40 there's a fine Modernist building with wrought balcony, art nouveau statues and pargeted façade. A little further on lies a rarely used bullring.

A craft market with wooden toys, brooches and ceramics is located in the Plaça Major. The Tourist Information Office is located on C. Bisbe Lorenz Ana 15.

The Fair of Sant Lluc with its spectacular firework display is held on 7–11 September. Olot is a good base for the endless touring possibilities whether culinary jaunts to the superb country restaurants (such as the one set in glorious countryside at the Fonda Can Mulleres in Sant Privat d'En Bas) or walking or cycling tours through the very beautiful countryside.

The three hills surrounding the town are extinct volcanoes. Montsacopa (also called Sant Francesc) lies on the right shoulder of the town as we approach, its crescent summit easily reached on foot in 20 minutes. On the outskirts of town, springs, woods and ponds along the Carrer La Moixina provide a favourite spot for wedding parties. The squat houses at the far end with their rectangular central turrets are typical of the region. Parc Nou is a large lush English style park containing the **Casal dels Volcans**, a museum with exhibitions on the volcanic park housed in the 19th-Century Palladian style La Torre d'en Castanys. Passing the old railway station which opened in 1911 and closed in 1969, and crossing the Riu Fluvià on the Pg d'Olot, you arrive at Olot's most exclusive residential suburb, Eixample Malagrida with its exotic South American street names. This residencia was designed by the *indiano*, Snr Malagrida, whose own ostentatious property fronts the main road (now a youth hostel). The road leads to Parc Vell.

The Santa Pau road (C153) out of town is only a stone's throw away and takes you through Catalonia's largest beech forest **La Fageda d'en Jordà**. The Mas Ventós farm house immediately on your right after the crossroads is built on one of the many hot air vents in the park. The great boon for the owners is that they need neither refrigeration in the summer nor heating in the winter as the temperature is regulated by their private natural thermostat. At the entrance to the wood is a monolith on which is carved a poem by Joan Maragall extolling the beauties of the forest. You pass the park's most famous volcano, Santa Margarida, with a crater nearly 350m across on the right. Approximately 7km further on at a right bend in the road, you'll see a notice board beside a bar on the left that provides information on the park (it's also one of the starting points for the horse-drawn carriage tours). A detour on the dirt track here provides a fascinating geological lesson in the open cast volcanoa mine with its layers of multi coloured ash.

Santa Pau (pop. 1263) is only a few kilometres further on, and well worth a visit.

The fortified town (with baronial castle) has a fine collection of medieval buildings (mostly 13th–15th century) in the old quarter and arcaded Plaça Firal dels Bous in which is found The Church of Santa Maria. There is a tourist office in the old quarter and a museum devoted to the volcanic park. To the east of the town on the Plaça de Reixac stands a megalithic basalt menhir known as La Pedra del Diable (the Devil's Stone). There's also a collection of religious exhibits in the parish church. The town's main festival is held between 14 and 17 August. Continuing further would take you back to Banyoles; instead, retrace your steps to Olot.

From Olot the most interesting way to travel the 30km to **Camprodon** (pop. 2376) would be on the daily train but if you prefer to drive, take the C153 and speedy N151. The 12th-century Romanesque monastic church of St Pere de Camprodon whose octagonal belfry dominates the skyline is one of three such monasteries that grace the River Ter's upper reaches. However, it is the Gothic convent and the pot-pourri of the turn-of-the-century Modernist villas, cramped medieval homes and palatial haciendas of the *indianos* (those who made their fortunes in the Americas and Caribbean before re-settling in their homeland) that gives the town its distinctive flavour. A maze of medieval alleyways leads to the Cerdanya Gate and the Pont Nou (the 'New Bridge', so named after it was rebuilt in the 16th century). Below the bridge to the right is the Carrer Isaac Albeniz with its cured meat shops and delightful bakery, Forn Sant Roc. At the latter you may be offered muscatel and biscuits whilst buying bread. Camprodon is famed for its biscuits – try *pinya* (marzipan with pine kernels) and *tocinets*. Below the bridge the River Ter swirls, suddenly disturbed by its convergence with the Ritort, before cutting a swathe southwards through lush green meadow pasture. Major festivals are on 21–23 June and 15–16 August.

The Forn Sant Roc in Camprodon.

Travelling north from Camprodon would quickly bring you to the French border at Coll d'Ares (1500m) just 18km away, but instead, detour north-west 11km to **Setcases** (Sept casas) whose 'seven houses' have long since grown to over a hundred, nestled at the foot of Pic de l'Infern and the Puig del Gegant. This is a popular base, close to the source of the River Ter, for skiers who don't wish to stay at the anonymous purpose-built resort of Vallter (2400m). The parish church of St Michael pre-dates the 12th century but has been rebuilt on a number of occasions. Its Baroque altar dates back to the 17th century.

Return to Camprodon, and turn southwards to follow the River Ter on its 200km journey to the sea. It may not be the province's prettiest river but it is the most typically Catalan in all its extraordinary diversity. The Ter snakes its way beneath Moorish castles, Romanesque chapels, industrial colonies and fortified medieval towns; through luxuriant alpine meadows and forests of beech, oak and cork; from a trickle to a roar and on through a series of reservoirs to the ocean.

Lush meadow pastures first lead you to **St Joan de les Abadesses** which boasts perhaps the most perfect of the Romanesque trinity of monasteries of the upper Ter. In 885 a Benedictine convent (Emma, the first abbess, was the daughter of Count Guifré el Pilós, Wilfrid the Hairy) was founded and its consecration as an Augustinian monastery took place in 1150. Only recently restored (1975), the church takes the form of a Latin cross with five apses. The most important exhibit is the 12th-century wooden figure behind the high altar depicting 'The Descent from the Cross'. The 15th-century Gothic cloister, museum (open June–September 10am–2pm and 4pm–7pm daily; and 4pm–7pm October–May weekends only at same times) and adjacent 18th-Century Baroque Chapel of La Pietat complete the ecclesiastical tour, though the town's Old Quarter with its arcaded square and medieval warren of streets running off it is worthy of an hour's stroll. Major festivals take place on the 24 June and 14–15 September.

Ripoll (pop. 12,000) lies just 10km away at the confluence of the Ter and the Freser, the capital of the comarca of the same name. The town grew up round the Benedictine **Monastery of Santa Maria de Ripoll** which, like Catalonia itself, was founded by Wilfred the Hairy (the first Catalonian count-king) in 879 following the expulsion of the Moors. The present building dates from 1032 and owes most to the entrepreunurial zeal of Abbot Oliba (later Bishop of Vic) when its reputation as a centre of learning was established (by the year of his death the library had 246 important volumes covering all aspects of learning from poetry to astronomy). Its ecclesiastical pre-eminence during the Middle Ages led Catalonia's most important poet, Jacint Verdaguer (1845–1902) to call it 'the cradle of Catalan civilisation'. It survived an earthquake in 1428, fire and looting in 1855 and similar treatment during the Civil War to remain Catalonia's most complete example of an 11th-century Romanesque church. Unfortunately the town itself has fared less well and there is little apart from the monastery to detain the visitor.

The Gateway of the Monastery disappoints those who have eagerly awaited their first glimpse of this celebrated example of Romanesque sculpture. There are two problems: one is the crumbling stone of which it is built – this is already badly disfigured and one day will erode completely – the other is the protective glass window officials have sensibly placed around it that stops one from closely viewing the whole. Built in the 12th century, the gateway is divided into seven horizontal layers sculpted with allegorical biblical scenes called by Verdaguer, 'The Bible printed on the heart of Catalonia' and 'The Triumphal Arch of Christendom'. The gateway leads into the great barrel-vaulted nave. A succession of sublime symmetrical arches lead down either aisle to the marble Virgin, donated by the Vatican. The church takes the form of a Latin cross, has five aisles in total and a transept with seven apses. When I visited, Snr Modest Moreno was playing a heavenly organ to a congregation of two.

In the two storey cloister are a number of intriguing secular images sculpted on the double capitals. The garden is dotted with cypresses and the belfry can be visited from the cloister.

In the adjacent Arxiu-Museum (open daily 9am–1pm and 3pm–7pm except Monday afternoons) is the Farga Catalana which is a typical example of the hundred such forges Ripoll boasted in the 18th century. The major industry was the production of nails but Ripoll also became one of Europe's most important weapon manufacturers. Ripoll was the undisputed capital of Catalonia's metal industry. Another room displays the weapons themselves manufactured in the city between the 16th and 17th centuries.

Alongside the museum is the Tourist Information Office. A market is held in Ripoll on Saturdays and trains stop here en route from Barcelona to Puigcerdà. A major festival is held here on 11 and 12 May. Outside the city are the metallurgical, textile and electrical industries on which much of the city's present wealth and employment rests.

If you intend continuing westwards along the Pyrenees then you should skip the rest of this chapter and proceed to the Tour 15. This tour, however, continues southwards on the N152, following the river past abandoned textile mills that bear testimony to the Ter's importance to Catalonia's industrial revolution. The river was exploited mercilessly by the entreprenuerial Catalans, and was the means of much of the nation's industrial wealth. Occasionally you'll come across a delapidated *colonie* a short distance from a mill – isolated terraced cottages built by the owners for their dependent workforce. A few of the mills still operate and other industries, particularly the paper mills, continue to pump polluted waste into the river despite the evidence of banks laden with dead fish and public campaigns for tighter controls. A short distance outside Vic you enter the important comarca of Osona, dotted with ancient bridges, castles and 11th-century early Lombard Romanesque architecture instigated largely by Abbot Oliba, bishop of Vic 1018–1046 (the best examples are the tower at Vic cathedral, Sant Pere de Casserres monastery, Tavernoles, el Brul, and Savassona). Many of the villages grew up round the large *masies* (examples are les Masies de Roda, el Brul, Gurb). *Rovellons* (mushrooms) in the hills here sell for 2000pts a kilo in Barcelona.

Vic (pop. 30,000), capital of the comarca of Osona, is set in the great Plain of Vic. The city experiences very cold winters by Spanish standards with temperatures falling below zero (Barcelona is often ten degrees centigrade warmer than Vic in the winter), concentrated periods of heavy rainfall and early morning fogs followed by brilliant sunshine. It is a prosperous city, its wealth based on textiles and leather-

The main square in Vic.

ware. Capital of the Ausetans in the 3rd century BC, it became a Roman city and then an important diocese.

Vic is worth visiting for its splendid main square alone, the **Mercadal** – perhaps the largest and loveliest in Catalonia – lined with a pot-pourri of Gothic, Baroque and Modernist façades above the porticoed passageway. This is where the large twice-weekly market (Tuesdays and Saturdays) has been operating for over a thousand years. In one corner of the square is the Tourist Information Office, located in the 14th-century Gothic Town Hall.

Leaving the square by the C. de la Riera (the corner with the ostentatious Modernist casino), proceed past some specialist shops. At No. 22 is the Renaissance Casa de Cultura, an old Jesuit building that was once an important seminary. Turning left along C. les Basses, you come to an intersection and find the Baroque Casa Estrada-Vilarresa. The C. de la Ramada eventually brings you into Plaça Catedral. Immediately to your left are early 19th-century and Modernist buildings. There is also a Carmelite monastery (silent order) in the square. For good reason Vic is known as the city of saints, nuns and priests and the city was in fact the base from which the austere Carmelite order spread throughout Spain. The city still has three such silent orders.

Opposite is the neo-classical façade of the **Cathedral** itself. The most unusual feature of the mostly 18th-century construction (built on an earlier Gothic structure), apart from its Romanesque crypt and impressive bell-tower 46m high, is that it was painted by Josep Maria Sert (1874–1945), not once but three times. His epic biblical murals with their teeming muscular hordes and gold and sepia painted columns create the effect of a junior school set for a nativity play.

Sert first painted the cathedral in 1920 but the bishop wasn't happy with the result and had him do it again. During the Civil War the cathedral was razed and so in the 1940s Sert in his sixties, returned to paint it once more. The artist is buried in the 14th-century cloister which, like the one at Lleida, has one of its aisles open on both sides (though less dramatically than Lleida – Vic's merely overlooks the busy Rambla del Bisbatet).

Returning out into the daylight, head down the C. Santa Maria which terminates at the Plaça de Jaume Balmes where the Parc of the same name is located. Turning left on the Rambla del Bisbatet, you are accompanied by the trickle of river that is the Riu Meder. Beyond the 11th-century Pont de Queralt, one of the original portals of the medieval city, you will see the old industrial mills and warehouses. Skirting the 14th-century town walls, behind which are the gardens of artistocratic mansions, follow the Rambla dels Montcada to its busy intersection with the Plaça de Santa Teresa. Immediately on the right is the 17th-century **Convent of Santa Teresa** at No. 10. Visits are restricted to 10.30am on Mondays for mass unless you make a special request at the hatch in the porch. Here too you may leave promises of gifts in return for miracles. The one I saw promised 'twelve eggs for sunshine on the 23rd'. No doubt a major party or wedding was planned. Indeed there is a tradition for brides to visit the convent on their wedding day.

The convent's baroque interior is as gaudy as one would expect of the period but nonetheless manages a certain majesty. Its most important treasure is the 17th-century Baroque retable of the main altar. The nuns can talk (at the abbess' discretion) to visitors through the grill that separates their austere Carmelite retreat from our world but you'll need Catalan or Spanish. The nun I spoke to, once released from silence, was a river in full spate, finally terminating our conversation with a request that I make it clear in my book that she was behind bars voluntarily.

On the other side of the road is the Esglesia i Convent de les Germanes Carmelites. Next to it is Casa Vilarrubia and then the city's best value restaurant, Cal'u. The daughter of the owner speaks good English and the Hostel offers basic rooms for those who prefer something a little more authentic than air conditioned muzak. The food is superb and the place is always packed, at luncthime by businessmen and at night by families.

Crossing back across the street, resume your tour on the other side of the city walls proceeding down C. de Dues Soles past a number of fine baroque aristocratic mansions including the Palau Bojons where Jaume Balmes, the respected 19th-century local philosopher and politician, died. The Restaurant La Taula on the left is elegant, modern and serves expensive international cuisine. On the right is an impressive recently refurbished Modernist house with pargeted façade, stained glass windows, wrought iron balconies and tiled roof. The four statues on the garden wall are of the four sons of the Masferrer family. The house backs on to a recently reconstructed sandstone 2nd-century **Roman Temple** and the remains of the 11th-century **Castell de Montcada** whose walls enclose two sides of the temple's garden. Immediately after passing the temple, turn left opposite the Baroque Esglesia de la Pietat through a maze of medieval alleyways lined by the most fragile-looking of homes until you arrive in the Plaça Bisbe Oliba. You are now once more in front of the Cathedral and it is in this square that you will find the Episcopal Museum.

The **Episcopal Museum**, located in the Archdeacon's House, is renowned for its

Romanesque and Gothic art collection. Upstairs is a mixed bag of first editions of the poetry, and the personal effects of, Jacint Verdaguer, 1845–1902, the city's most famous son, (born in nearby Folgueroles) alongside stamps, coins, tiles, pirons and religious artefacts. The museum was founded in 1868 and today is one of Catalonia's most important. The cloister contains the ancient lapidary museum.

Leave the square via the C. St. Miguel Arcàngel and turn left up the C. Corretgers into the Plaça St Felip which has the Gothic Town Hall's finest façade. It's worth asking permission to visit the upper floors to see 'The Gallery of the Distinguished Vigatans', Vic's own Hall of Fame. You can exit from the Town Hall back in the main square.

Vic's calcereous stone weathers quickly and so constant refurbishment is essential if the city is to retain its architectural heritage. Many of the city's palaus have recently been refurbished – one particularly fine example is the Modernist building on C. de Cardona that now houses the English School. Vic's major festivals take place on 5 July and during the week before Easter.

The modern Parador (1978) is located 17km away, to the northeast, and is dramatically set, overlooking the **Pantànó de Sau**, one of three reservoirs that swell the Ter's girth and provide both Barcelona and the Costa Brava with most of their water supply. (Miquel Fananas' novel *Susqueda*, in the best traditions of the disaster movie, gives a fictional account of a chaotic mass exodus from Girona when the Pantànó dam wall bursts. In 1983 it was broadcast over the radio and the ensuing panic (the production omitted to tell the listeners it was fiction) was a re-run of the bedlam that followed Orson Welles' April Fool broadcast of *The War of the Worlds*. It is easy to sympathise with Gironins panic reaction – records tell of 123 genuine floods since the 12th century. Rooms in the Parador overlook the swimming pool and reservoir. The scene is not the customary one of the Spanish interior during summer months when rivers trickle, streams die and soil grows parched and cracked like a crocodile's hide. Below the large oval pool, dense vegetation creeps half a mile down the hillside to the great lake. Windsurfers trace furrows below the extraordinary sculpted clay Cingles Mountains that border its northern banks. The reservoir is the headquarters of the Vic-Sau Nautical Club who offer water-skiing and sailing instruction on the lake. The parador's service and cuisine do not match the beauty of its location, but a few kilometres back along the Vic road, is an excellent restaurant, the Hostel Fussimanya, again superbly located.

Above the parador is the 11th-century Benedictine monastery (and former castle) of **Sant Pere de Casserres**. You reach it either on foot from the parador (an arduous near-vertical hike) or along an easier footpath from the Hostel Fussimanya.

From the parador this route leaves the river and re-joins it again 18km from Girona. A few kilometres from Vic, turn left for **Sant Julià de Vilatorta**, a charming village with large Modernist pargeted mansions where Vic's wealthiest natives live. The Romanesque church of Santa Julià dates from the 11th century and the village also contains the ruins of the Castle of Bellpuig. From the town, follow the minor road that climbs in a series of hairpins through cork and oak forests that threaten to engulf you at any moment, so dense is the vegetation. Umbrella pines, ash and chestnuts can also be seen along this stretch. **St Hilari Sacalm** is known as 'the village of 100 fountains' and its innumerable springs provide the province with its Font Vella and Font Picant bottle water. Located between the Guilleries and Montseny Mountains, the town has a flora and fauna exhibition in the Museu de les Guilleries.

From St Hilari, take the road to **Anglès** where you re-join the river. The town has a charming old quarter. Worth a visit are the castle and church of Sant Miquel and the chapel of Santa Barbara. Girona is now just 18km away. This region between Lleida and Girona has traditionally been isolated because of its poor road network but this will no doubt change shortly when the super highway, 'The Axle', is built linking Lleida through Tarrega, Manresa and Vic to Girona. Anglès' main festival is held on the first Sunday in September.

After Girona the tour crosses the Ter for the last time at Torroella de Montgri. Here the river will appear substantial and full of intent as it passes through the marshy flatlands of the Baix Empordà but just a few kilometres further eastward it will turn and turn again, like a trapped animal before finally dissolving its personality into the Mediterranean at Platja de Pals.

Girona

Situated just an hour's drive from Barcelona, half an hour from the Garrotxa Natural Park, less than forty minutes from the coast and half an hour from the border with France, GIRONA is the best sited of all Catalonia's cities. Unfortunately, as the first city on the autopiste south, Girona has traditionally been called 'The Gateway to Spain' and people seem to have taken the soubriquet literally, simply passing through and missing out on one of Europe's truly fascinating cities.

The river Onyar flowing through Girona.

In bygone days the invading hordes pouring across the border were of a different ilk, but they too only stayed long enough to storm the town before moving on to Barcelona. This role as Barcelona's first line of defence has left Girona with a history decorated by brave resistance. In the 19th century Napoleon's troops had to starve the populace into submission and similar tales can be traced back to early settlements.

Gironins are proud of their history and of their entrepreneurial zeal. Theirs was the first city on the Iberian peninsular to have electric street lighting and the city claims to be the third richest in Spain. Several multi-nationals (Coca-cola, Panasonic, Nescafé) have set up here in recent years. Gironins also claim to be the most Catalan people of all. Jealousies and prejudices declare Barcelonans as brash and overly self-obsessed (as indeed inhabitants of Madrid are considered to be by Barcelonans) whilst Barcelonans themselves view Gironins as conservative and inflexible (one Barcelonan friend called them 'the hard crust on the bread'). The heavy Catalan accents, impenetrable city walls and silence of the innumerable convents and churches reinforce this impression of a sober, sombre people.

Apart from the military invasions, Girona has also had to contend with regular floods: 123 such inundations have been documented in the city's records. One bar, the Mora on Cort Reial, proudly displays the various high water marks on a wall. Such a history does not create a party-minded, gregarious people and their sobriety leaves little enthusiasm for night life. Mists are common and the city is damp in winter.

Surprisingly, in view of its military struggles, Girona shows none of the beleaguered aspect found in Lleida and Tortosa. The compact Casc Antic (old

Exquisite craftsmanship is commonplace in Girona.

quarter) nestles in a triangle formed by the confluence of the Ter and the Onyar. Like Catalonia's other major cities, Girona has its Gothic cathedral. Unlike its neighbours', however, Girona's old quarter can rival even Barcelona's superbly preserved Barri Gòtic and contains perhaps the finest medieval Jewish quarter in Europe.

The city has a population of 67,000, boosted by a further 20,000 living in the ugly overspill of Salt, on the far bank of the river. Girona's modern sector, like much of Spain's 60's developments, was thrown up without a glance backwards, nor indeed forwards. The best you can say for it is that it is anonymous.

I stayed in the Bellmirall, a Gothic mansion in the heart of the old barri. Here you

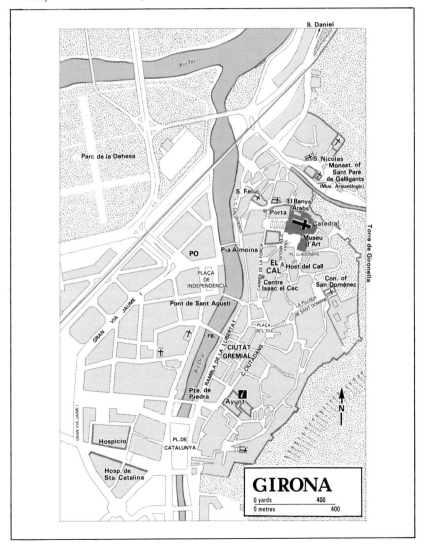

may walk the medieval alleyways at night under the warm glow of coach lamps abutting the walls. As the cathedral bells boom out, a delicious eerie chill like an electric current cuts through the balmy evening and you may catch a refrain from a sephardic song coming from the patio of the Museu d'Isaac el Cec in the C. Sant Llorenç. Each summer concerts are held here to commemorate those halcyon days when Girona was Europe's most important Cabalistic mystical centre before the final Jewish expulsion in 1492.

The following city tour I suggest can take anything between three hours to a full day, depending on whether you zoom through or linger over things. I would suggest starting the tour in the most typical of the city's warren of guild streets, Carrer de l'Argentería (Silversmiths' Street). The shops on either side of the street were once either silversmiths' workshops or jewellery shops. This practice of concentrating a trade in one street grew in the middle ages and detours to C. de Mercaders (Merchants' Street), C. de les Ferreries Velles (Smiths' Street), Plaça de les Olles (Cooking Pot Square) and Plaça dels Raims (Grapes Square) can offer further examples of this tradition. The C. de l'Argentería leads directly into **Rambla de la Libertat**. Off to the right is the Pont dels Peixateries (Fishmongers' Bridge) which leads over the River Onyar into the modern sector. The Rambla, as you might expect, is a good place to sit and watch. Unlike most ramblas however, it is entirely pedestrianised (Girona is a nightmare for parking) and offers a leafy canopy over the terraced cafés. Running along one side is a Gothic arcade which in the week is a chic shopping mall but which on Sunday mornings is transformed by the weekly flower market.

At the head of the Rambla is the Tourist Office and a statue commemorating the execution by the Nationalists in 1939 of Carles Rahola, an important Gironin writer. The Pont de Pedra again spans the Onyar to the right, but here turn left into the C. Nou del Teatre and then into C. de Auriga past the 17th-century Monastery La Mercè (now an Arts and Crafts school) and up the steps built in 1985 to provide access to the medieval ramparts. The 17th-century homes nestling below the steps do not appear to be old enough to have been granted funds for renovation and are in a very poor state.

A walk along the 14th-century eastern ramparts, the **Passeig de les Muralles**, offers the perfect opportunity to orientate yourself with a panoramic view over the city and Devesa Park. Across on the far side of the river the ugly, noisy congestion of the Eixample (Extension) spills from the city but on this, the near side, the old city is a symphony of bell towers, domes and tiled roofs.

At the Gothic convent of Sant Domènec, we descend the ramparts to visit its superb cloister. Until 1988 the convent served as an army barracks but plans are now afoot to convert it into part of the university that already occupies the 16th-century Les Aguiles building opposite. Every May the church opens its doors to the public and is richly decorated with flowers for its annual festival.

Continuing through the square, you will pass under the **Porta Rufina**, one of the gateways into the city whose ramparts' successive layers take you from the 1st century BC Roman Republic's rough limestone blocks, through late Imperial 3rd-century sandstone and 11th-century medieval brickwork which in turn was again built on between the 13th and 15th centuries. The gateway leads into the C. dels

Alemanys whose name commemorates the billeting of German troops here in the 17th century.

This is just the first of many such delightful medieval streets you now walk through in the **Casc Antic** whose rough-hewn stone has a warm glow even when denied sun. The C. Bellmirall possesses the best value hostel in the city located in an old *palau* that has been beautifully restored. The only disadvantage to staying here is that the cathedral bells insist on telling you the time every quarter of an hour round the clock.

The C. de l'Escola Pia leads into the Trav. d'en Miquel which in turn takes you to the steeply sloping stone steps of the C. de Sant Llorenc. We are now in **El Call**, the Jewish Quarter (see The Jews of Catalonia box p. 47), where in the 12th century was founded the first Cabalistic School in the Iberian Peninsula. It is in this, the narrowest of alleyways, and perhaps the most extraordinary street in the whole city (it was bricked away until only a couple of years ago) that we find the **Centre Isaac el Cec**. The centre has literature and exhibitions charting the 600-year history (from 890 to the final expulsion in 1492) of the Jewish community here, which was second only to Barcelona's in size. There's a café on the patio where the concerts are held and stairs lead down to three garden levels and out into the city's most famous street, C. de la Força, once part of the mythical 'Path of Hercules' which linked the Iberian Peninsula to the rest of Europe and which the Romans made into their own Via Augusta. The street runs between the city's northern (still standing) and southern (no longer standing) gates. On La Força you find sumptuous patios, gardens staggering several floors and stunning stone stairways such as the ones located in the 16th-century Casa Burges and Casa Ribas Crehuet opposite. At the southern end is the **Museu d'Historia de la Ciutat** at Casa Cartella House (an 18th-century Capuchin monastery) with exhibits dating back to Catalonia's first ancient settlers of Puig d'en Roca.

Eventaully you arrive at the **Plaça de la Catedral** with its ornate 17th-century Rococo *escalinata*, Catalonia's grandest stairway consisting of 90 steps in three flights standing free from surrounding buildings and providing the cathedral with its triumphal approach. In the square is the most beautiful Gothic **Pia Almoina** (almshouse) which now houses the lucky draughtsmen of the Association of Architects of Girona.

The **Cathedral**'s Baroque façade is carved from Girona stone (you can see the fossils if you look closely enough). The most stunning feature inside is the world's broadest unsupported Gothic nave spanning 22.98m and in width second only in any style to St Peter's in Rome. This architectural marvel was begun at the beginning of the 14th century and has created a rather dark, forbidding place, broken only by the occasional stained glass window (the rose is particularly lovely). Those rare occasions when the church is illuminated are worth waiting for, for then the cathedral is transformed into perhaps Catalonia's loveliest. Above the altar are the province's oldest examples of polychrome glass.

Other notable features are the 11th-century high altarstone and the marble Catedra Episcopal, the Bishop's Chair (also inexplicably known as Charlemagne's Chair despite the fact that he liberated the city from the Moors more than 200 years earlier). The Capella de Sant Pere is a 1975 reconstruction of the Romanesque church that pre-dated the cathedral and it is reached through a side door in the nave. Above the chapel entrance is the 14th-century sarcophagus of Ramón Berenguer II. His parents must have been short of imagination for they had already named his brother Berenguer Ramón. Ramón Berenguer clearly never recovered from the slight and murdered his brother on a hunting trip in an attempt to grab power for himself. It is in this chapel that mass is now heard as it rarely draws crowds big enough to fill the main nave. When I visited there were five present and they were all either priests or canons.

The Romanesque cloister is reached through a side door next to the Chapel of Hope. The double columns and capitals are decorated with the Creation story and other tales from the old testament. On one, Adam and Eve are tempted by the serpent, on another sinners are manhandled into a cauldron where three unfortunates are already being boiled alive. The pillar carvings are better preserved than those on the capitals. From the far side of the cloister there is an excellent view of the 12th-century Charlemagne's Tower (which is reminiscent of Barcelona's Plaça del Rei) and the cathedral's angular, abrupt buttresses. Near the roof of Charlemagne's Tower is a rather sinister gargoyle known locally as La Bruixa, The Witch, who supposedly turned the angel on the roof to stone.

The **Cathedral Museum** boasts two very important pieces and a fine supporting cast. The first is the Codex del Beatus, the beautiful illuminated manuscript of the Apocalypse originally written by Beato de Liébano and copied out painstakingly by Nun Eude around 1000AD. The manuscript contains a number of vibrant miniatures in the Mozarabic style. The most important exhibit of all is the Tapis de la Creacio (tapestry of Creation), a unique Romanesque embroidered tapestry from the 11th or 12th century. Measuring 12sq m, the tapestry has Christ at the centre with the Holy Spirit above him. On the left is the Angel of Darkness ('In the beginning darkness covered everything') and on the right, the Angel of Light ('God made light'). This stunning depiction of the Creation story with encircling firmament provides a marvellous insight to the medieval cosmos with the separation of the waters clearly shown (people believed there was an upper as well as lower sea and cited rain as evidence of this). Other interesting exhibits include the Llit de la Mare de Deu (Mother of God's Bed), the gold-plated Corpus Cristi Monstrance (a Flemish Gothic miniature of the Cathedral around which the elderly canons now process during the Corpus Cristi celebrations, finding it too heavy to cart around with them according to the tradition), the 10th-century Arabic chest – Arqueta d'Hixem II – and the recently restored Sant Helena's altarpiece.

The impressive Porta dels Apòstols with its intricate Gothic filigree at its base leads out onto the cathedral terrace, **La Plaça dels Apostols**. There is a simple font at the centre of the square and a fine view over the nearby St. Feliu. The terrace is flanked by the upper rear of the Pia Almoina, the 16th-century **Casa de l'Ardiaca** (Archdeacon's House) and the **Episcopal Palace**. The latter is a delightful pot-pourri of architectural styles spanning the 9th to 16th centuries and housing the much acclaimed **Museu d'Art de Girona**. Within a radius of 200m of the square are at least five working convents with nuns in residence.

Passing under the portal between the museum and the cathedral, ascend the C. Cartana (whose balustrade, incidentally, is made from tombstones) to the rear of the cathedral to view its cemetery, buttressed walls, spires, cornices and gargoyles. Passing the **Jardins de la Francesa** (donated by a French lady to the city when her house collapsed), descend through the 18th-century Portal de Sant Cristòfol. On the right you can see on the **Castel de Montjuïc** (Mountain of the Jews) the remains of the 12th-century Gironella Tower, blown up by Napoleon's troops as they left the city. Further off down the Ter Valley you will see the smoking columns of a paper factory that has had protracted wrangles with the council over pollution.

At the bottom of the steps are the **Arabic Baths** which were built in the 13th century by Christians in the traditional Arabic style (the Moors left in 785). The single-storey baths have been impressively restored and have an ingenious caldarium (paved floor over which water is heated by a hot air cavity below), a tepidarium (warm bath) and frigidarium (cold bath). The latter is the first room one enters and has light pouring in through an overhead window which surmounts a central octagonal marble well. The baths are open 10am–1pm, 4.30pm–7pm, (but mornings only on holidays) closed Monday.

If you turn left on leaving the baths, the C. Ferràn el Catòlic leads into C. de Santa Llucia and to the exquisite Romanesque **Monastir de Sant Pere de Galligants** which houses **El Museu Arqueològic de Girona** with exhibits from the Paleolithic to Visigothic periods. The 12th-century Benedictine abbey has an unusual three-storey bell tower, the upper two octagonal shaped and the lower, rectangular shaped. The doorway is most intriguing with its primitive motifs that are almost certainly part of an earlier structure. The cloister is also impressive with Hebrew-inscribed stones from the Jewish cemetery leaning up against the walls. Inside the church a replica of the rose window bears the following legend carved round its edge, 'I want everyone to know Peter carved a window.'

Across the street is the charming Romanesque **L'Eglesia de Sant Nicolau** whose structure most closely resembles a Greek Orthodox cruciform church with its three naves and short apses. Retracing your steps past the Baths, turn right down C. Ferran el Catòlic to Girona's second major Gothic landmark, **L'Eglesia de Sant Feliu**, built between the 14th and 17th centuries. The church contains the tomb of the 4th-century Christian martyr Sant Feliu of Africa and eight other sarcophagi of both Christian and pagan Gironins dating back to the 2nd century. A large arch in the left hand aisle leads into the marble-walled 18th-century Capella de Sant Narcis whose vaulted ceiling was painted by Francesc Tramulles. The chapel contains the mausoleum of General Alvarez de Castro, Governor of Girona during the Napoleonic siege. There's also a monument to 'Les heroines de Santa Barbara' in memory of Girona's female militia during the siege.

The C. dels Calderers leads from the Plaça de Feliu to the **Pont d'En Gomez** where you can view the pot-pourri of 18th- and 19th-century back terrace balconies and verandas that overlook the River Onyar (an even better view is offered by the next bridge up, the Pont de Sant Agustí). The houses were restored in 1983.

A few hundred yards downstream the Onyar converges with the Ter. You'll see fat carp swimming below the bridge but few Gironins would risk eating them. Carp, unlike the trout we find up near the source of the Ter, seem to thrive in polluted tepid waters. Across the river you immediately find yourself at the entrance to the neo-Classical **Plaça de la Independència**. The five-storey buildings, the tallest in any

19th-century Catalan square, consist of arcaded ground floors, three upper floors and attics. The arcade itself contains a number of restaurants, cafés and bars. Turning right, you arrive at the Noucentiste Post Office (1916) with sculptures by Frederic Marès. Continuing down the Av. Ramon Folc brings you to the city's lungs, **El Parc de la Devesa**, the largest urban park in Catalonia. At any time of day you'll see people jogging under the leafy canopy provided by more than 2500 mature plane trees (some reaching heights of 55m). A 19th-century garden is separated from the rest of the park by a small stream. The woodland was donated to the city by the king in the 15th century. A weekly open air market is held here on Saturdays.

Tour 15
The Pyrenees

This inland tour starts at Ripoll and travels through Catalonia's most important ski resorts and the bizarre Spanish enclave of Llivia before crossing the verdant Cerdanya to La Seu d'Urgell, the capital of the Catalonian Pyrenees. From La Seu the route crosses a high pass to the National Park, Aigües Tortes, and visits the lush Vall d'Aran and Boi Valley where the province's most celebrated Romanesque chapels nestle. Finally, leaving the Pyrenean peaks behind, the tour burrows through dramatic sandstone gorges carved out by the Noguera Pallaresa to the dusty plains surrounding Balaguer.

The tour straddles both the Girona and Lleida regions and the distinctive personality you meet here is the cumulative effect of a series of occupations by Iberians, Carthaginians, Romans, Visigoths and Moors. Today's culture may owe more to the occupation of the high valleys by ski resorts and shopping centres for French and Andorran day-trippers but nevertheless in the foothills you will still find Moorish castles rubbing shoulders with medieval monasteries consecrated after the Islamic expulsion by Ramón Berenguer IV. The region's long military history stretches almost to the present for it was not until the early 1960s that the Pyrenees ceased to be a battlefield for the exiled *maquis* (ex Republican troops) who made sporadic incursions across the border to occupy valleys and do battle with the Guardia Civil.

From Ripoll, take the N152 north alongside the River Freser. At **Ribes de Freser** (pop. 2810) those with ski slopes on their mind may take Spain's only rack and pinion railway to **Nuria** (1964m) 12km away. Nuria was the first ski resort to open in the Catalonian Pyrenees back in the 1920s and there are still a few original posters from those days to be seen. The Nuria monastery is set in a valley surrounded by the highest peaks of the eastern Pyrenees. The Virgin of Nuria statue is the village's most cherished possession — it took refuge in a Swiss safe deposit box during the Civil War.

Nuria has an artificial lake in front of the parish church, a smattering of hotels and restaurants but as you'd expect it's a seasonal centre (the fixed population is only 17). The village's main festival is on 8 September.

Returning to Ribes de Freser, pick up the N152 switchback once more and proceed to the Catalonia's principal ski resort, **La Molina**, where the first cablecars in Spain was installed in 1948. Make sure you don't miss the turning left by the petrol station 25km from Ribes, as this provides a faster and far more pleasant drive across to Puigcerdà via the resort than remaining on the N152. This route also has another advantage in that it hugs the eastern border of the Cadí-Moixeró Natural Park along the Riu d'Alp (see page 173).

Puigcerdà (pop. 5818), despite being the capital of the Cerdanya, does not have a whole lot going for it apart from its tree-lined artificial lake surrounded by fine villas as you approach Schierbeck Park; the town need not detain you for more than an hour or two (though the King likes it well enough to spend his summers here). The town, which is sited on the River Segre, was established in 1177 by King Alfons I, received its charter in 1182 and its Sunday market has operated ever since. Park by the side of the theatre and enter the Plaça dels Herois with its obelisk memorial to those who died in the Carlist Wars. On the left is the Kennedy Restaurant which has a pleasant location on the first floor overlooking the square, if you're looking for something quicker, then the Bar Sol i Sombra on the right offers snacks. The 42m bell-tower of the Gothic former parish church of Santa Maria stands forlornly in the inter-connecting square.

The Tourist Office is in the Plaça de l'Ajuntament which has a mirador overlooking the hills of the Cerdanya. The Gothic Church of Sant Domènech (a former convent) in Pg 10 d'Abril has had its sculpted capitals ruined and has a hideous modern stained glass window set in generally poor recent restoration work. Fortunately the cloister seems to have escaped this treatment. A new museum was about to open next door when I visited.

The town has a covered ice-rink and has traditionally been one of Spain's leading ice-skating and ice-hockey centres. Major festivals are held on the first Sunday in July and on 8 September.

Llivia (pop. 921) is a bizarre Spanish enclave located 5km from Puigcerdà and totally surrounded by France. Soon after you leave Puigcerda a redundant checkpoint declares that you are entering France and the SNCF line trundling alongside the road confirms the claim. Three kilometres later another sign announces that you have re-entered Spain (you'll notice the tree trunks are suddenly no longer painted white) and yet you are still surrounded by France.

Llivia was a Roman settlement and the traditional capital of the Cerdanya before Puigcerdà stole its thunder. Mythology has it that Llivia, like so many other towns, was founded by Hercules. Under the Treaty of the Pyrenees in 1659, 33 Catalan villages were ceded to France by Spain but as Llivia had traditionally been known as 'vila' instead of 'village' it managed to exclude itself from the hand-over.

Apart from its novelty value, Llivia is worth an hour or two of your time. It is set in glorious countryside, has some delightful old houses, particularly in the Plaça Major (including the Can Ventura restaurant) and a partially fortified church with attractive clock tower. Over the entrance to the parish church is the date 1617 but the building

The Catalonian enclave of Llivia.

dates back to the 14th century. Llivia's much vaunted 'oldest pharmacy in Europe', founded in 1592 and operated by the same family for two hundred years, is a huge disappointment: in my opinion, a few apothecary bottles in rather lovely cabinets were not really worth the price of admission. A number of Barcelonans have their second homes in Llivia and ski chalets litter the lower valley. The main festival is the Pasquetes on the Sunday after Ascension Day.

Returning to Puigcerdà and heading out on the C1313, the road improves dramatically as you exchange Lleida for Girona province, and pass through the heart of the glorious **Cerdanya**. If they have 50 different words for white in the ice fields of Alaska, then the Cerdanya needs 50 for its different greens. The roofs grow steeper, the churches more Nordic with slate witches' hats for towers, cattle graze with bells round their necks, many of their rough stone barns converted into fashionable new homes. Everything proclaims that you are now really in the mountains. The peaks rise to just under 3000m; there are caves, lakes and more than twenty mountain shelters for hikers (some very well equipped and all free of charge – the best are at Meranges, Tartera, Urus, Cortal d'en Vidal and Riu).

Pass the rustic delights of Bolvir, Ger and All, on the banks of the Segre, before taking a dirt road off on the left to **Tallo** (not on the Michelin map). The Romanesque *catedral cerdana* (the cathedral of the Cerdanya), was the seat of the ancient canonry where the archdeacons of the Cerdanya lived. The belfry has been almost totally requisitioned by pigeons. When I dropped in, pears were ripening on a table in one of the farmhouse gardens and there was not a person to be seen in this rural idyll just a stone's throw from the main road.

The next port-of-call is **Bellver de Cerdanya**, another medieval delight with the remains of 13th-century fortifications overlooking the Segre. The main square is a blueprint for Pyrenean arcaded perfection with flowers and creepers spilling over the wooden balconies beneath the Gothic parish church. Many of the homes here seem to have been abandoned and it's mostly the elderly who still inhabit the town; the young no doubt having been drawn to the resort towns and cities by employment.

The road south from Bellver de Cerdanya leads through pine forests to the Tunel del Cadí which leads down to Bagà and the southern slopes of the **Cadí-Moixeró Natural Park**. There are also two forest tracks from Bellver into the park and a number of other roads and tracks further west along the C1313. This, the Cerdanya side, is the most popular for summer homes particularly around Alp, Martinet, Das, Urus and Bellver. The northern side has skiing, climbing and a number of other sports activities to complement the good camping and accommodation facilities.

The park was established in 1983 and borders three comarcas (Berguedà, Alt Urgell and Cerdanya) and covers 385 sq km including the pre-Pyrenean ranges of Cadí and Moixeró.

The park information office just before the tunnel lists a number of walking itineraries and suggested climbs. Trout and barbel are plentiful in the park's three rivers but fishing is prohibited. Many northern European species of plant are found in the park because of the high humidity and low temperatures. The Alpine meadows found above 2200m are a riot of gentian in spring. Larger herds of chamois are found in this park than in the Aigües Tortes Park further west. Red deer and roe deer, which had died out, were recently successfully re-introduced to the park. Great golden eagles may be glimpsed and other bird species date back to the Ice Age. Unlike in Aigües Tortes, the villages which rely on the cattle and forests, are a natural part of the park, rather than outside it.

Five kilometres from Bellver west along the C1313 is **Martinet** which has the thermal baths of Sanilles nearby. The Sanctuary of the Mother of God of Bastanist has a Romanesque apse but it is the 4-star Hotel Boix, which many claim to be the best hotel and restaurant in the Spanish Pyrenees, that draws most people to the resort. Continuing westwards along the C1313, as you near La Seu d'Urgell, the plain opens out and terraced orchards appear.

LA SEU D'URGELL (pop. 10,681) is located just 20km from Andorra and is the undisputed capital of the comarca of l'Alt Urgell and indeed the whole Catalonian Pyrenees. La Seu d'Urgell claims to date back to pre-historic times and was already a bishopric in the 6th century. Through some bizarre anachronism its present bishop still retains the title joint-prince (with the President of France) of Andorra, an honour first bestowed in the 12th century.

With its ecclesiastically sombre mood, its darkened medieval nooks and crannies, La Seu d'Urgell is, with Girona, the most fascinating of all Old Catalonia's cathedral cities. If you have the time, I would suggest spending at least two days here, making excursions into the Cadí Moixeró or just sitting in the cathedral cloister, browsing in its hugely impressive museum or wandering under its broad Gothic arcades.

La Seu d'Urgell's long history as an episcopal see was only briefly interrupted by the Moorish occupation which ended with the town's recapture by the Francs in the 11th century. The best place to start your tour has to be the **Cathedral of Santa Maria**, a national monument that dominates not only the town, but the whole valley.

La Seu d'Urgell.

Compared to most of Catalonia's other cathedrals, La Seu is well preserved considering the harsh Pyrenean climate; neither does it seem to have suffered the level of vandalism that has occurred elsewhere. This is not to suggest the cathedral has not been attacked. In a matter of just three hundred years from its inception it was re-built a staggering three times. The cathedral standing today dates back to the 12th century.

Approaching the cathedral from the west-front you can see the lombard arches of the campanile rising gracefully above the geometric frieze of the pediment. Below it, above the main entranceway, gruesome Romanesque beasts stand guard. Also interesting to note on the exterior walls of the side aisles (and indeed on the pillars inside) are the Romanesque 'bread rolls' which seem so 'surreal' on Dalí's museum in Figueres (supporting Dalí's assertion that above all else he was a 'classicist').

The unusually tall granite cathedral (21m high) follows an Italian model and is unique among the province's Romanesque architecture with three aisles and a large transept whose rear wall has four of the five apses embedded in it. The nave is also impressively long (38m) creating a powerful impression of grandeur and endurance. Few would doubt that the cathedral will see at least another 700 years' service. The central apse is particularly beautiful and houses the revered Romanesque statue of St Mary of Urgell. The upper galleries are well illuminated and decorated with floral capitals.

The cloister is particularly peaceful and harmonious. The finely preserved secular imagery on the capitals take us into the western portico where piped monastic chants in turn draw us into the sublime purple-stoned 11th-century chapel of Sant Pere (also known as Sant Miquel), perhaps the most perfect of all the Romanesque chapels in the Pyrenees. Next door is the excellent **Diocesan Museum** (whose stark glass mirador rudely interrupts the continuity of brick above the cloister). Inside is a papyrus papal bull from 1001 and a most beautiful 10th-century copy of the Apocalipsis of Beato (there's also one in the cathedral museum in Girona). The wooden Majesties on the second floor are enchanting in their rough naivety and there are important paintings from the same period on the first floor. The ground floor contains a most memorable 16th-century wooden sculpture of 'the Virgin asleep' by J. Sanxo, housed in the beautiful old cathedral chapel.

Leave the museum by the far gateway, entering the square that houses the Bishop's Palace. Turning right, make your way to the dark arcaded Carrer Major which seems to have been locked in a time capsule. Under the broad ancient arcade are a number of wonderfully bizarre shopfronts beneath which owners somehow seem to be earning a living selling unknowable things. Along the C. Major there are also ancient, sturdy grain measures dating from the 14th and 18th centuries. The Carrer Major leads eventually back to the cathedral where there are a cluster of outstanding buildings: private homes of the Borxi family, the delightfully named Antipope Luna and Casa del Pelegrí. There's also the 19th-century Episcopal palace which houses valuable archives as well as the Bishop of Urgell.

Beyond the Casc Antic is the Rambla shaded by broad plane trees. Here you'll find the majority of the restaurants and hotels.

To get an overview of the town walk to the rear of the Cathedral (where there's a playground and mirador where families gather in the evenings) and out into the valley. The magnificent granite exterior of the Sanctuary of the Cathedral blends harmoniously with the medieval walls below which kitchen gardens run down to the river bank.

If you're not staying at the parador (which is one of the best despite its lack of view and lowly three star status) then at least pay a visit to see the extraordinary hanging gardens in the glass roofed atrium created out of an old cloister. It may be the least impressive of all the paradors from the outside but it is certainly one of the most beautiful inside. Its restaurant, in my opinion, is the best of the Catalan paradors with the possible exception of the one at Tortosa.

Another impressive building is the 19th-century red stone council seminary beyond the parador with an important library dating back to 1860. From a distance it looks like three separate buildings but on closer inspection you realise it is a vast single building forming a letter 'E'.

A market is held in La Seu d'Urgell on Tuesdays and Fridays. Within a stone's throw of the town lie the ruined citadel of Castellciutat and castle ruins at Castellbo. Festivals are the last Sunday in August and the Fair of Sant Ermengol on 1 November.

A short distance out of town on the C1313, you pass the 4-star El Castell built into the remains of a castle. Shortly a secondary road (the C146) leads off to the right signposted to Sort. As you climb the hills, you are rewarded with a view of the Segre snaking its way through the valley. This 52km potholed rollercoaster offers stunning views (and possibly punctures) all the way to **Sort** (pop. 1496) where there are the ruins of the 11th-century castle of the counts of Pallars and some fine mansions of the nobility; anything else there once was, has long since been buried under modern

Aigües Tortes, Catalonia's only national park.

hotels or chalets. Sort is the capital of the Pallars Sobirà comarca and has an important canoeing school which hosts national and international events.

Before turning northwards again towards the majestic peaks of the Pyrenees, a 13km detour left down the Riu Noguera Pallaresa to **Gerri de la Sal** beckons. On the outskirts of town are salt beds that have existed since the middle ages. This, surprisingly, is the only salt extraction project in the Catalan Pyrenees despite the abundant saltwater springs. The village is bisected by the main road. On the left is an ancient gateway that leads via a steep cobbled alleyway to the main bridge across the river. A path beneath a leafy canopy leads along the bank of the river to the abandoned 12th-century Monestir de Santa Maria. Unfortunately the frescoes on the ceilings of the three apses are in poor condition as is the exterior of the church. Alongside is a charming cemetery.

Although it's tempting to follow the C1313 further south to la Pobla de Segur through the Collegats Gorge, the tour now returns via Sort along the C147 and then follows the C142 to **Aigües Tortes National Park**. (You will not miss Pobla de Segur, it comes up later in the tour.) Despite the beauty of Catalonia's slice of the Pyrenees, only one sector has been designated a national park and as you might expect, it is very special indeed. 'Aigües Tortes' – 'Tortuous Waters' – is located at the junction of five mountain ranges. Its two valleys, La Vall de Boi and La Vall d'Espot, are connected by a walkable pass or a 100km road detour through the Port de la Bonaigua.

The 100sq km the park covers are blessed with more than 50 lakes nestling in alpine meadows surrounded by awesome granite and slate peaks. Waterfalls cascade out of hanging valleys into streams that spread like veins across the parkland. There are Pyrenean chamois roaming the meadows, golden eagles gliding overhead and along the river banks wild roses, lilies, periwinkles and a plethora of rare mushrooms grow. Dotting the park are eight refuges where walkers can stop overnight and eat cheaply. To enter the park, a fleet of jeep taxis transports walkers at moderate cost, usually dropping them at Lake Sant Maurici from which the major treks radiate. The park's highest peaks are Subenuix (2949m) and Pic Peguera (2982m). (For more details on jeep hire and refuges see p. 182).

To the north a necklace of lakes lead up to 'Agulles d'Amitges', 'the needles', so named because of the prismatic effect of the splintered mountain peaks. This is a popular climbing spot, but one which has claimed a number of lives. The most dramatic alpine scenery however is to be found in the south skirting the darkest and highest tarn, Estany Negre.

I was fortunate to arrive at **Espot** (pop. 250), the eastern gateway to the park, on the most important day in the village's calendar, the Fete of Sant Maurici, (22 September). The festival commemorated a fateful day in the village's calendar when two huntsmen, warned in a vision against shooting chamois, predictably enough went outside and shot the first one they came across. Their twin petrified forms, Els Encantats, now dominate the park towering above Lake Sant Maurici. The modern festival however seemed to have little to do with chamois or mountains. Instead organisers showed a steely determination to involve visitors in the celebrations by directing the speakers of the World's Worst Band, 'Montse Joe and Transfer', directly at the hotel and blasting everybody out of their beds till four in the morning. Another bizarre cabalistic ritual involved throwing flour over visitor's cars and then tracing the conciliatory message 'Hola!' in the muck.

The village itself is still split into two distinct hamlets, Salou and Obago, on either bank of the river. During the Civil War the right and left political divide followed the geographic division. The village consists of a few hotels, a typical Pyrenean parish church that appears to be permanently closed, a couple of bars and a gaggle of farm buildings.

Returning to the C147, the road embarks on the long climb to the 2000m Bonaigua pass detouring en route through the delightful Vall d'Àneu. The first port of call along this road is **Esterri d'Aneu** (pop. 559), the valley's capital and the starting point for mountain hikes in this region. Festivals are on 22 January and 8 September. The road now follows the upper reaches of the Riu Noguera Pallaresa through Borén, Gil and Alós de Gil – all charming villages with their churches surmounted with the typical slate Pyrenean tower.

At the crest of the Bonaigua pass you start to descend the equally breathtaking, lush **Vall d'Àran**. This is another major sports centre with national and international ski events (plus a unique annual international horse race over snow at the beginning of January), canoeing, hiking and the hunting of wild boar, Pyrenean goats and grouse (some of Spain's most important game reserves are located here). The most important ski resorts are Baqueira-Beret and Tuca-Betrén (see list of ski resorts on pages 200–201).

The Vall d'Àran lies in the upper basin of the River Garona surrounded by soaring sierras known as *tucs*. Across the French border the river becomes the Garonne and travels all the way to the Atlantic at Bordeaux. The 600sq km the valley covers is criss-crossed by two other rivers, the Noguera Pallaresa and Noguera Ribagorçana. But it is along the banks of the Garona that the majority of the valley's 6000 inhabitants live. The Vall d'Aràn is the only Catalan valley on the northern slopes of the Pyrenees opening to the cooler Atlantic climate. With more rain and snow than the rest of the Pyrenees, it is hardly surprising that the Vall d'Aràn is considered the greenest of all the valleys.

It is worth stopping at the pretty village of **Tredós** with its hot baths and 12th-century Cap d'Aràn church which has managed to preserve its wooden roof to the present day. The old village is reached by a small road on the left just before you enter **Salardú** (pop. 227). At the latter I followed a trail of Pyrenean folk music to its source, a speaker in the belfry of the 12th-13th century Romanesque Sant Andreu parish church. The bell-tower itself was a 15th-century addition. Inside the church is an important 13th-century polychrome wooden crucifix. Salardú's festival is 3 May (the Feast of the Holy Cross).

Your next stop is at **Artíes** (pop. 387) which grew up round a Knights Templar castle. The village is graced with charming old cottages overlooking a stream. A mixture of slate, stone and wood create a far more distinctive Catalonian feel to the mountains than the imitation Tyrolean chalets that seem to be sprouting up everywhere. The simple 12th-century Romanesque parish church of Santa Maria has a 16th-century tower and houses statues and paintings from the 12th–17th centuries. Nearby is the Parador Nacional Don Gaspar de Portola (three star) located in the valley's finest building and offering a spectacular view. Artíes' main festival is on 24 June.

At the head of the valley, where the C132 meets the N230, you arrive at **Viella** (pop. 2961) whose parador has an even more stunning location overlooking the spires of four churches through the valley. The parador, located in a modern building may claim better facilities and fine outdoor swimming pool but the cuisine does not compare with that offered at Artíes and La Seu d'Urgell (tinned fruit and artificial cream, poor service and a distinct lack of Catalan dishes). One service it does provide though is free buses to Spain's best (and most expensive) ski slopes at Baqueira.

Viella is the capital of the region and, like all the towns and villages in the valley, possesses an old quarter; unfortunately this is bisected by the main road. Most of the town however, consists of modern shops servicing the French who pour across the border at weekends. Over the past twenty-five years Viella has been transformed from poor peasant farming to a hugely wealthy tourist centre (though shrewd day-shoppers go to nearby Les and Bossost which are considerably cheaper). In school children have a choice of Aranese, Catalan or Castillian as their medium of instruction. Aranese belongs to the linguistic family of the langue d'Oc and is a variant of the Gascon spoken in the Comminge region across the border. Nonetheless it remains a close relative to Catalan.

The most important church is also the most prominent: the 12th-century church of Sant Miquel with its most beautiful sculpted doorway and Baroque altars in both wings of the transept (which like the belfry, was added in the 14th century), either side of a memorable 15th-century Gothic high altar. The church has been well restored recently. Across the road is the most helpful Tourist Office whose window proclaims 'Parlo toto Aranese' ('We all speak Aranese'). The irony is that Miguel Alvarez, who runs it, is from Seville and doesn't speak a word of the language! The Museu d'Era Val D'Aran is housed in an 18th century mansion on the main road and charts the geology, glaciology and every other -ology of the region.

Apart from the skiing and shopping, the area is popular with walkers particularly to the north of Viella. As one might expect of such a resort, there are also excursions to nearby towns and natural attractions. The main festival is on 8 September.

The Tunel de Viella, 8km south of Viella, opened to normal traffic in 1965 and is 5.165km long. Once through it, follow the Riu Noguera Ribagorçana for half an hour until you turn left up the **Boï Valley** 3km before Pont de Suert. Now follow the River Tort past Catalonia's finest collection of Romanesque churches (twelve in all) to the western gateway to the Aigües Tortes Park. This section of the tour should not be omitted from anyone's itinerary: every hamlet has its cluster of medieval homes nestled round a 12th- or 13th-century parish church surmounted by perfectly preserved campaniles. Again the countryside is glorious; there's a number of artificial lakes and even the Hydro-electric plant looks like a Romanesque church!

At **Barruera**, there's a camp site (open 1 April to 30 September) and a Tourist Information Office as well as, naturally, a parish church (Sant Feliu). The finest Lombard Romanesque churches however are Santa Eulàlia at **Erill La Vall** and **Sant Climent de Taüll**, 3km above Boï. Both boast exquisite six-storey campaniles, Santa Eulàlia just winning by a head. But it's Sant Climent that has become the shrine drawing the crowds, particularly now that has been converted into a museum (the original celebrated fresco of the Pantocrator is in the Museum of Catalonian Art in Barcelona but there is a faithful reproduction in the central apse). Gracing the main square in Taüll is another, larger 12th-century Romanesque church, the Santa Maria.

Further up the valley, just 2km before **Caldes de Boï** (with a 4-star hotel built round the thermal spa) is the western gateway to the Aigües Tortes Park. Jeeps run from many of the villages into the park where a number of treks await the walkers who flock here particularly in the summer (though the park is at its finest in spring and autumn). Franco once made a visit to the park in 1955 to stay in a house that had been given to him. The road he had built to get him there, like the dictator himself, has disappeared.

Retrace your steps through the valley back to the main road, and turn left into **El Pont de Suert** (pop. 2879), an interesting mix of old and new (the modern church was built in 1955). The town produces rather lovely blankets that can be bought cheaply. Major festivals are on 20 January and 9 August.

Just after the tunnel leading out of town (on the C144), one catches sight of the ruins of the 8th-century Monestir de Lavaix rising from the waters of the Panta d'Escales reservoir (part of the building, has been submerged). The road eventually joins the C147 at **La Pobla de Segur** (pop. 3356), whose Modernist mansions are complemented by a rather charming old quarter. La Pobla de Segur has an important hydro-electric industry surrounded by orchards. You can pick up excursions back up the Collegats gorge to Gerri de la Sal from the town centre. Pobla's main festival is on 25 and 26 July.

From La Pobla de Segur the C147 south follows a series of man-made lakes along the Riu Noguera Pallaresa to Balaguer. Just before Tremp is **Talarn**, a medieval town with fortified walls, ancient homes and castle remains. **Tremp** itself (pop. 5603), capital of the comarque of El Pallars Jussà, is situated in a large plain and has both a modern bustling commercial centre and old quarter surrounded by what's left of its medieval walls. The parish church, dating back to the 9th century and restored in the 17th century, and the Tower of Forques are worth a look. Monday is market day and Spring fairs are held in May.

About 9km south of Tremp turn right to **Guardia de Noguera** to visit the 10th-century Mur Castle ruins (another national monument) and the 11th-century Romanesque Santa Maria church. This can be followed by a lakeside lunch at **Cellers'** Hostal del Llac, overlooking the Pantà de Terradets with the Serra de Montsec providing the backdrop (plans are afoot to make the whole range a protected park).

The drive through the honeycomb gorge gouged out by the Noguera Pallaresa and then the Segre is one of the great Catalonian trips and truly stunning. This again is popular trekking country with a path carved 60m above the Noguera Pallaresa running the length of the Mont-Rebei gorge.

Having passed through the Portell dels Terradets, near the 11th-century church and castle of La Baronia de Sant Oïsme you must decide whether to continue due south or head off the C147 route westwards. The latter will take longer but you will be compensated with stunning views over the Ager Pass, the ancient collegiate church of Sant Pere, the Roman tomb in the parish church at Ager and the beautiful old abbey of Bellpuig de les Avellanes (with 12th-century cloister). If you continue due south however, the road splits again just below Camarasa (ruins of 12th-century Romanesque church of Sant Miquel del Castell). Keep to the fast new road (left fork) – it offers the most spectacular views high above the Segre.

Whichever route you take leads you to **Balaguer** (pop. 12,432), the capital of La Noguera comarca, and a town of split personality. Dominating the skyline is the 13th-century Santuari del Sant Crist – the patron of the city (at the back of the church is a terraced café offering a view over the plain), the old Moorish fortifications and castle (Castell Formós – later used as the residence of the Counts of Urgell) and the considerable bulk of the 15th-century Gothic Santa Maria, crumbling quietly at the southern end and concealing the town's most prized possession – the charred feet and head of an icon of Christ that saw the rest of its body meet its maker during the Civil War.

Dropping below this noble brow however, we find a warren of absolutely filthy streets where modern buildings are crumbling with far less dignity. This area is inhabited by a fixed gypsy population who have ceased their nomadic ways.

Eventually the streets lead into the enchanting medieval quarter where the town's finest shops sit under Gothic arcades. At the centre of the old quarter is one of the province's largest squares, the vast colonnaded Plaça del Mercadel where you can sit at terraced cafés under plane trees serenaded by the cacophony of birds. Running off the square are the delightful Carrer Major and Carrer d'Avall with their modern patisseries and delicatessens alongside ancient shops selling anachronistic, intriguing products. Running parallel with these streets are the riverfront arcades.

Crossing the river, another ugly aspect of the town's personality stretches its banal modern concrete skin along the eastern bank. Smoking chimneys, cranes and apartment blocks now fill the skyline. The endless, characterless Pg de l'Estació is where the modern shops are. At its head is a statue to the moustachioed Captain Don Gaspar de Portolà, born in Balaguer, discoverer of the bay of San Francisco and founder of the towns of San Diego and Monterey in California.

The monastery of Sant Domènec beside the upper bridge is certainly worth visiting with its unusual low supporting arch bisecting the vast nave and fine Gothic cloister (a national monument). Opposite is the vastly overpriced parador-collaborador. The main road that separates them is the major artery out of town linking up with the speedy N1313 road to Lleida, 29km away.

The town's major museum has a variety of pottery, ironwork, sculpture and glass gathered from the far-flung corners of the comarca. Balaguer's chief festivals take place on the last Saturday in May and on 9 November.

The North: Practical Information

The Consorci de Promocio Turistica, Pg de Gràcia 112, 08008 Barcelona (tel. 415 16 17), provides useful guides and literature on the region. A full list of Catalonian tourist offices is given under Further Information at the back of the book.

Useful telephone numbers

International telephone information: 9398
Telephone information within Spain: 003

GIRONA
Rail travel information: 20 70 93
Airport information: (972) 20 23 50
Taxis: 20 33 02/20 32 87/20 29 80
Telegrams: 20 00 00

Aigues Tortes Park

JEEP HIRE
Can easily be arranged on arrival. Jeeps take up to eight passengers. Sant Maurici Lake c.£23, half-day hire c.£65, full day c.£95, from Hotel Sarrat (tel. 65 50 63). For jeeps on the Boï side of the park, tel. 69 60 36.

WALKING IN THE PARK
There are eight *refugis*, which accommodate 30–80 people and provide mattresses, blankets and food. Spartan but adequate and cheap: c.£3.50 per night, breakfast c.£2, lunch and evening meals c.£6. Book through C.E.C., Paradis 10, 08002 Barcelona (tel. 315 23 11).

Restaurants and accommodation

Restaurant (R) prices: cheap = under 1500pts; moderate = 1500–2700pts; expensive = 2700–4000pts; very expensive = over 4000pts.
Accommodation (A) prices (per double room with bathroom, per night): cheap = under 3000pts; moderate = 3000–6000pts; expensive = 6000–18,000pts; very expensive = over 18,000pts.

AIGUABLAVA
A/R. **Parador Aiguablava** (4-star). Book through Keytel in UK (071 402 8182) or book direct (972-62 61 62). Stunning location. Expensive.
A/R. **Hotel Aiguablava** (4-star). (tel. 972 62 20 58). Highly recommended. Expensive, but less so than the Parador.

ARTÍES
A/R. **Parador Turisme Don Gaspar de Portolà** (4-star), Afores (tel. 64 08 01). Expensive.
R. **Restaurant Patxiku Quintana**, Remeis (tel. 64 16 13). Good fish menu. Expensive.
R. **Restaurant El Restrillé**, Pca. Canera (tel. 64 15 39). On the road from Artíes to Viella at Garós, offering very good Aranese cuisine. Moderate.

BALAGUER
A/R. **Parador Colaborador Comte Jaume d'Urgel**, Apdo 25, Urgüell 2 (tel. 44 56 04). Moderate.
R. **Restaurant Cal Morell**, Pg de l'Estació, 18 (tel. 44 56 66). Snails, rabbit and other Catalan delicacies. Moderate.

BANYOLES
A. **Victoria** (2-star), Dr Isern 22 (tel. 57 12 79). Moderate.
A. **Hostal l'Ast**, small pool, quiet tree-lined street leading to lake. Moderate.
A/R. **Can Xabanet** (Rancho Grande) (Hostel), Plaça del Carme 24 (tel. 57 02 52). Popular restaurant offering home cooking. Moderate.

BAQUEIRA BERET
A. **Hotel Montarto** (4-star), Nucleo Baqueira beret, Apdo 110 (tel. 64 50 75). Open winter and August only. They can provide packages with ski passes. Expensive.

BLANES
A. **Hotel Horitzó** (3-star), Pg Maritim Sabanell 11 (tel. 33 04 00). Moderate.
R. **Can Flores II**, Esplanada del Port 3 (tel. 33 16 33). Recommended for fish and shellfish fans. Moderate.

BESALU
A/R. **La Curia Real** (1-star), Plaça de la Llibertat 14 (tel. 59 02 63). Located in former convent with restaurant offering cheap good value local dishes. Moderate.
R. **Fonda Xiques 'Cal Parent'**, Av. Lluis

Companys 6 (tel. 59 01 10). On main Banyoles-Olot road on outskirts of town. The hostel has cheap rooms and a very popular cheap-moderate restaurant.

BOÏ
A. **Hotel Beneria** (2-star), Plaça Treio (tel. 69 60 30). Cheap.

CADAQUÈS
A. **Hotel Llane Petit** (3-star), Platja Llaner Petit (tel. 25 80 50). Moderate.
R. **La Galiota**, Monturiol 9 (tel. 25 81 87), run by the Riberas sisters, has a very good name in the town. Baked fish are their speciality. Moderate-expensive.

CALDES DE BOÏ
A/R. **Hotel Manantial** (4-star) 25528 Boï (Tel. 69 01 91). Expensive. The hotel also has a good, moderately priced restaurant.

CALELLA DE PALAFRUGELL
A. **Hotel Garbí** (3-star), De la Murtra (tel. 31 01 00). Moderate-expensive. See Palafrugell for restaurants.

CAMPRODON
A. **Edelweiss** (3-star), Ctra Sant Joan 28 (tel. 74 09 13). Expensive.
A. **Güell** (1-star), Plaça d'Espanya 8 (tel. 74 00 11). Moderate.
A. **Hotel Rigat** (2-star), Plaça del Dr Robert 14 (tel. 74 00 13). Moderate.

CELLERS
A. **Hotel Terradets** (2-star), Ctra Tremp, located beside the lake. Moderate.
A/R. **Hostal del Llac** next door to the Terradets (tel. 65 03 50). Lakeside with a good restaurant (the paella is excellent here). Cheap.

COLERA
A. **Hotel Lido** (1-star) Plaça de Port 2 (tel. 38 90 10). Moderate.

L'ESCALA
A. **Hotel Voramar** (3-star), Pg Lluis Albert 2 (tel. 77 01 08). Moderate.

A. **El Rem** (2-star), Av. Maria 3 (tel. 77 02 45), Moderate.

R. **Els Pescadors**, Port d'en Perris 3 (tel. 77 07 28). Great seafood cooking. Moderate.

ESPOT

A/R. **Hotel Saurat** (2-star) S. Martí, 25597 Espot (tel. 62 60 00). Closed October and November. Moderate.

R. **Restaurant Casa Palmira** (tel. 63 50 72). Trout, wild boar, chamois. Cheap.

L'ESTARTIT

A. **Bell Aire** (3-star), Plaça de l'Eglesia 39 (tel. 75 81 62). Moderate.

R. **La Gaviota**, Pg Maritim (tel. 75 84 19). Regional cooking offered on the terrace. Moderate-expensive.

ESTERRI D'ÀNEU

A. **Hostal Vall** 6' Aneu, Ctra. Balaguer (tel. 62 60 97). Cheap.

FIGUERES

A/R. **Ampurdan** (3-star), Ctra NII, km 763 (tel. 50 05 66). Excellent restaurant offering Empordà cuisine. Accommodation expensive, meals moderate.

A/R. **Hotel Duran** (3-star), Lausaca 5 (tel. 50 12 50). Managed and owned by renowned Duran family. The restaurant serves traditional paellas and Empordà dishes. Accommodation expensive, meals moderate.

R. **Mas Pau**, Avinyonet de Puigventós, km 4 (tel. 54 61 54). Former country mansion, elegant with covered terrace. Catalan cuisine. Expensive.

GIRONA

A. **Costabella** (3-star), Av. França 61 (tel. 20 25 24). Moderate-expensive.

A. **Europa** (2-star), Carrer Jul Garreta 23 (tel. 20 27 50). Moderate.

A. **Bellmirall** (1-star), Bellmirall 3 (tel. 20 40 09). Central and excellent value. Cheap.

R. **Bromsom's**, Av. Sant Francesc 7 (tel. 21 24 93) offers home cooking delights such as zarzuela perdiu a la col (partridge in cabbage). Moderate.

R. **Cal Ros**, Cort Reial 9 (tel. 20 10 11). Traditional Catalan cuisine. Moderate.

LLAFRANC

A. **Hotel Llevant** (2-star), Francesc de Blanes 5 (tel. 30 03 66). Family run, overlooking beach. Recommended. Moderate-expensive.

R. **Restaurant Faro** (the lighthouse) on top of the hill (tel. 30 05 86). Fabulous views and good food, recommended. Moderate.

LLÍVIA

A/R. **Hotel Llivia** (3-star), Ctra Puigcerdà (tel. 89 60 00). Moderate.

R. **Restaurant Can Ventura**, Plaça Major 1 (tel. 89 61 78). Local cuisine. Moderate.

LLORET DE MAR

A. **Hotel Monterrey** (4-star), Ctra Tossa (tel. 36 40 50). Expensive.

A. **Bonanza Park Hotel** (2-star), Narcís Fors 22 (tel. 36 52 50). Moderate.

A. **Roca Grossa**, Platja de Santa Cristina (tel. 36 51 09). Seafood. Moderate.

R. **La Bodega Vella**, Marina 4 (tel. 36 74 78). Meat dishes. Expensive.

R. **Casino Lloret de Mar** (tel. 36 64 54) has a running buffet on Fridays and Saturdays; the casino's Dafne Restaurant offers French and Catalan cuisine. Expensive.

MARTINET

A/R. **Hotel Boix** (3-star), Ctra Lleida-Puigcerdà (tel. 51 50 50). On the Segre, equidistant between Puigcerdà and La Seu d'Urgell. Highly recommended – the hotel restaurant is possibly the best in the Catalonian Pyrenees. A gourmet's delight (even the breakfasts are magnificent). Expensive.

OLOT

A. **Montsacopa** (2-star), Mulleres (tel. 26 92 92). Moderate.

A. **Stop** (hostel), Sant Pere Màrtir 29 (tel. 26 10 48). Cheap.

R. **Font Moixina**, Pg de la Moixina (tel. 26 10 00). Imaginative local cuisine in fine country suburb. Moderate.

R. **Hostal La Perla** (1km out of town on Vic road). A highly recommended, good-value restaurant. Cheap-moderate.

PALAFRUGELL
For accommodation see Calella de Palafrugell and Llafranc.

R. **La Xicra**, Carrer Estret 17 (tel. 30 56 30). Recommended Empordà cuisine. Expensive.

R. **Reig**, Jonama 53 (tel. 30 00 04) also highly recommended Empordà cuisine. Expensive.

PALAMOS
A. **Hotel Trias** (3-star), Pg del Mar (tel. 31 41 00). Expensive.

A. **Hostal Francia**, Pere Joan 18 (tel. 31 41 09). Cheap-moderate.

R. **Maria de Cadaquès**, Notaries 39 (tel. 31 40 09). Recommended seafood. Expensive.

PERELADA
R. **Casino Castell de Perelada** (tel. 53 81 25) has a restaurant offering some of the lesser known dishes of the excellent Empordà cuisine such as goose liver in sour apples. Expensive.

PLATJA D'ARO
A. **Hotel Columbus** (4-star), Pg del Mar (tel. 81 71 66). Expensive.

A. **Hotel Costa Brava** (2-star), Punta d'en Ramis (tel. 81 73 08). Expensive-moderate.

A. **La Marina** (hostel), C. Major 36 (tel. 81 71 82) Cheap-moderate.

R. **Carles Camós**, Barri de Canals 5 (tel. 81 80 12). One of the leading Costa Brava restaurants offering lighter Empordà cuisine than is usually found elsewhere. Expensive-very expensive.

LA POBLA DE SEGUR
A/R. **Can Solé** (pension) Av. de l'Estació 44 (tel. 68 04 52). Moderate. The Can Solé also has a reasonable restaurant offering local trout and game dishes in a cheap menu del día. Cheap-moderate.

EL PORT DE LA SELVA
A. **Hotel Porto Cristo** (2-star), Major 48 (tel. 38 70 62). Moderate.

R. **Ca l'Herminda**, L'Illa 7 (tel. 38 70 75). Seafood. Expensive.

EL PORT DE LLANÇÀ
A. **Hotel Grimar** (2-star), Ctra Portbou, (tel. 38 01 67). Moderate.

R. **Can Manel**, Plaça del Port 5 (tel. 38 01 12). Probably the best place for moderately priced sea food.

PUIGCERDÀ
A/R. **Hotel Del Lago** (2-star), Av Dr Piguillem (tel. 88 10 00). Cheap.

Can Borrell, Retorn 3 (tel. 88 00 33). Just out of town at Meranges offering large local dishes in a pleasant location. Highly thought of. Moderate-expensive.

RIPOLL
A/R. **Solana del Ter** (2-star), Ctra Barcelona-Ripoll (tel. 70 10 62). The hotel has a good Catalan restaurant. Moderate-expensive.

A. **Monasterio** (1-star), Plaça Gran 4 (tel. 70 01 50). Moderate.

A. **Ripollès** (Hostel), Plaça Nova 11 (tel. 70 02 15). Cheap.

ROSES
A. **Almadrava Park** (4-star), Platja Almadrava (tel. 25 65 50). Expensive.

A. **Hotel Marítim** (3-star), Platja Salatar (tel. 25 63 90). Moderate.

R. **Hacienda el Bulli**, Cala Montjoi 30 (tel. 25 76 51). The best gourmet restaurant along the coast and with a fabulous isolated setting overlooking the sea. Very expensive.

SANT FELIU DE GUÍXOLS
A. **Reina Elisenda** (4-star), Pg de Guíxols 8 (tel. 32 07 00). Moderate-expensive.

A/R. **Avenida** (2-star), Girona 10 (tel. 32 08 00). Moderate.

R. **Eldorado Petit**, Rambla Vidal 23 (tel. 32 18 18). Twin of the more famous family member of the same name in Barcelona and recently totally refurbished. Highly recommended. Very expensive.

R. Cheaper and almost as good is the seafare offered at **Can Toni**, Sant Martirià 19 (tel. 32 10 26). Expensive.

SANT PRIVAT D'EN BAS (hamlet 20km from Olot)

A/R. **Fonda Can Mulleres** (tel. 69 32 57). Good value accommodation and heavenly local cuisine. Cheap.

LA SEU D'URGELL

A/R. **Parador Nacional** (3-star but worthy of more). Sant Domènec (tel. 35 20 00). Good food. Accommodation expensive, meals moderate.

Castell Motel (4-star), Ctra La Seu-Lleida (tel. 35 07 04). Just outside town, also recommended. Its restaurant has built up a very good reputation for Empordà country cuisine. Very expensive.

A. **Hotel Andria** (1-star), Pg Brudieu 24 (tel. 35 03 00). Comfortable. Moderate.

R. **Can Ton** restaurant in Carrer de la Font is very popular with local workforce. It provides gargantuan meals ridiculously cheaply.

SORT

A. **Hotel Pessets II** (2-star), Ctra la Seu (tel. 62 00 00). Moderate.

R. **Restaurant Les Collades**, Major 5 (tel. 62 02 89). Trout and barbecued meats. Cheap.

TOSSA DE MAR

A. **Gran Hotel Reymar**, Platja Mar Menuda (tel. 34 03 12). Expensive.

A. **Avenida** (2-star), Av. de la Palma 16 (tel. 34 07 56). Moderate.

A. **Hotel Rovira** (2-star), Pou de la Vila 14 (tel. 34 07 55). Moderate.

R. **Castell Vell** Pintor Roig i Soler (tel. 34 10 30). Worth visiting for a meal just to savour its setting in the Old Town. Seafood. Expensive-very expensive.

R. **Restaurant Can Tonet**, Plaça de l'Eglesia 2 (tel. 34 05 11). Opened in 1900, very popular good fish restaurant. Moderate.

TREMP

A/R. **Hotel Siglo XX** (2-star), Plaça de la Creu 32 (tel. 65 00 00). Has a good restaurant serving local dishes. Accommodation moderate, meals cheap-moderate.

VIC

A. **Hotel Can Pamplona** (3-star), Ctra Nal 152 Vic-Puigcerda (tel. 885 36 12). Moderate.

A/R. **Hostal Cal U**, Rambla de Santa Teresa 4 (tel. 885 00 45) has clean, basic, rooms (sharing bathroom) and an earthy, very popular, restaurant offering local dishes. Recommended for those who want to live in the city and taste local life. The owner's daughter speaks very good English. Cheap.

A/R. **The Parador** (4-star), Pantà de Sau (tel. 888 72 11). Paradors can be booked through Keytel in the UK, (tel. 071 402 8182). Superbly located out of town overlooking El Pantà de Sau reservoir. Expensive.

A/R. **Hostal Fussimanya** (13kms from Vic a few kilometres from the parador in a superb location), Ctra Parador Nacional de Vic, km 7 (tel 888 73 77). The hostel has good value rooms and a marvellous restaurant offering local specialities. Accommodation cheap, restaurant cheap-moderate.

VIELLA

A. **Hotel Adyal Neu** (2-star). Ctra Gausac (tel. 64 02 75). Moderate.

R. **Restaurante Antonio**, Deth Casteth (tel. 64 08 87). Good local food. Moderate.

Further Information

Spanish government tourist offices abroad

ARGENTINA
Buenos Aires Oficina Nacional Española de Turismo, Florida, 744, 1,°
(1005) Buenos Aires, tel. (541) 3225923/3327264, telex 21660 EMBES AR

AUSTRIA
Wien Spanisches Fremdenverkehrsamt, Rotenturmstrasse, 27. 1010 Wien 1,
tel. (43222) 5353191, telex 047/13 63 31 ONET WA

BELGIUM
Bruxelles Office National Espagnol du Tourisme, 18, rue de la Montagne,
100 Bruxelles, 1, tel. (322) 512 57 35, telex 046/64151 TURESP-B

CANADA
Toronto Spanish National Tourist Office, 60 Bloor Street West, 201. Toronto,
Ontario M4W 3B8, tel. (1416) 961 31 31, telex 021/06 21 82 06

DENMARK
København Spanish Nationale Turisbureau, Store Kongensgade, 1-3, København,
K 1264, tel. (451) 14 70 96/15 11 65, telex 055/16165 SPATUR DK

FINLAND
Helsinki Espanjan Valtion Matkailutoimisto, Mikonkatu 6C 24. 00100 Helsinki,
10, tel. (3580) 441992, telex 057/12 21 93 ESPAN-SF

FRANCE
Paris Office National Espagnol du Tourisme, 43 ter. Av. Pierre 1 de Serbie.
75381 Paris 08, tel. (331) 7209054, telex 042/28 06 89

GERMANY
Düsseldorf Spanisches Fremdenverkehrsamt, Graf. Adolfstrasse, 81. 4000
Düsseldorf, tel. (49211) 37 04 67/68, telex IBERIA 858 63 51 TURE
Frankfurt/Main Spanisches Fremdenverkehrsamt, Steinweg, 5.6000 Frankfurt/
Main, tel. (4969) 725033, telex 041/41 3087 TURES E
München Spanisches Fremdenverkehrsamt, Oberanger, 6–8, München 2,
tel. (4989) 2609570, telex 041/5213678 ONET D

ITALY
Roma Ufficio Nazionale Spagnolo del Turismo, Piazza di Spagna, 55. 00187 Roma, tel. (396) 679 82 72-678 31 06, telex 043/620841
Milano Ufficio Nazionale Spagnolo del Turismo, Via del Don, 5. Milano 20123, tel. (392) 837 74 39/38, telex 043/320602

JAPAN
Tokio National Tourist Office of Spain, Daini Toranomon Denki Bldg., 4F, 1–10, Toranomon, 3-chome Minatu-ku, TOKIO 105, tel. (813) 432 61 41-432 61 44, telex TURISPAN J 26939

MEXICO
Mexico Oficina Nacional Española de Turismo, Alejandro Dumas 11560 Mexico D.F., tel. (525) 531 17 85-545 73 22, telex 1763489 ONET ME

THE NETHERLANDS
Gravenhague Spaans National Bureau Voor Vreembelingenverkeer, 4 Laan van Meerdervoort, 8. 2517 Gravenhague, tel. (3170) 346 59 00/346 5901, telex 044/33435 ONET HL

NORWAY
Oslo Den Spanske Stats Tursbyra, Ruselokkveien, 26 Vika-Torvet. 0251 Oslo 2, tel. (472) 834092, telex 056/74861

PORTUGAL
Lisboa Delegaçao Oficial do Turismo Espanhol, Camilo Costelo Branco, 34, Lisboa, 1, 1900 Portugal, tel. (3511) 54 53 29, telex 0404/12106 ONET P

SWEDEN
Stockholm Spanska Statens Turistbyra, Birger Jarlsgatan, 15 ltr. S-11145 Stockholm, tel. (468) 20 71 26-36, telex 054/17606 TURSPAN-G

SWITZERLAND
Génève Office National Espagnol du Tourisme, 40 Bld Helvétique/67 rue du Rhône, 1207 Génève, tel. (412) 35 95 94 95, telex 045/23485 ONET CH
Zürich Spanisches Fremdenverkehrsamt, Seefeldstrasse, 19. Zürich 8008, tel. (411) 2527931/30, telex 045/816718 SFVACH

UNITED KINGDOM
London Spanish National Tourist Office, 57-58 St. James Street, London SW1A 1LD, tel. (441) 499 10 95/493 57 60/499 11 69/491 12 74, telex 051/88 81 38 TURESP-G

USA
Chicago Spanish National Tourist Office, 845 North Michigan Avenue, Water Tower Place-Suite, 915 East. Illinois 60611 Chicago, tel. (1312) 944 02 15/16; 280 90 25, telex 023/033 20 20 NTOS
Houston National Tourist Office of Spain, 5085 Westheimer, 4800. The Galleria, HOUSTON, Texas 77056, tel. (713) 840 74 11/12 – Director: 840 74 13; telex 023/0790753 TURISOMO HOU

New York Spanish National Tourist Office, 665 Fifth Avenue, New York, NY 10022, tel. (1212) 759 88 22/23/24/25/26/27/28, telex 023/426782 SNTO UI. Spanish National Tourist Office, Casa del Hidalgo Hypolita and St. George, San Agustin, Florida 32084, tel. (1904) 829 64 60, telex 023/079753 **Los Angeles** Spanish National Tourist Office, 8383 Wilshire Blvd. Suite, 960, Beverly Hills, C.A. 90211, tel. (213) 658 71 88-658 71 93/95

Tourist Offices in Catalonia

ALTAFULLA
Centre d'Iniciatives Turistiques, 43893 Plaça dels Vents, tel. (977) 65 00 08

L'AMETLLA DE MAR
Oficina Municipal de Turisme, 43860 Av. Amistat Hispano-italiana, tel. (977) 45 63 29

ARBÚCLES
Oficina Municipal d'Informació Turistica, 17401 Major, 2, tel. (972) 86 00 01

ARENYS DE MAR
Oficina de Turisme del CIT, 08350 Rambla Bisbe Pol, 8, tel. (93) 792 02 42

BANYOLES
Oficina Municipal de Turisme, 17820 Pg de la Indústria, 25, tel. (972) 57 55 73

BARCELONA
Oficina Municipal d'Informació, 08002 Plaça de Sant Jaume, tel. (93) 010; Oficina de Turisme, 08010 Gran Via de les Corts Catalanes, 658, tel. (93) 301 74 43; Patronat Municipal de Turisme, 08007 Pg de Gràcia, 35, pral. (Casa Lleó Morera), tel. (93) 215 44 77; Patronat Municipal de Turisme, 08014 Estació de Sants, tel. (93) 490 91 71; Patronat Municipal de Turisme, 08004 Plaça de l'Univers, tel. (93) 325 52 35; Patronat Municipal de Turisme, 08002 Moll de la Fusta (Port), tel. (93) 310 37 16.

BARRUERA
Oficina de Turisme del Patronat de la Vall de Boi, 25527 Ajuntament de Barruera, tel. (973) 69 60 00

BEGUR
Oficina Municipal de Turisme, 17255 Av. Onze de Setembre s/n. Ed. Casa Gran, tel. (972) 62 34 79

BELLMUNT DEL PRIORAT
Oficina de Turisme del CIT, 43738 Major, 49, tel. (977) 83 03 79

BELLVER DE CERDANYA
Oficina de Turisme, 25720 Plaça Sant Roc, 9, tel. (973) 51 02 29; Oficina d'Informació, 25720 Area del Cadl, tel. (973) 51 02 33

BERGA
Oficina Municipal de Turisme, 08600 Carrer dels Angels, 7, tel. (93) 821 03 04

BESALÚ
Oficina Municipal de Turisme, 17850 Plaça de la Libertat, 1, tel. (972) 59 12 40

LA BISBAL D'EMPORDÀ
Oficina Municipal de Turisme, 17100 Plaça Francesc Macià, 10, tel. (972) 64 25 93

BLANES
Patronat Municipal de Turisme, 17300 Plaça Catalunya, s/n, tel. (972) 33 03 48

BOSSÒST
Oficina d'Informació Turistica, 25550 Passeig de Bossòst, tel. (973) 64 81 57

CADEQUÉS
Oficina de Turisme del CIT, 17488 Cotxe, 2-A, tel. (972) 25 83 15

CALAFELL
Oficina de Turisme del CIT, 43820 Vilamar, 1, tel. (977) 69 17 59

CALDES D'ESTRAC
Oficina de Turisme del CIT, 08393 Baixada de l'Estació, 3, tel. (93) 791 02 89

CALELLA
Oficina Municipal de Turisme, 08730 Sant Jaume, tel. (93) 769 05 59

CALELLA DE PALAFRUGELL (PALAFRUGELL)
Oficina Municipal de Turisme, 17210 Colom, s/n, tel. (972) 30 36 75

CALONGE DE MAR
Oficino Muncipal de Turisme, 17251 Pl. d'Espanya, s/n, tel. (972) 65 24 76

CAMBRILS
Patronat Municipal de Turisme, 43850 Plaça Creu de Missió, s/n, tel. (977) 36 11 59

CAMPRODON
Oficina de Turisme del CIT, 17867 Plaça d'Espanya, 1, tel. (972) 74 00 10

CANET DE MAR
Oficina de Turisma del CIT, 08360 Ctra. Nacional II, s/n, tel. (93) 794 08 98

CARDONA
Oficina de Turisma, 08261 Plaça de la Fira, 1, tel. (93) 869 27 98

LES CASES D'ALCANAR (ALCANAR)
Oficina Municipal de Turisme, 43569 Carretera Barcelona-València, s/n, tel. (977) 73 71 31

CASTELLDEFELS
Oficina de Turisme del CIT, 08860 Plaça Rosa dels Vents, s/n, tel. (93) 664 23 01/61

CASTELLÓ D'EMPÚRIES
Oficina de Turisme, 17486 Carretera Besalú a Roses, tel. (972) 45 08 02

COMA-RUGA
Oficina de Turisme, 43800 Plaça Germans Trillas, s/n, tel. (977) 68 00 10

DELTEBRE
Oficina Municipal de Turisme, 43580 Plaça del 20 de Maig, tel. (977) 48 96 79

EMPÚRIA-BRAVA (CASTELLÓ D'EMPÚRIES)
Oficina Municipal de Turisme, 17486 Urbanització Empúriabrava, Sector Puigmal, 1, tel. (972) 45 08 02

L'ESCALA
Oficina de Turisme del CIT, 17130 Plaça de les Escoles, 1, tel. (972) 77 06 03

L'ESPLUGA DE FRANCOLI
Oficina Municipal de Turisme, 43440 Torres Jordi, 16, tel. (977) 87 00 05

L'ESTARTIT (TORROELLA DE MONTGRÍ)
Oficina Municipal de Turisme, 17258 Pg Maritim, 47, tel. (972) 75 89 10

FIGUERES
Oficina Municipal de Turisme, 17660 Plaça del Sol, tel. (972) 50 31 55; Oficina Municipal de Turisme, 17600 Plaça de l'Estació, tel. (972) 50 31 55

GIRONA
Oficina de Turisme, 17004 Rambla Llibertat, 1, tel. (972) 20 26 79; Oficina Municipal de Turisme, 17007 Estació RENFE, tel. (972) 21 62 96

LA JONQUERA
Porta Catalana, 17700 Area de Peatge de la Jonquera Autopista A-7, tel. (972) 55 40 00

LLAFRANC (PALAFRUGELL)
Oficina Municipal de Turisme, 17211 Roger de Llúria, s/n, tel. (972) 30 50 08

LLANÇA
Oficina del Patronat Municipal de Turisme, 17490 Avinguda d'Europa, s/n, Edifici Ajuntament, tel. (972) 38 08 55

LLAVORSÍ
Oficina de Turisme del CIT, 25595 Cra. de la Vall d'Aran, tel. (973) 63 00 08

LLEIDA
Oficina d'Informació Turistica, 25007 Arc del Pont, s/n, tel. (973) 24 81 20

LLORET DE MAR
Oficina Municipal de Turisme, 17310 Plaça de la Vila, tel. (972) 36 47 35; Serveis de Turisme, 17310 Terminal d'autobusos a la Cra. de Blanes, tel. (972) 35 57 88

MALGRAT DE MAR
Oficina Municipal de Turisme, 08380 Carme, 30, tel. (93) 765 40 82

MANRESA
Oficina Municipal d'Informació, 08240 Plaça Major, 1, tel. (93) 872 53 78

MATARÓ
Oficina d'Informació Municipal, 08301 Carrer de la Riera, 48, tel. (93) 796 01 08

MIRAVET
Oficina Municipal de Turisme, 43747 Casal, s/n, tel. (977) 40 72 39

MONTBLANC
Oficina Municipal de Turisme, 43400 Plaça de l'Ajuntament, 1,
tel. (977) 86 00 09

MONT-ROIG DEL CAMP
Oficina Municipal de Turisme, 43300 Cra. N-340, km. 227, tel. (977) 83 79 68

OLOT
Oficina de Turisme del CIT, 17800 Mulleres, s/n, (Edifici plaça del Mercat),
tel. (972) 26 01 41

ORGANYÀ
Oficina Municipal de Turisme, 25794 Pl. Homilies, s/n, tel. (973) 38 30 07

PALAFRUGELL
Oficina Municipal de Turisme, 17200 Carrilet, 2, tel. (972) 30 02 28,
telex 570 77

PALAMÓS
Oficina Municipal d'Informació Turistica, 17230 Passeig del Mar, 8,
tel. (972) 31 43 90

PALS
Oficina Municipal de Turisme, 17256 Plaça d'Espanya, 7, tel. (972) 66 78 57

PINEDA DE MAR
Oficina d'Informació de Turisme, 08397 Carretera Nacional II,
tel. (93) 762 34 90

PLATJA D'ARO (CASTELL-PLATJA D'ARO)
Oficina Municipal de Turisme, 17853 Carrer Verdaguer, 11, tel. (972) 81 71 79,
telex 57 098

LA POBLA DE SEGUR
Oficina de Turisme de la Junta Municipal, 25500 Avinguda Verdaguer, 12,
tel. (973) 68 02 57; Centre d'Iniciatives Turistiques del Pallars Jussà «CITPJ»,
25500 Avinguda Verdaguer, 37, tel. (973) 68 04 27

EL PONT DE SUERT
Oficina Municipal de Turisme, 25520, Pl, Mercadel, 7, tel. (73) 69 00 05

PORTBOU (G)
Oficina Municipal de Turisme, 17497 Passeig de la Sardana (Edifici Ajuntament),
tel. (972) 39 02 84; Oficina d'Informació Turistica, 17497 Estació RENFE,
tel. (972) 39 05 07

EL PRAT DE LLOBREGAT
Oficina de Turisme de l'Aeroport de Barcelona, 08820 Aeroport de Barcelona,
tel. (93) 325 58 29

PUIGCERDÀ
Oficina de Turisme del CIT, 17520 Querol (baixos de l'Ajuntament),
tel. (972) 88 05 42

REUS
Oficina Municipal de Turisme, 43201 Plaça Mercadel, 1, tel. (77) 30 57 40
Oficina d'Informació Municipal, 43201 St. Joan, 36, tel. (977) 34 41 53; Oficina
de Turisme, Plaça de la Llibertat, tel. (977) 75 96 33

RIBES DE FRESER
Oficina Municipal de Turisme, 17534 Casa Consistorial, baixos,
tel (972) 72 77 28

RIPOLL
Oficina de Turisme del CIT, de Ripoll, 17500 Plaça Abat Oliva, s/n,
tel. (972) 70 23 51

ROSES
Oficina Municipal de Turisme, 17480 Avinguda de Rhode, s/n,
tel. (972) 25 77 31

SALOU (VILA-SECA I SALOU)
Oficina Municipal de Turisme, 43840 Carrer Montblanc, 1, tel. (977) 36 01 36;
Oficina Municipal de Turisme, 43840 Espigó del Moll, tel. (977) 38 02 33; La
Pineda, 43840 Av. Pau Casals, s/n, tel. (977) 37 17 12

SANT ANTONI DE CALONGE (CALONGE DE MAR)
Oficina Municipal d'Informació Turistica, 17251 Avinguda de Catalunya, s/n,
tel. (972) 65 17 14

SANT CARLES DE LA RÀPITA
Oficina Municipal de Turisme, 43540 Plaça Carles III, tel. (977) 74 01 00

SANT CELONI
Oficina de Turisme, 08470 Plaça de la Vila, s/n, tel. (93) 867 04 25

SANT CUGAT DEL VALLÈS
Oficina Municipal de Turisme, 08190 Plaça de Barcelona, 17,
tel. (93) 674 09 50

SANT FELIU DE GUÍXOLS
Oficina Municipal de Turisme, 17220 Plaça d'Espanya, 6-9, tel. (972) 82 00 51

SANT HILARI SACALM
Oficina Municipal de Turisme, 17403 Cra. d'Arbúcies, s/n, tel. (972) 86 88 26

SANT JOAN DE LES ABADESSES
Oficina de Turisme del CIT, 17860 Rambla Comte Guifre, 5, tel. (972) 72 05 99

SANT LLORENÇ DE MORUNYS
Oficina de Turisme, 08230 Cra. de Berga, 15, tel. (973) 49 22 30

SANT SADURNI D'ANOIA
Oficina Municipal de Promoció i Turisme, 08770 Pl. Ajuntament, 1, tel. (93) 891 12 12

SANTA COLOMA DE QUERALT
Oficina de Turisme del CIT, 43420 Pati d'Armes del Castell, s/n, tel. (977) 88 00 88

SANT PAU
17811 Carrer Major, s/n, tel. (972) 68 00 02

SEGUR DE CALAFELL (CALAFELL)
Oficina de Turisme del CIT, 43882, Vistula, 1, tel. (977) 69 05 02

SEU D'URGELL, LA
Oficina Municipal de Turisme, 25700 Av. de la Valira, s/n, tel. (973) 35 15 11

SITGES
Oficina Municipal de Turisme, 08870 Pg. Vilafranca, Bus Terminal Oasis, tel. (93) 894 12 30

SOLSONA
Oficina Municipal, 25280 Castell, 20, tel. (973) 48 23 10/48 00 50

TAMARIU (PALAFRUGELL)
Oficina Municipal de Turisme, 17212 Riera, s/n, tel. (972) 30 50 07

TARRAGONA
Oficina de Turisme de Tarragona, 43001 Fortuny, 4, tel. (977) 23 34 15; Patronat Municipal de Turisme, Centre Comercial PRYCA, tel. (977) 23 89 22; Patronat Municipal de Turisme, 43003 Major, 39, tel. (977) 23 89 22; Patronat Municipal de Turisme, 43003 Plaça de la Font, 1, tel. (977) 29 61 98

TÀRREGA
Oficina Municipal de Turisme, 25300 Les Piques, 1, tel. (973) 31 07 31

TORREDEMBARRA
Oficina de Turisme del CIT, 43830 Avinguda de Pompeu Fabra, 3, tel. (977) 64 03 31; Oficina Municipal de Turisme, 43830 Pg Mediterrani, 1, tel. (977) 64 06 38/64 21 10

TORROELLA DE MONTGRI
Oficina Municipal de Turisme, 17257 Avinguda Lluis Companys, 51, tel. (972) 75 89 10

TORTOSA
Oficina Municipal de Turisme, 43500 Plaça d'Espanya, s/n, tel. (977) 44 00 00

TOSSA DE MAR
Oficina Municipal de Turisme, 17320 Cra. de Lloret «Terminal»,
tel. (972) 34 01 08

VALLFOGONA DE RIPOLLÈS
Oficina Municipal de Turisme, 17862 Puig Estela, s/n, tel. (972) 70 19 09

VALLS
Oficina d'Informació Municipal, 43800 Plaça del Blat, 1, tel. (977) 60 10 50

EL VENDRELL
Oficina de Turisme del CIT del Vendrell, 43700 Doctor Robert, 33,
tel. (977) 66 02 92

VIC
Oficina Municipal de Turisme, 08500 Plaça Major, 1, tel. (93) 886 20 91

VIELLA (VIELHA E MIJARAN)
Oficina del CIT de la Vall d'Aran, 25530 Av. Castièro, 15, tel. (973) 64 09 79;
Ofincina d'Informació Turistica, 25530 Sarriulera, 6, tel. (973) 64 01 10

VILAFRANCA DEL PENEDÈS
Patronat Municipal de Turisme, 08720 Cort, 14, tel. (93) 892 03 58

VILANOVA I LA GELTRÚ
Patraont Municipal de Turisme, 08800 Passeig Ribes Roges, s/n,
tel. (93) 815 45 17; Oficina Municipal de Turisme, 08800 Plaça de la Vila, 8,
tel. (93) 893 00 00.

Consulates

BARCELONA
Argentina Pg de Gràcia, 11 (08007) tel. (93) 317 58 82, telex 54029 CGRA E
Austria Mallorca, 286 (08037) tel. 257 36 14
Belgium Diputació, 303 (08009) tel. 318 98 99, telex 50203 COSB E
Bolivia Pl. Francesc Marià, 8 (08029) tel. 322 62 12
Brazil Consell de Cent, 357 (08007) tel. 215 16 15, telex 54100 CBRA E
Cambodia Pg Sant Gervasi, 3 (08022) tel. 417 42 67
Canada Via Augusta, 125 (08006) tel. 209 06 34
Colombia Pl. Doctor Letamendi, 5 (08007) tel. 254 02 48
Costa Rica Av. Diagonal, 482 (08006) tel. 217 73 92
Cuba Pg de Gràcia, 34 (08007) tel. 318 19 36
Chad Tuset, 5-11 (08006) tel. 200 66 99, telex 59306 NART E
Chile Gran Via Corts Catalanes, 591 (08007) tel. 318 85 86, telex 98817 CGBN E
Denmark Compte d'Urgell, 240, tel. 419 04 28

195

Dominican Republic Paris, 211 (08008) tel. 237 92 13, telex 98566
Ecuador pge. Josep Llovera, 3 (08021) tel. 209 57 31
El Salvador Muntaner, 260 (08021) tel. 209 36 58
Finland Av. Diagonal, 613, tel. 419 77 00
France Pg de Gràcia, 11 (08007) tel. 317 81 50, telex 52938 FRAB E
Gabon Rosselló, 257 (08008) tel. 237 01 61, telex 98096 BNR E
Germany Pg de Gràcia, 111 (08008) tel. 218 36 96, telex 54768 AABCL E
Greece Nàpols, 122 (08013) tel. 246 22 90
Guatemala Gran Via Carles III, 94 (08028) tel. 330 65 59, telex 52220 ARTRA E
Haiti Viaducte de Vallcarca, 3 (08023) tel. 213 81 50
Iceland Sardenya, 229 (08013) tel. 232 58 10, telex 52886 COBEG E
India Teodor Roviralta, 21–23, tel. 212 04 22
Indonesia Pintor Fortuny, 3 (08001) tel. 317 75 31
Ireland Gran Via Carles III, 94 (08028) tel. 330 96 53, telex 52220 ARTRA E
Italy Mallorca, 270 (08037) tel. 215 16 54, telex 93419 CGIB E
Ivory Coast Av. Parel-lel, 21 (08004) tel. 329 69 16
Japan Diagonal, 662 (08034) tel. 204 72 24
Jordan Aragó, 174 (08011) tel. 254 48 50, telex 50474 YRT E
Korea Pg de Gràcia, 85, tel. 215 20 63
Lebanon Trav. de Gràcia, 64 (08006) tel. 209 03 99, telex 97005 VLTA
Liberia Viaducte de Vallcarca, 3 (08023) tel. 213 81 50
Luxembourg Tuset 8-10, (08006) tel. 237 37 01, telex 53115 FEX E
Malaysia Pg de Colom, 11 (08002) tel. 315 00 11, telex 54764 CODE M
Mexico Av. Diagonal, 626 (08021) tel. 201 18 22, telex 50473 MEEQ E
Monaco Via Augusta, 158 (08006) tel. 209 75 88, telex 50007 TRAS E
Morocco Rambla Catalunya, 78 (08007) tel. 215 34 70
Netherlands Pg de Gràcia, 111 (08008) tel. 217 37 00, telex 59018 HOLP E
Nicaragua Aribau, 195 (08006) tel. 210 90 59
Norway Provença, 284 (08008) tel. 215 00 94, telex 54775 LUTKN E
Pakistan Córsega, 366, tel. 257 42 30
Panama Pg Gràcia, 20, tel. 302 00 73
Paraguay Rambla de Catalunya, 90 (08008) tel. 215 05 26, telex 59033 VMIT E
Peru Av. Diagonal, 441 (08036) tel. 410 61 23
Philippines Pintor Fortony, 3, tel. 318 84 36
Portugal Ronda Sant Pere, 7 (08010) tel. 318 81 50
Sierra Leone Balmes, 92 (08008) tel. 215 90 54, telex 93068 CSLB E
South Africa Gran Via Corts Catalanes, 634 (08007) tel. 301 55 83,
Sweden Av. Diagonal 601, tel. 410 11 08
Switzerland Gran Via Carles III, 94 (08028) tel. 330 92 11, telex 52220 ARTRA
Thailand Av. Diagonal, 339, tel. 258 14 61
Tunisia Diputació, 400 (08013) tel. 231 53 79
United Kingdom Av. Diagonal, 477 (08036) tel. 322 21 51, telex 52799 BRE E
Uruguay Trafalgar, 4 (08010) tel. 412 27 33
USA Via Laietana, 33 (08003) tel. 319 95 50, telex 52672 CGBAR E
Venezuela Provença, 278 (08008) tel. 215 01 12

GIRONA
Belgium Ciutadans, 15 (17004) tel. 20 18 75
Bolivia Portal Nou, 16 (17004) tel. 20 04 07
France Ulltònia, 8, 5.ᵉ (17002) tel. 20 03 35
Germany Pg General Mendoza, 2 (17002) tel. 21 26 24
Ireland Carme, 79 (17004) tel. 20 22 28
Italy Pl Marquès de Camps, 18 (17006) tel. 20 13 76
Netherlands Devesa, 6 (17001) tel. 20 20 43
Norway Cra. de Barcelona, 31 (17001) tel. 21 34 08

TARRAGONA
Belgium Rambla Nova, 109 (43003) tel. (977) 21 70 64
Brazil Rambla Nova, 109 (43003) tel. 21 97 57
Colombia Real, 38 (43004) tel. 21 02 20
Costa Rica Rambla Nova, 42 (43004) tel. 23 75 13
Chile Mar, 1 (43004) tel. 21 05 04
Denmark Apodaca, 32 (43004) tel. 23 41 11
Finland Apodaca, 27 (43004) tel. 22 49 11
France Rambla Nova, 94 bis, 2n. 2a. tel. 23 37 31
Greece Plaça dels Carros, 12 (43004) tel. 21 01 13
Italy Via de l'Imperi Romà, 11 (43005) tel. 23 43 18
Netherlands Real, 38 (43004) tel. 21 02 20
Norway Apodaca, 32 (43004) tel. 23 41 11
Sweden Apodaca, 27 (43004) tel. 22 49 11
United Kingdom Real, 33 (43004) tel. 22 08 12, telex 56602 INTO

Dates of Major Festivals

January (sometimes February): Festival of Els Tres Tombs in Vilanova i la Geltrú.
February: Festival of Santa Eulàlia celebrating Barcelona's previous patron saint
and remembering the Spanish Inquisition.
February/March: Carnivals in Sitges, Vilanova i la Geltrú and Barcelona. Mardi
Gras is celebrated with the 'feast of the mad'.
March/April: Throughout the province the Easter Week (*Semana Santa*)
processions and *sardanas*. Vic's Mercat del Ram (Palm market) is held over the
three days preceding Palm Sunday. Throughout the province, the hanging of
the palm on balconies is carried out and there it remains, as protection against
evil, until the palm is replaced the following year.
    Castellers celebrate Sant Jordi (the province's patron saint) on 23 April in
Vilanova i la Geltrú and other celebrations mark the occasion throughout the
province. This was also the day Cervantes died and the day is marked also by
the National Day of the Book. This is particularly memorable in Barcelona
where roses and books are exchanged.
27 April sees the festival of the Virgin of Montserrat with the Salve sung by the
celebrated boys choir and outside sardanas are danced.

June: Three day Festa de la Patúm at Berga (see above).
23 June and particularly 24 June bonfires and celebrations mark Sant Joan day in Barcelona and along the coast and inland.
July: month-long open-air theatre, dance, music festival at Teatre Grec in Barcelona.
August/September: Most towns have their *festa majors*.
September: On September 11 Diada, the National day of Catalonia commemorated everywhere. The castellers move into Sant Sadurní d'Anoia. Coming up to 24 September Barcelona parties for several days before the actual Festa de la Verge de la Mercè which honours the patron saint of the city.
December: On 21 December there are Fira del Gall markets all over the province; particularly notable is the one in Vilafranca del Penedès. On 24 and 25 Christmas celebrations.

On the following holidays you are likely to find most museums, shops and banks closed throughout the province.

Cap d'Any (New Year's Day): 1 January
Els reis (Ephiphany): 6 January
Divendres Sant (Good Friday): March–April
Festa del Treball (May Day)
Sant Joan (Saint John's Day): 24 June
L'Assumpcío (Assumption): 15 August
La Diada (National Day): 11 September
Festa de la Hispanitat (Feast of the Hispanics): 12 October
Tots Sants (All Saints' Day): 1 November
La Immaculada (The Immaculate Conception): 8 December
Nadal (Christmas): 25 December
Sant Esteve (Saint Stephen's Day/Boxing Day): 26 December

Sailing Ports

The following list runs from north to south.

Portbou (Girona, L'Alt Empordà) Wharf. Club Nàutic de Portbou. Port Nàutic Portbou, tel. (972) 39 03 50/39 02 93
Colera (Girona, L'Alt Empordà) Wharf. Club Nàutic Sant Miquel de Colera. Badia, s/n, tel. (972) 38 90 95
Llançà (Girona, L'Alt Empordà) Sports dock. Club Nàutic de Llançà. Port, tel. (972) 38 07 10
El Port de la Selva (Girona, L'Alt Empordà) Sports dock. Club Nàutic de Port de la Selva. Mar, s/n, tel. (972) 38 70 00
Roses (Girona, L'Alt Empordà) Sports dock. Grup d'Esports Nàutics. Port, tel. (972) 25 70 03
Santa Margarida (Roses) (Girona, L'Alt Empordà) Marina. Canals de Santa Margarida. Urbanització Canals de Santa Margarida, tel. (972) 25 77 00

Empúria-brava (Castelló d'Empúries) (Girona, L'Alt Empordà) Marina. Club Nàutic de Ampuriabrava. Port, tel. (972) 25 05 04/45 12 39

L'Escala (Girona, L'Alt Empordà) Sports dock. Club Nàutic de l'Escala. Port, tel. (972) 77 00 16

L'Estartit (Girona, El Baix Empordà) Sports dock. Club Nàutic de l'Estartit, Port, tel. (972) 75 84 02

Aiguablava (Girona, El Baix Empordà) Wharf. Club Nàutic d'Aiguablava. Port, tel. (972) 62 31 61

Llafranc (Girona, El Baix Empordà) Wharf. Club Nàutic de Llafranc. Port, tel. (972) 30 07 54

Palamós (Girona, El Baix Empordà) Sports dock. Club Nàutic Costa Brava. Port, tel. (972) 31 43 24

Port d'Aro (Castell-Platja d'Aro) (Girona, El Baix Empordà) Marina. Sierra de Mias, S.A. Port, tel. (972) 81 89 29

Sant Feliu de Guíxols (Girona, El Baix Empordà) Sports dock. Club Nàutic de Sant Feliu de Guíxols. Passeig del mar, tel. (972) 32 17 00.

Cala Canyelles (Lloret) (Girona, La Selva) Wharf. Club Nàutic Cala Canyelles. Cala Canyelles tel. (972) 36 88 18

Blanes (Girona, La Selva) Sports dock. Club de Vela Blanes. Port, tel. (972) 33 14 98

Arenys de Mar (Barcelona, El Maresme) Sports dock. Club Nàutic d'Arenys de Mar. Port, tel. (93) 792 08 96

El Balís (Sant Andreu de Llavaneres) (Barcelona, El Maresme) Sports port. Club Nàutic El Balís. Port, tel. (93) 792 69 47

Premià de Mar (Barcelona, El Maresme) Wharf. Club Nàutic de Premià de Mar. Port, tel. (93) 751 14 45

El Masnou (Barcelona, El Maresme) Sport port. Promociones Portuarias, S.A. Port, tel. (93) 555 30 00

Barcelona (Barcelona, El Barcelonès) Sports dock. Reial Club Marítim de Barcelona, Reial Club Nàutic de Barcelona Port, tel. (93) 315 00 07, 315 11 61

Port Ginesta (Port La Ginesta-Sitges) tel. 664 3661

Garraf (Barcelona, El Garraf) Sports dock. Club Nàutic de Garraf. Port, tel. (93) 894 05 00/665 78 79

Alguadolç (Sitges) (Barcelona, El Garraf) Sports port. Port d'Aiguadolç-Sitges, S.A. Port, tel. (93) 894 26 00

Vilanova i la Geltrú (Barcelona, El Garraf) Sports dock. Club Nàutic de Vilanova i la Geltrú. Port, tel. (93) 893 07 58/815 02 67

Port Segur (Calafell) (Tarragona, El Baix Penedès) Wharf. Port Segur, S.A. Port, tel. (977) 69 35 50

Coma-ruga (El Vendrell) (Tarragona, El Baix Penedès) Wharf. Club Nàutic Coma-ruga. Port, tel. (977) 68 01 20

Tarragona (Tarragona, El Tarragonès) Sports dock. Club Nàutic de Tarragona. Port, tel. (977) 21 03 60

Salou (Tarragona, El Tarragonès) Wharf. Club Nàutic de Salou. Port, tel. (977) 38 21 66

Cambrils (Tarragona, El Baix Camp) Sports dock. Port, tel. (977) 36 05 31

L'Hospitalet de l'Infant (Tarragona, El Baix Camp) Sport dock. Club Nàutic L'Hospitalet-Vandellós. Port, tel. (977) 82 30 04
Sant Jordi d'Alfama (L'Ametlla de Mar) (Tarragona, El Baix Ebre) Wharf. Club Nàutic Sant Jordi d'Alfama. PO Box 84 (Tortosa), tel. (977) 45 60 63
L'Estany Gras (L'Ametlla de Mar) (Tarragona, El Baix Ebre) Wharf. Yacht International Club L'Ametlla de Mar. Port, tel. (977) 45 60 37
L'Ampolla (El Perelló) (Tarragona, El Baix Ebre) Sports dock. Club Nàutic de L'Ampolla. Port, tel. (977) 46 02 11
Sant Carles de la Ràpita (Tarragona, El Montsià) Sports dock. Club Nàutic Sant Carles de la Ràpita. Port, tel. (977) 74 11 03
Les Cases d'Alcaner (Tarragona, El Montsià) Sports dock. Club Nàutic Les Cases d'Alcanar. Port, tel. (977) 73 70 06

Major Ski Resorts

Baqueira Beret
Naut Aràn (La Vall d'Aràn). 1500–2510m. 22 lifts; 4 black runs, 20 red, 16 blue, 3 green.

Boï-Taüll
Vall de Boï. 2038–2457m. 7 lifts (mostly cross country); 2 black runs, 4 red, 5 blue, 3 green.

La Molina
Alp (La Cerdanya). 1590–2465m, the gateway to the Cerdanya: 19 lifts; 4 black runs, 9 red, 8 blue, 8 green.

Llessui
Sort (El Pallars Sobirà). 1445–2430m, 6 lifts; 7 black runs, 10 red, 2 blue, 3 green.

Masella
Alp (La Cerdanya) 1600–2530m, 11 lifts; 10 black runs, 38 red, 31 blue, 9 green.

Port Ainé
Pic de l'Orri (Rialp). 1650–2440m, 6 lifts; 1 black run, 9 red, 3 blue, 5 green.

Port del Comte
La Coma i la Pedra Solsona (El Solsones) 1690–2400m, 15 lifts; 5 black runs, 14 red, 4 blue, 8 green.

Rasos de Pegeuera
Berga (El Bergueda) 1895–2050m, 4 lifts; 5 red runs, 2 blue, 2 green.

Espot
Super Espot (El Pallars Sobirà) 1490–2320m, 6 lifts; 3 black runs, 7 red, 10 blue, 4 green.

Tuca-Mall Blanc
Veilla-Mig Aràn (La Vall d'Aràn) 1000–2250m, 9 lifts; 3 black runs, 9 red, 5 blue, 3 green.

Vall de Nuria
Queralbs (El Ripollès). No road access but delightful rack railway from Ribes de Freser. 1963–2268m, 4 lifts; 1 black run, 4 red, 2 blue, 2 green.

Vallter 2000
Setcases (El Ripollès) 2010–2500m, 7 lifts; 2 black runs, 4 red, 4 blue, 2 green.

Language

Glossary

bodega	wine-vault or cellar
carreterra (ctra)	major road
castellers	performers in the traditional human pyramid displays
comarca	administrative region of which there are 37, governed by the Generalitat (Catalonia's parliament)
escorxador	abattoir
gralla	primitive wind instrument played as an accompaniment to the performances of the *castellers*
horchata	traditional Catalonian (and Castillian) drink of milk flavoured with almonds
maquis	Republican activists exiled in France during the Civil War
masia	farmstead, often fortified, and often a mini-community in itself rather than just a farmhouse. Many now offer accommodation and/or meals
mirador	observatory
mudéjar	Muslim under Christian rule
parador	castle or palace converted into a hotel (not necessarily very expensive)
sardana	traditional Catalonian dance
teulat	tiled roof
trencadis	mosaic of tiles

Survival Catalan

GREETINGS AND COURTESIES

si	yes
no	no
gràcies	thank you
moltes gràcies	thank you very much
per favor/si us plau	please
parla anglès	do you speak English?
no ho entenc	I don't understand

203

bon dia	good morning
bona tarda	good afternoon
bona nit	good evening
adeu	goodbye
ahir	yesterday
avui	today
demà	tomorrow
com està?	how are you?
estic be	I'm well
estic malament	not well
perdoni	excuse me
perdó	pardon

DIRECTIONS

a la dreta	on the right
a l'esquerra	on the left
prop	near
lluny	far

BANKS AND SERVICES

diners	money
banc	bank
xec de viatge	traveller's cheque
pagar	to pay
preu	price
quant	how much?
car	expensive
barat	cheap
obert	open
tancat	closed
gasolina	petrol
taller	garage
malalt	sick
metge	doctor
ambulància	ambulance
hospital	hospital
dentista	dentist
farmàcia	chemist

ACCOMMODATION

habitació	room
habitació senzilla	single room
habitació doble	double room
llit	bed
llavabo	toilet
bany	bath room
compte	bill

FOOD AND DRINK

forn	bakery
pastisseria	cake shop
cambrer	waiter
carta	menu
cervesa	beer
vi	wine
aigua mineral	mineral water
got	glass
plat	plate
cullera	spoon
ganivet	knife
forquilla	fork
panet/pa	bread
mantega	butter
llet	milk
tè	tea
cafè	coffee
sucre	sugar
oli	oil
all	garlic
peix	fish
formatge	cheese
olives	olives
arròs	rice
patates	potatoes
amanida	salad
fruita	fruit
verdura	vegetables
sal	salt
pasta	pasta
entremesos	hors-d'oeuvres
sopa	soup
marisc	seafood
postres	dessert
gelat	ice cream
pera	pear
poma	apple
maduixes	strawberries
banana	banana
taronja	orange
meló	melon
prèssec	peach
raïm	grapes
xai	lamb
vedella	veal

porc	pork
conill	rabbit
xuleta	chop
truita	trout
salmó	salmon
bacallà	cod
ostres	oysters
llagosta	lobster
gambes	prawns
cargols	snails
mongetes	haricot beans
espàrrecs	asparagus
pastanagues	carrots
pèsols	peas
bolets	mushrooms
cebes	onions

Publications

periòdic	newspaper
guia	guide book
revistes	magazines
mapa	map

Numbers

un	one
dos	two
tres	three
quatre	four
cinc	five
sis	six
set	seven
vuit	eight
nou	nine
deu	ten
onze	eleven
dotze	twelve
tretze	thirteen
catorze	fourteen
quinze	fifteen
setze	sixteen
disset	seventeen
divuit	eighteen
dinou	nineteen
vint	twenty
trent	thirty
quaranta	forty

cinquanta	fifty
seixenta	sixty
setanta	seventy
vuitanta	eighty
noranta	ninety
cent	one hundred
mil	one thousand
mig	half
terç	a third
quart	a quarter

DAYS AND MONTHS

dilluns	Monday
dimarts	Tuesday
dimecres	Wednesday
dijous	Thursday
divendres	Friday
dissabte	Saturday
diumenge	Sunday
nit	night
tarda	evening
matí	morning
migdia	midday
dia	day
setmana	week
mes	month
any	year
gener	January
febrer	February
març	March
abril	April
maig	May
juny	June
juliol	July
agost	August
setembre	September
octubre	October
novembre	November
desembre	December

Index

BARCELONA & CATALONIA